The Lifegiving Table

THE *Life* GIVING TABLE

Nurturing faith through feasting,
ONE MEAL AT A TIME

SALLY CLARKSON

A Tyndale nonfiction imprint

Visit Tyndale online at www.tyndale.com.

Visit Tyndale Momentum online at www.tyndalemomentum.com.

Visit Sally Clarkson at www.sallyclarkson.com, www.momheart.com, and www.wholeheart.org.

Tyndale, Tyndale's quill logo, *Tyndale Momentum*, and the Tyndale Momentum logo are registered trademarks of Tyndale House Ministries. Tyndale Momentum is a nonfiction imprint of Tyndale House Publishers, Carol Stream, Illinois.

The Lifegiving Table: Nurturing Faith through Feasting, One Meal at a Time

Designed by Mark Anthony Lane II

Edited by Anne Christian Buchanan

Unless otherwise indicated, all Scripture quotations are taken from the *Holy Bible*, New Living Translation, copyright © 1996, 2004, 2015 by Tyndale House Foundation. Used by permission of Tyndale House Publishers, Inc., Carol Stream, Illinois 60188. All rights reserved.

Scripture quotations marked NASB are taken from the New American Standard Bible,® copyright © 1960, 1962, 1963, 1968, 1971, 1972, 1973, 1975, 1977, 1995 by The Lockman Foundation. Used by permission.

Scripture quotations marked NIV are taken from the Holy Bible, *New International Version*,® *NIV*.® Copyright © 1973, 1978, 1984, 2011 by Biblica, Inc.® Used by permission. All rights reserved worldwide.

Scripture quotations marked NKJV are taken from the New King James Version,® copyright © 1982 by Thomas Nelson, Inc. Used by permission. All rights reserved.

For information about special discounts for bulk purchases, please contact Tyndale House Publishers at csresponse@tyndale.com, or call 1-800-323-9400.

Library of Congress Cataloging-in-Publication Data
Names: Clarkson, Sally, author.
Title: The lifegiving table : nurturing faith through feasting, one meal at a
   time / Sally Clarkson.
Description: Carol Stream, Illinois : Tyndale House Publishers, Inc., 2017. |
   Includes bibliographical references and index.
Identifiers: LCCN 2017025414| ISBN 9781496430632 (hc) | ISBN 9781496431547
   (sc) | ISBN 9781496414205 (sc)
Subjects: LCSH: Dinners and dining—Religious aspects—Christianity.
Classification: LCC BR115.N87 C63 2017 | DDC 248.4/6—dc23 LC record available at
https://lccn.loc.gov/2017025414

Printed in the United States of America

28   27   26   25   24   23   22
8   7   6   5   4   3   2

Heartfelt thanks to You, sweet Lord, for creating us with the need to eat. Thank You for designing our bodies with the need for constant nourishment every day, so that we might be drawn into regular rhythms of delight for the multitude of delectable ways You satisfy our hunger.

Thank You for the friendships You knew those rhythms would create, pulling us into a vibrant dance of worship together for the bounty of Your grace.

———————————— �֍ ————————————

Deep gratitude to Joy, who used her skill to help me make this book come to life.

Contents

CHAPTER I

DISCIPLES AROUND MY TABLE
The Feasting-Faith Connection

*If the home is a body, the table is the heart, the beating
center, the sustainer of life and health.*
SHAUNA NIEQUIST

*The LORD of hosts will prepare a lavish banquet for all peoples on this mountain;
A banquet of aged wine, choice pieces with marrow,
And refined, aged wine.*
ISAIAH 25:6, NASB

Table-Discipleship Principle:

All table-talk discussions, love given, and beauty
cultivated at our table are for the purpose of
making real our Savior and calling those who
share life with us to serve Him their whole lives.

CANDLES FLICKERED with the brush of the evening breeze floating through our Colorado deck, awash with the fragrances of geraniums and roses. It was a beautiful evening, and our table was beautiful as well. Multiple shades of green lettuce in our salad bowl provided a lovely backdrop for the dark-rose cranberries, salted and roasted mahogany pecans, stark-white goat cheese, pungent red onions, and chartreuse chunks of avocado sprinkled here and there. Twice-baked potatoes stuffed full with spinach and bacon adorned each plate next to sizzling chicken, hot from the grill. Crisp homemade whole-grain rolls shone with their glaze of butter. Sparkling cider bubbled in the cut-glass wineglasses.

The stage was set for the occasion of having all my young-adult children home together to celebrate my sixtieth birthday. And as is usual for us, we did our celebrating with a feast.

The excitement of being together once again spilled over into smiles and laughter, rousing conversation, and even tears as we celebrated, once again, what it meant to be *us*.

My firstborn, Sarah, was home after a summer as a teacher/counselor at an apologetics seminar at a Colorado mountain retreat center.

Joel, her musician/writer brother, was living in Los Angeles, trying to establish a career as a composer of film scores.

Nathan, our "outside the box" boy, was also in LA, working as an actor in TV and commercials and taking his first steps toward becoming a filmmaker.

And Joy, our cherished "caboose," had just finished her freshman year at Biola University.

Clay, my husband, was there, too, of course—my beloved longtime partner in ministry, in business, in creating and nurturing a family. And beside him was our beloved, ever-present golden retriever, Kelsey, hoping for a few crumbs from our table.

"This is what I think of when I think of home." Sarah smiled as she looked around at the bounty of treasured faces and favorite foods. The others nodded. And I couldn't stop smiling as we sat down once more around the table that had always been such a source of life to all of us.

It happened again just last summer. Days before converging on our home for a family gathering together, both of my boys called me.

"Mama, I can hardly wait to get there."

"What is your favorite expectation about coming home?" I asked each of them.

Both answered with almost the same words, even though they were now separated by two thousand miles!

"It is the feasting every night around the table with delicious home-cooked food, being each other's best friends, talking about every possible subject and sharing in each others' lives, needs, stories, and fun—that is my favorite part. I need *my* people. I want a place to belong. I miss playing with my pack." (Since choosing our first golden retriever puppy years ago and watching her frolic with her little dog family, we have often referred to our own family as our "pack.")

A Table Ministry

It's no accident that they feel this way. Creating a lifegiving table in our home was a priority for Clay and me from the very beginning, and we both put effort and intention into making it happen. Actually, when I think of it, I was doing it even before I had a family.

As a young woman, I was captivated by the heart of Jesus—His compassion to see and meet the needs of those He rubbed shoulders with and His desire for many workers to carry out His loving purpose.

> Jesus traveled through all the towns and villages of that area,
> teaching in the synagogues and announcing the Good News
> about the Kingdom. And he healed every kind of disease and
> illness. When he saw the crowds, he had compassion on them
> because they were confused and helpless, like sheep without
> a shepherd. He said to his disciples, "The harvest is great, but
> the workers are few. So pray to the Lord who is in charge of the
> harvest; ask him to send more workers into his fields."
> MATTHEW 9:35-38

From the time I read that passage in college, I said a passionate yes to the call to follow Jesus into the fields of harvest. That passion to follow stayed with me and eventually prompted me to pursue mission work both in the United States and abroad—even behind what was then the Iron Curtain. And I quickly learned that my table was an effective tool for sharing my faith and building relationships with others.

As a single woman almost until age thirty, I hosted many people in my home for snack-meal Bible studies, celebratory holiday gatherings and dinner evenings with friends, picnics outdoors, and a procession of one-on-one sessions with friends over strong tea or coffee. Over the years I learned more and more about how to make my table a place where His life would be shared, His love offered, His encouragement given to anchor those around us and to provide hope in a dark world.

After Clay and I met and married, we felt that God wanted us to give ourselves as a couple to seeking ways to reach out into the harvest fields of our own lives to find those who longed for truth, who needed the love and forgiveness of Christ. We found that inviting people we met in our neighborhood, at work, and through friends into our home to feast at our table gave us many unthreatening opportunities to share His love with those who longed for it. And so our table was also a strategic place of ministry as we served His love and truth through sharing meals in a cozy environment.

This dynamic of faith and feasting—or perhaps faith *through* feasting—took on an added dimension when our children came along. When we had only littles, our approach to meals and snack times had to consider the individual personalities of our children, their love of delight, their short attention spans. But we still sought to make our table a place of influence. With a heart for mentoring and discipleship, I would whip up a meal, and Clay and I together would seek to capture the imaginations of our children and friends with table talk that inspired and stimulated conversation.

And we continued to do so through the years. Almost every night, without fail, we would gather round the dining table, light candles, turn on music—whether dinner was a simple bowl of soup or a beef roast with all the trimmings—and we would participate in the comfort and pleasure of each other's friendship over a meal shared together.

The soul satisfaction of belonging to one another, the anchor of commonly held traditions, and the understanding that our home was a sanctuary from all the pressures and storms of life—all these knit our hearts together into tight bonds that will not easily be broken. And all these we cultivated carefully through years and years of sitting down together, through multiple hours of cooking and baking and preparing meal after meal, through the disciplines of teaching manners and fostering conversation. Our determination to incarnate the life of Christ in every detail of our time together, even our meals, had forged a legacy of love.

Feasting, Family, and Faith

In all the years that the Clarksons have been a family, feasting together has been a lifegiving activity for us. And we've always *called* it feasting, whether it involves a full-blown banquet, a one-on-one treat of milk and cookies, or a bowl of fresh-popped popcorn enjoyed around the fire. The word *feasting* reminds us of God's bounty, the gift of our relationships, and the response of pleasure and thanksgiving that the act of sharing a meal requires of us. Somehow it makes "eating" sound more significant.

When God created the world and pronounced it good, He lavishly provided an abundance of delights to please every possible palate. His artistic hand can be seen in all of the food He provided, not just to satisfy our basic need for calories, but also to gratify our senses with color, aroma, texture, and taste—orange carrots and red peppers, purple-black eggplant, rust-colored cinnamon, yellow and green squash, golden honey, sweet green and red and purple grapes, yellow and multicolored corn, brown rice and pale grains of wheat, pink sea salt, speckled trout, crunchy pecans and bumpy walnuts, rich maple syrup, mild hominy, spicy green and red chilies.

God created all these and more for our pleasure and our satisfaction. And He created us in such a way that we make emotional and spiritual connections in the process of enjoying them, especially when we share them around the table with people we love.

Breaking bread together, sharing food, sitting at table eye to eye is essential to individual growth and relationship. Adults and children are not just bodies to be fed, but also minds to be challenged, hearts that depend on emotional input to survive and to grow as healthy human beings, and spirits that long for connection with God and purpose in life. Feasting together is a powerful way to fulfill physical, emotional, and spiritual needs.

Perhaps an exhausted, fussy toddler needs small snacks of chicken, nuts, fruit, or cheese to fuel his little body and settle his emotions. A hormonal teen might brighten up with a cup of coffee or tea, a hot piece of homemade toast awash with butter and jam, and a set-apart time together that communicates, "I am here to listen to your heart." And for a stressed-out adult, there's nothing like coming home to a pot of potato-cheese soup bubbling on the stove, bread warming in the oven, candles lit, the table set. (Thank you, Joel, for recently saving my own day!)

A Model for Discipleship

Feasting is not only a way to meet physical and emotional needs. It's also a powerful tool for making disciples. And discipleship has always been the focus of my heart for my children. My longing for them to catch the love of Christ, the life of His Spirit, and the redeeming truth of His words was at the core of all of my planning and practices as a mom. And I learned long ago, from pondering Christ, how strategic shared meals can be to this purpose.

Biblical tradition underlines the physical, emotional, and spiritual significance of food and feasting. In fact, Jesus ushered in His ministry as our Messiah by providing new wine—the best of wine—at a wedding celebration. He also inaugurated His coming as our Redeemer in a setting of food and drink abounding. And the way He went about this can tell us a lot about how He would have us create our own lifegiving tables.

The final evening before Jesus was to be crucified, He strategically set the stage for His most profound messages to be shared with His inner circle. This evening, unique in Scripture, shows the God of all creation preparing a feast for His own.

He began with preparation. Jesus picked a room where the Passover meal would be celebrated and then dispatched two trusted disciples to make the arrangements for the traditional feast. Luke 22:7-8 records Jesus' instructions: "Now the Festival of Unleavened Bread arrived, when the Passover lamb is sacrificed. Jesus sent Peter and John ahead and said, 'Go and prepare the Passover meal, so we can eat it together.'"

Preparation for a meal indicates thoughtfulness, caring, and intentionality. We show others their worth to us by considering how to best meet their needs and by intentionally arranging the environment to provide comfort and pleasure.

Then came the moment when Jesus assumed the role of a servant. His desire to pour out His love and affection to those who would eventually give their lives for His Kingdom purposes is shown clearly in His loving actions.

> So he got up from the table, took off his robe, wrapped a towel
> around his waist, and poured water into a basin. Then he
> began to wash the disciples' feet, drying them with the towel
> he had around him.   JOHN 13:4-5

Touching one another is a sign of personal intimacy, an expression of friendship, kinship, affection, or close connection. For Jesus to bow His knees on the dusty floor is a personal choice of deep humility. As tenderly as a mother comforting her children, He personally washed one hundred twenty dirty man toes and wiped rough, callused feet with all the love of a doting parent.

This unexpected act surely gave a surprise relief to those who had walked the dusty roads in the sweltering heat of the day. The flooding rush of therapeutic pleasure as their feet were massaged and wiped dry, the nerve endings soothed under the hands of their friend, soon to be their Savior, must have been impressed on their memories forever. He, the Savior, had bowed to attend His closest friends, His beloved companions through years of ministry, and to minister to them with the intimate gift of touch.

Next came the food—the traditional Passover feast with the delectable aroma of herbs and spices wafting through the air. Hungry men must have eagerly gobbled up the familiar feast.

Because of Jesus' careful preparation, His loving service, and His provision to satiate the hunger of this gang of friends, His beloved Twelve were ready to hear the final words and admonitions He was about to deliver before He left them. Having their physical and emotional needs met opened the disciples' hearts to receive the Master's spiritual instruction. And seeing their Lord's profound model of humble servant leadership helped shape the direction their future ministries would take.

Communion of heart, soul, and mind was at the center of Jesus' aim for His last earthly evening with the band of men who had walked with Him through all the days of His ministry. And it all happened around a table. His years of discipling them, punctuated by many meals together, culminated with a feast they would always remember—a feast that His followers reenact to this day.

God's desire, you see, is always for intimacy and communion with His beloved children. The feasting table sets the stage for heightened intimacy with Him as He shares His heart, mind, and soul. Initiating love, providing enjoyment through delicious food and drink, sustaining hearts with words of friendship, granting hope, giving courage and comfort, and speaking words of life were all a part of His message in this last place He lingered with them on the night before He gave His life.

I believe this is the example we must follow if we want to cultivate disciples around our tables. Through our careful preparations, our attention to tone and atmosphere, our gifts of loving touch, our example of humble service, and the provision of satisfying food, we can bring ourselves and those we love closer to Christ and foster growth of body, mind, and spirit.

Your Lifegiving Table

To my delight, I have been able to watch as my own grown children carry what we have taught them about faith and feasting, food and service and discipling into their own homes and their own lives. I've also had the satisfaction of sharing some of my insights and experience with other men and women who hunger to gather around a lifegiving table and share their hearts. And now, in this book, I'd like to share them with you.

In the pages to come you will find personal stories, practical guidance, ideas to try, plus a little bit of Bible study to anchor you, and some practical ideas for creating your own lifegiving table. With each chapter I have suggested a table-discipleship principle to help keep you focused on the real purpose behind your own lifegiving table. And at the end of most chapters, I have shared a couple of favorite recipes that my family has enjoyed through the years.

Most of these recipes are family favorites—family tested and intended to please a broad audience. I have worked and traveled throughout the world and enjoyed a variety of sophisticated cuisines. But for this book, I've chosen my simplest comfort food—easy to make and tested crowd-pleasers.

My own habits of cooking involve what I call *real* food—food that has not been highly processed or prepared with lots of chemicals or additives—and I avoid anything that has been bleached, such as flour or sugar. I lived in Europe at a time when there was much less fast food available, so I learned the value and joy of doing my own cooking from scratch, which has become a sort of hobby for me. As I learned more about how food affects our bodies and minds, I moved more and more toward a natural diet. I try to cook with fresh, wholesome, organic ingredients and whole grains, and I strive to make food that is as healthy *and tasty* as possible.

A little shop in a market near my house in Austria ground kernels of wheat into flour, and I soon became hooked on the superior taste of baked goods made from freshly ground flour. So when I returned to America, I bought my own grain mill. I use it often to grind my own wheat or grains to make flour. I also invested in a heavy-duty Bosch mixer that allows me to make and bake our own bread easily and quickly.

All of this, you will find, is reflected in these recipes. But don't worry if you don't have some of the specialized equipment to follow them exactly. Just use the alternative ingredients and instructions given in the recipe. There is such freedom and grace for each of us to pick and choose how we will cook according to our own unique personalities, preferences, and dietary needs. Individual cuisine brings distinct life art to different tables. If the recipes in this book don't appeal to you, I hope you will take them as inspiration from our own family culinary preferences and either find or create recipes that work for your own version of the lifegiving table.

Although "cooking healthy" is important to me, you'll note that I've also included recipes for treats—some sweets and even my special fried chicken. They're not for every day—we usually reserve such goodies for weekend teatimes, holidays, or company meals. But we *do* enjoy them, and I hope you will too.

Whatever your specific circumstances, it is my sincere hope that this book will stimulate your own appreciation of how significant your shared meals can be in shaping the legacy of faith celebrated, embraced, and offered through the seasons of your own home. I also hope you'll feel free to use it any way that works best for you. This isn't the kind of book you have to read cover to cover, although you can do that if you want to. Each chapter is complete in itself, so you can read them in any order. If you're interested in a theological and philosophical ground-work for table ministry, start with chapters 2 through 5. If you're ready to start some new table traditions in your family's life, flip through chapters 6 through 14. Each chapter focuses on a specific aspect of table discipleship or a table tradition our family enjoys.

However you read it, I hope you'll learn, as we have, that your table can be one of your most potent discipling tools as well as a source of great joy in relationships. And may you be inspired to cultivate feast-ing in your own home as a powerful way of influencing the hearts and minds of your children, friends, neighbors, and even strangers with the sacrificial love and boundless servant heart of Jesus.

Bon appétit!

CHAPTER 2

TABLEOLOGY
Biblical and Spiritual Foundations for Faith by Feasting

❈

by Clay Clarkson

For Jesus the home is not what defines the table;
the table is what defines the home.
LEONARD SWEET, *FROM TABLET TO TABLE*

For he satisfies the thirsty
and fills the hungry with good things.
PSALM 107:9

Table-Discipleship Principle

Creating a lifegiving table is an
intentional act of gathering, blessing,
eating, sharing, and serving.

SUMMER EVENINGS often find us sitting in white wooden rockers on our front porch, sipping something cool and munching on a summer-fare dinner of salad or my own version of tomato basil bruschetta. Our home faces the front range of the Rocky Mountains, and we love to sit and rock and chew while watching the sun go down.

One evening I was chatting away with Clay, my husband, about how this book was progressing. Our conversation took many twists and turns as we remembered stories from our life together and reminisced about the important ways our family table traditions had shaped our history together—meals shared in foreign countries where we lived, mission trips to places where we ministered, outdoor picnics shared on our deck, and countless Clarkson dinnertime "discussions."

As we talked, Clay suggested that I give a short biblical discussion of the role that the table played through the stories of God.

"Why don't you write me one chapter of your thoughts on this," I ventured. After all, Clay is our resident theologian. "In fact, it would be great if you write a little from your own perspective about what the table means in our family and what its spiritual significance is."

"I will!" he agreed.

And so now I give you Clay's view on the Bible, our family, and the lifegiving table.

Reclaiming the Family Table

The story of the Clarkson family has been written at tables. Not with pen and paper, but with words and people, food and fellowship, talk and time. Whatever kind of table it might be—breakfast, lunch, dinner; picnic or deck; plain or fancy; small, tall, wood, metal, or rock; bare or cloth-covered; even the ground—it becomes our family table when we sit down together to eat and drink and be and belong. The delightful fruits of God's creation we share together fill and fuel us as God's life-breathed and image-bearing creatures, and our shared story grows from the table's Spirit-infused life coming alive in us.

I believe that's true for all of us.

When we sit at our tables, we're not just an aggregate of individual family members eating and drinking to stay alive; we're a congregation of communing souls hungering and thirsting to experience the goodness and beauty of the life God has designed just for us. Even the simplest supper, meal, snack, or teatime can become, in some way, a feast—a lavish celebration of the living God's life and goodness. It's not just about the physical act of eating, but about sharing and enjoying life as God designed and gave it to us. That is the essence of the lifegiving table.

Now you may be thinking, *That doesn't sound like any table where my family sits. We're doing well just to get four kids sitting in chairs, with cereal and milk in bowls, all at the same time. Most of the "life" at our breakfast table comes from a family-size cereal box.* Maybe you see yourself among the growing number of families who eat fewer meals together at home, spend less time at the table when they do, and consume less real food made at home and more manufactured or take-out food made somewhere else by some unknown makers.

The unfortunate reality of modern American culture is that it has robbed too many homes of the once-central role of the table in family life and has stolen the goodness of eating real, home-cooked foods. When asked, most parents will respond that of course it's important for families to eat regular meals together. At the same time, many will sheepishly admit that they don't. If there is life to be found at the table today, it is life that must be intentionally rescued and reclaimed from its cultural exile.

According to statistics gathered on The Six O'Clock Scramble website (thescramble.com), the frequency of family dinners has declined 33 percent over just the last twenty years. The average time spent at a dinner table has shrunk from ninety minutes in the middle of the last century to less than twelve minutes today. And the real effects of these trends cannot be ignored. Kids and teens who share fewer than three family dinners each week are less likely to eat healthier foods and *more* likely to be overweight, perform poorly academically, engage in risky behaviors such as substance abuse, and have poor relationships with their parents.[1]

And make no mistake—this trend applies to Christian families as much as to nonbelievers. Christian homes tend to be just as busy, meals just as rushed or fragmented, food just as likely to be eaten out or carried in or microwaved straight from the freezer. And the diminishing presence of the table in Christian homes can affect the quality of discipling in the home as well as its biblical role as a source of hospitality to others. Christian futurist Leonard Sweet puts it this way: "An untabled faith is an unstable faith."[2]

Tables can give life, in other words, but only if we choose to let them.

This book is all about how we Clarksons chose to experience life at our various tables through thirty-five years of marriage and family. It's about the variety of feasts and fellowship that formed our family, fed our faith, filled our souls, and fueled our visions for God's work in us and in the world. It is not an exaggeration to say that who we are—our essential identities in Christ and our collective family identity—was shaped as much by what happened at our family table as by any other influences.

In particular, this book looks back on many of the personal and practical ways that Sally and I used the experience of eating together as an opportunity to spiritually influence our children and others through what we call "faith by feasting." We took the table seriously, purposely using it to disciple our children—creating faith-shaped habits, patterns, priorities, and traditions. We wanted our family tables to be truly lifegiving tables. And we believed—we still believe—that this desire is deeply scriptural.

The Table in the Bible

To my knowledge, no one has ever written a formal "tableology"—or theology of the table. But that doesn't mean the ideas and intentions shared in this book are unbiblical or unrelated to what God is doing in the world. In fact, the opposite is true. They are built on a biblical and theological framework that gives the table an eternal significance.

Scripture depicts the table as something woven into the fabric of creation by the divine mind and imagination of our creator God, who always creates with purpose and intentionally imbues His creation with meaning. That means it is there for our good. It is there, in some way, to give life. But to understand how this is true, you might need to approach the Scriptures with what the Bible calls the "eyes of your heart."

If you've studied Scripture for long, then you know that there is always more in the words of God's Word than meets your eye or ear. The apostle Paul prays for the Ephesian believers that "the eyes of your heart may be enlightened" (1:18, NASB)—so that they would know all that God had done for them spiritually, even things their physical eyes could not see. When God opens the "eyes of your heart," you're able to see the glory that is often hidden in the seemingly ordinary things of life. Things like tables. Like food. Like daily time together.

Exploring the more-than-meets-the-eye nature of the table and food in Scripture is a book-length task, as deep as it is wide, so all we can do here is skim the surface. Perhaps a good place to start is with this statement by biblical scholar and author N. T. Wright: "When Jesus wanted to explain to his followers the meaning of his death, he didn't give them a theory; he gave them a meal."[3]

In other words, Jesus (who made us) knew that we learn truth through illustration as much as we do by instruction. Metaphor and analogy are not just literary devices, but gateways of understanding. They are often the way we're able to see truth with the eyes of our heart.

But our "heart sight" requires more than just illustration. It also requires illumination—when the light of Jesus lights up all reality so we can see what is true in what is real. As Jesus celebrated His final Passover meal in the Upper Room with His disciples, He turned a common table and familiar food into what would become known as "the *Lord's* Table" (1 Corinthians 10:21) and "the *Lord's* Supper" (11:20). He gave the Passover table and its familiar food and rituals an eternal and spiritual significance beyond their temporary and physical natures, pointing His disciples to the future day when they would one day "eat and drink at my table" (Luke 22:30)—a real feast at a real table in the new Kingdom to come.

That last meal Jesus ate with His disciples—the meal His followers have emulated to this date in our practice of Communion—is perhaps the most powerful expression of biblical tableology. But the assumption that there is spiritual significance in the acts of preparing and sharing food runs throughout the Bible from beginning to end.

The Old Testament, for instance, is filled with tables, foods, and feasts—stories of God's provision of food and drink and of God's people gathered together to enjoy it. We see stories of Abraham's hospitality to strangers and the Israelites' first Passover meal together—both table gatherings with profound spiritual significance. And consider just a few tasty passages from the books of poetry and prophecy:

> You prepare a table before me in the presence of my enemies . . .
> My cup overflows.
>
> PSALM 23:5, NASB

> For he satisfies the thirsty
>   and fills the hungry with good things.
>
> PSALM 107:9

> The eyes of all look to You,
> And You give them their food in due time.
>
> PSALM 145:15, NASB

> The LORD . . .
>   will spread a wonderful feast
>   for all the people of the world.
> It will be a delicious banquet
>   with clear, well-aged wine and choice meat. . . .
> He will swallow up death forever!
>
> ISAIAH 25:6, 8

You'll also find tables and food everywhere in the Gospels. Jesus often ate and reclined at tables with others. Many of His parables involve food, eating, and tables. Some of His best miracles involve food and drink, and some of His best teaching takes place at tables.

In John's Gospel, the first miracle of Jesus' public ministry was turning water into the finest wine at the wedding in Cana (John 2:1-11). The last miracle of His postresurrection ministry was Peter's net-breaking catch of fish—followed by a seaside picnic that Jesus cooked for some of the disciples (21:1-14). In Luke, the final appearance of Jesus includes breaking bread with the two disciples He taught on the road to Emmaus and then eating broiled fish with the disciples to prove His presence (Luke 24:13-43). Even Matthew's more instructional narrative of Jesus' life and ministry is flavored throughout with tastes of tables and food.

In fact, Jesus' apparent love for feasting—sometimes in company that some considered questionable—became a scandalous part of His reputation. Jesus noted this Himself: "The Son of Man has come eating and drinking, and you say, 'Behold, a gluttonous man and a drunkard, a friend of tax collectors and sinners!'" (Luke 7:34, NASB). He was quoting a slanderous taunt apparently being spread by the Pharisees, and yet He did not seem to think it needed correction; rather, He unapologetically affirmed His reputation for "eating and drinking"—and immediately afterward accepted the Pharisee's dinner invitation.

But Jesus didn't simply use food as a tool in His ministry. He made it integral to His explanation of who He was and what He had come to do. When challenged to give a sign better than the manna in the wilderness, Jesus said, "I am the bread of life. Whoever comes to me will never be hungry again. Whoever believes in me will never be thirsty" (John 6:35). That statement took on added resonance at that final Passover table the night before He died. Jesus transformed some of the food and drink He consumed with His disciples into symbols of His sacrifice. Bread and wine, the physical food and drink that gives us physical life, represented His body and blood, the spiritual food that gives us eternal life.

After Jesus' resurrection and ascension, the act of sharing food and drink continued to carry heavy spiritual significance for His followers. The New Testament accounts indicate that sharing meals was integral to the growing church. The table, where those early Christians partook of both the physical and the spiritual food and drink, came to represent the unity we all share in Christ (1 Corinthians 10:16-17). Even John's description of the end of time in Revelation includes a great wedding feast (19:9) and trees laden with nourishing fruit (22:2).

There are far too many other references to food and tables to mention here, so let me share a helpful summary by Leonard Sweet:

> The first word God speaks to human beings in the Bible—God's very first commandment—is "Eat freely" (Genesis 2:16, NASB). The last words out of God's mouth in the Bible—his final command? "Drink freely" (see Revelation 22:17). These bookends to the Bible are reflective of the whole of the Scriptures: Everything in between these two commands is a table, and on that table is served a life-course meal, where we feast in our hearts with thanksgiving on the very Bread of Life and the Cup of Salvation: Jesus the Christ.[4]

The Table in the Home

So what is the point? you might be thinking. *I get it. I can see that Scripture has something meaningful to say about tables and foods and feasts. But what is the meaning of all this for my family? How does this impact us personally and practically as believers?*

The original drive behind this book was to explore the idea of dinner-table discipleship. Although quality of food has always been important to us Clarksons, sharing a meal was rarely *only* about eating food. It was also about feasting together on Scripture, stories, ideas, concepts, experiences, thoughts, feelings, news, philosophy, insights, and so much more. We purposefully planned a table experience that would fill not just our children's hungry bodies, but also their spirits and minds. We even coined the slogan "faith by feasting" to describe the kind of discipleship that took place regularly, one meal at a time, at our tables.

A secondary purpose for our family tables involved both mission and hospitality—the practice of welcoming others to share our home, our table, and hopefully a taste of God's Kingdom as well. This practice—and teaching it to our children—was an integral part of our commitment to faith by feasting. It was something we sought to teach our children through our words and our example. We discipled them in this specific practice even while we discipled others at our table.

This book is an "in our home" look at the various ways we set out to accomplish these purposes for our tables—to create the kinds of meal-centered feasts that would feed and form growing bodies and growing faith and allow us to touch the lives of those outside the home as well. As Sally and I look at what our children have become at age twenty-one, twenty-six, thirty, and thirty-two, we are more convinced than ever that what took place at our tables was critical to the formation of their emerging identities, faith, intelligence, and confidence. Today we find it enormously satisfying to hear each of them affirm the shaping influence of our tables on their lives and to see them creating lifegiving tables of their own.

A lifegiving table, like a lifegiving home, doesn't just happen—it is intentionally cultivated and created. Like a beautiful musical composition, its elements must be carefully arranged, thoughtfully directed, and passionately played in order for the music to fulfill its purpose. But it's not really that difficult. In fact, if you can keep five key elements or goals in mind—gather, bless, eat, share, and serve—you can make the music happen wherever there are food and people.

Gather: We Come Together around the Table

The idea of gathering to eat is a somewhat fluid one. We can gather in the kitchen to graze on food options. We can gather in the living room with plates in laps. We can gather in the family room to eat in front of a screen. We can gather in a yard for a barbecue and wander around with plates in hand—or no plates at all. And any of these gatherings can contain elements of the family table. But the furniture does make a difference. When we gather around a physical table, we uniquely maximize the opportunity to create something the Bible calls *koinonia*.

Think about the relational dynamics of a table for a moment. First, it creates a physical unity—all who sit at the table become, in a sense, one with the table, and so one with each other while at the table. Second, the table creates an experiential unity—you are sharing an experience of food and fellowship. Third, the table fosters interaction with other people—it is natural to look into others' eyes at a table, to engage in conversation, and to communicate nonverbally. Finally, the table becomes an anchor; it anchors everyone to a static spot and thus discourages wandering. It is hard to avoid the natural, communal dynamic of a physical table. And that in turn helps to create koinonia, which means fellowship or partnership with others.

For Christians, koinonia specifically describes the unique communion we share with others who are also "in Christ." It shows up often in the New Testament descriptions of the early church, beginning with Acts 2:42, which describes the early church in Jerusalem as "continually devoting themselves to the apostles' teaching and to fellowship [koinonia], to the breaking of bread and to prayer" (NASB). They "had all things in common" (verse 44, NASB) and daily were "breaking bread from house to house . . . taking their meals together with gladness and sincerity of heart" (verse 46, NASB). They were experiencing koinonia by gathering at lifegiving tables to feast with other believers.

When we gather at a lifegiving table in our home, our goal is not just to be together, but to experience koinonia—both in the general sense and in the uniquely Christian sense. We gather to be together as a family and also to connect as spiritual beings and followers of Christ. But making that happen requires a certain amount of work and attention. If there are relational problems such as anger, those need to be resolved before we gather at the table. If there are distractions—cell phones, tablets, noises from other rooms, pets—we minimize them. If there are competing schedules, we try to work around them as best we can.

Everyone in the Clarkson family has strong opinions and convictions, so it is not unusual for lively dinnertime discussions to become increasingly vociferous. When that discussion deteriorates into emotional or insensitive argument, we have to discipline ourselves to take a step back. That's not easy, but we like to remember the time when four-year-old Joy single-handedly ended such an overly spirited table discussion about Tarzan (don't ask). When she had had enough of the older kids' loud discussion, she stood up, raised her arms straight into the air, closed her eyes, and proclaimed with great conviction and assertiveness, "Everybody stop! Take a deep breath, and think about Jesus."

It worked. We had a good laugh and got back to our koinonia.

Bless: We Thank God

American culture has, unfortunately, trivialized and minimalized the practice of giving thanks before a meal. In our rush to get to the eating, the blessing often gets dropped under the table. I confess this can be true even in our own home. And this is unfortunate because the ritual of giving thanks can transform our experience of a meal. It helps those of us who have gathered together make the connection between feasting and faith.

When we thank God for a meal, we are decisively turning our hearts away from focusing just on our own needs to focusing on the Giver of the good gifts we are about to enjoy. We're allowing gratitude to change our attitude. Saying a blessing is a way of acknowledging that God is the source of life in our lifegiving table.

Author Norman Wirzba suggests that a blessing can also be a way for us to tune in to the sacrifice that is necessary for any of us to eat. Growing and living things in creation—plants and animals—must die in order to give us life. As Wirzba puts it, "Eating is the daily reminder of creaturely mortality."[5]

If that sounds familiar, it should. Consider the foods at the Last Supper that Jesus blessed and that became sacraments of His coming death. Bread and wine both require someone to "make" them; there is no bread bush to eat from, no wine pool to dip a cup in. Bread and wine come only from effort, work, and even acts of violence. Bread requires picking grain, crushing it, kneading dough, baking, and breaking. Wine calls for picking grapes, smashing them, fermenting, bottling, and pouring out. There is a rich poetic and spiritual meaning in the human-prepared foods Jesus selected that can enrich us if we stop to see it.

This hidden truth about food is not something that needs to be repeatedly rehearsed at every table—especially not with little children—but it can add a depth of meaning and a truer sense of gratitude to the act of feasting. God has designed us to be interdependent creatures with His creation, to the point that our physical life is entirely dependent on something in creation dying so that we can live. And in the same way, our spiritual life is dependent on Jesus' death, which we share in the broken bread and poured-out wine. An awareness of this dynamic enriches the act of asking a blessing at the table.

The point is, we lose something important, something significant, when we skip the blessing. And we should never be content with rote and spiritless "God is great; God is good" type recitations. Instead, our blessing should provide a moment to contemplate the meaning of God's provision, the reality of service and sacrifice, the gift of table fellowship, and the abundance of beauty and joy we are privileged to experience in our bodies on this earth.

That's not to say that every blessing needs to be long-winded and complicated, especially at a table with little ones present. But it should be intentional and thoughtful, not rushed and random.

Some families have found it helpful to write their own meaningful blessings or even create a kind of mealtime liturgy. Reciting or reading aloud a thoughtfully written family blessing can bring a whole new life to the table blessing. Such composed blessings can reflect different seasons, events, and topics. They can even consist of personalized Scripture readings.

If you're not a writer type, a quick Internet search will reveal numerous possible collections of mealtime blessings. Our family loves William S. Kervin's *A Year of Grace*,[6] an anthology of Scriptures, quotes, poems, and original blessings to be used at mealtime, but there are many other mealtime blessing collections that are worth the search. If you're willing to make a minor exception to the "no devices at the table" rule, Kindle versions can keep the blessings quickly available no matter where you are.

Eat: We Break Bread

We gather. We bless. We eat. Or alternatively, we just eat—gathered or not, blessed or not. We do it three times a day and in between. In this country, it seems, we're surrounded by food all the time. We eat instinctively, habitually, regularly, compulsively, guiltily, joyfully. We eat too much. We eat too little. We eat because we must, but also because we can, and we want to.

We eat to live. We live to eat. We love to eat. We eat what we love.

We are what we eat. We eat because we are.

Adam and Eve were created hungry and thirsty. As soon as God had blessed and commissioned His new human creatures as His vice regents over the new creation, He told them where to get food (Genesis 1:30; 2:9). And it's been that way ever since, for every one of the 108.2 billion (or so) humans who have ever lived on the earth.[7] After an "I'm here" scream exiting the womb, the first thing we do is eat and drink. From that first taste of mother's milk, our lives are driven and defined by the universal cry of the human soul, "What is there to eat?"

The creation narrative in Genesis 1–2 is a description of God creating a food-filled home for His new creatures that would be as lavish and abundant as He Himself is, a reflection of His own beauty and goodness. Every one of our human senses is fine-tuned by God to resonate with our physical appetite: eyes see the beauty of food, noses pick up the tantalizing aromas, hands feel the shapes and textures, ears hear the crunches and sizzling of preparation and service, and of course our taste buds revel in the sensory journey of eating.

God placed us in an edible creation, not just to make sure we'd have sufficient foodstuff to stay alive, but also to make sure we would be enlivened by enjoying the goodness of His creation that we depend on for life. When God, after each wave of creative activity, looked at what He'd done and declared it good, He was essentially saying, "This works, and it pleases Me." It was an act of divine love that covered our physical reality, eating included. If we think that our ultimate and best reality is exclusively spiritual, we've missed the bigger-picture realities of the creation story.

In the same way that we are dependent on God for spiritual life, we are dependent on God's creation for physical life. We are not just spirits stuck in physical bodies awaiting release. Our bodily existence, with all its senses, needs, and appetites, is an expression of God's ultimate good for us and for Him.

Don't forget that God eventually became incarnate—literally "enfleshed"—in the same kind of body He created for us. When Jesus walked this earth, He never seemed to neglect an opportunity to enjoy a good meal with others. As He said of Himself, He came "eating and drinking" (Matthew 11:19, NASB), and that was good.

So how does this understanding of the act of eating contribute to a lifegiving table? In simplest terms, I think it means we never take food for granted. We try to find ways to acknowledge and treat all food served at our tables as a gift for us from the loving heart of God to be enjoyed for all its divinely designed goodness and beauty. Even more, we put the same kind of thought and creativity into presenting food on our tables as God did in creating and providing it in His creation for us. We make it a goal to say of every meal served at our table, "It is good . . . this pleases me."

C. S. Lewis's book *Prince Caspian* (in the Chronicles of Narnia series) describes a fierce battle between the citizens of Narnia, led by the lion king Aslan (a Christ figure) and enemies called the Telmarines. After the Telmarines have been defeated, Aslan throws a great victory feast. In his long description of the meal, Lewis describes smells, sights, textures, tastes, and more. And he closes the feast narrative with an evocative sentence: "Thus Aslan feasted the Narnians."[8] He didn't just carelessly put out some food for the Narnians to eat. He lavishly "feasted" them, providing joy for all their senses.

Perhaps that is how we need to come to the table to eat. When we "break bread," we are symbolically breaking open all the creative glory of God expressed in His creation. We are not just consumers of food when we come to a lifegiving table; we are guests of the One who has feasted us with food and drink that please our God-created senses and make us all want to cry out with the psalmist, "O taste and see that the LORD is good" (Psalm 34:8, NASB).

Let's eat!

Share: We Open Hearts

Sharing food is an intimate human act. Sharing something from our plate at the dinner table, sharing a favorite entrée at a restaurant, sharing the last granola bar while lost in the woods—each is an interpersonal exchange involving a complex mix of feelings. Children know this instinctively. Just think of a cookie-possessed child asked to share with a cookie-deprived child. Whatever the response, it's easy to see the complex forces at work in the interaction.

Obviously, the lifegiving table model involves sharing of this kind. We pass around the serving dishes, and we make sure that each person is fed. But this intimate act of sharing is actually an invitation to a much more significant one—the sharing of ourselves. In the same way that we give and receive portions of food to feed our bodies, we can also give and receive portions of our hearts to feed our spirits—hopes, fears, joys, failures, loves, desires, wonders, faith, victories. We share food to stay alive physically. We share hearts to stay alive emotionally and spiritually.

But there is a catch. Opening our hands to share food comes much more naturally and easily to most of us than opening our hearts to share our spirits. We need quite a bit more encouragement, it seems, to share our hearts, even at the table. The gathering helps. The blessing helps. The act of sharing good food and drink definitely helps. All of these experiences can set the stage. But the kind of interpersonal sharing that is truly lifegiving usually requires something more.

Through four decades of life and ministry in all sorts of groups and all variety of tables, Sally and I have become very aware of how this dynamic works. Sharing spiritually from open hearts around a table almost never happens unless someone in the group is intentional and initiating. Someone has to lead the way, to begin the act of sharing and to prompt others to share as well.

This is similar but not really the same as initiating conversation with "icebreaker" questions. The point is not just to let people get acquainted by giving out random facts, but to encourage the sharing of stories. People, after all, are not static collections of information;

they are stories waiting and wanting to be told. Our stories are what define us and help to locate us within the greater story of what God is doing in us and in the world—the slow but steady progress of the Kingdom spreading across all creation. The more each person is able to see their life in that context, the more they will find hope, exercise faith, and risk love.

Henri Nouwen, the Dutch Catholic priest who gave his last years to working with people who had intellectual disabilities, suggests a helpful way of thinking about our stories that might be helpful in this regard. In his book *Life of the Beloved,*[9] he observes a pattern in his celebration of Communion that echoes in each person's spiritual journey. This pattern revolves around four simple words: *taken, blessed, broken,* and *given.*

This pattern can clearly be seen in four Gospel passages: the feeding of the five thousand (Luke 9:16), the feeding of the four thousand (Mark 8:6), the Last Supper in the Upper Room (Matthew 26:26), and Jesus' postresurrection meal with two disciples on the road to Emmaus (Luke 24:30). In each of the passages, Jesus' actions are described by variants of the same four verbs. For example, Matthew's account of the Last Supper says, "While they were eating, Jesus *took* some bread, and after a *blessing,* He *broke* it and *gave* it to the disciples" (NASB, emphasis added).

In those four words—*taken, blessed, broken, given*—Nouwen sees a summary of the life of Jesus, who was taken, blessed by God, broken on the cross, and given to the world. But he also sees in them a summary of the life of a believer, who is also taken (chosen by God), blessed (declared good), broken (to embrace pain), and given (to be spiritually fruitful).

Perhaps that is a good pattern for the kind of story sharing that makes an ordinary meal into a lifegiving table. As we gather, bless, and eat, we can also connect by sharing ways we each have been taken, blessed, broken, and given. It is this kind of sharing that brings spiritual life to a lifegiving table.

How can we initiate that kind of sharing? That depends on the personality and gifts of the initiator and the diners. One might feel comfortable simply steering conversation into deeper waters or modeling the process by telling a bit of her own story. Another might lead with a gesture—picking up a loaf of bread, breaking it, serving a piece to each person, and inviting reflections on how each person has experienced being taken, blessed, broken, or given that week. Yet another might bring a prepared list of questions or even devise a game. Young children might respond best to a brief, around-the-table telling of how God used them or blessed them in some way that day.

Whatever the initiator's approach, the goal is to facilitate the gentle but intentional sharing of spiritual life at your lifegiving table. When that happens, opened hearts will share the food of life with others at the table, because we are all taken, blessed, broken, and given.

Serve: We Give Ourselves

The final element in creating a lifegiving table is to serve. Each of the first four—gather, bless, eat, and share—starts with the table and then focuses on a corresponding truth about our inner spiritual life. This final one still focuses on the table and suggests an inner truth, but then it also points us outward, beyond the table, to the world.

Serving the world, in other words, begins with serving and being served in the home—and developing a right attitude about how and when to give and receive acts of loving service. And nowhere in the home, perhaps, is the concept of service more relevant than at the table.

The story of Jesus visiting His friends Martha and Mary in Bethany is a curious little interlude in Luke's Gospel (10:38-42). Twice in these five verses, Luke refers to Martha's chosen role with the Greek term for serving. Martha welcomes Jesus and His disciples into her home and throws herself into the task of preparing them a meal and serving it to them. She expects her younger sister, Mary, to pitch in and help with the work. But Mary chooses to sit at Jesus' feet instead and to listen to His teaching. Martha, distracted and anxious from the burden of serving alone, complains to Jesus and asks Him to tell her sister to come help her. But Jesus, to Martha's dismay, affirms Mary's choice and gently rebukes Martha for being focused on the wrong things.

Interestingly, John also records another visit by Jesus to that house.

"They made Him a supper there," we're told, "and Martha was serving" (12:2, NASB). Clearly, if meals were to happen in Martha's home, it was her service that made them happen. And what she did was important! Jesus never once indicated that Martha was wrong for working so hard to serve or even for wanting a little assistance. He never once intimated that her motivations were faulty. What He took issue with was her attitude and her priorities. Martha's focus that day was more on the task of serving and even on herself as server than on connecting with those she served.

What an important lesson for those of us who have taken on the important role of serving our families and others by planning meals, cooking food, and putting it on the table. Such loving service always requires a sacrifice of some kind. Yet the sacrifice is wasted if the attitude of serving is self-concerned and complaining in nature. *How* we serve, in other words, is just as important as *what* we serve.

The 1987 Danish film *Babette's Feast*, one of the Clarkson family's favorite movies, is a positive example of serving. Set in nineteenth-century Denmark, it tells the story of a woman who must flee her homeland of France. She becomes a servant in the home of two sisters in an austere religious community that rejects anything considered sensual. For fourteen years she serves the sisters their customary boiled fish and dry bread with the humble spirit of a servant. But then she wins ten thousand francs in the French lottery, and rather than using the money to return home, she spends the entire amount to prepare a sumptuous feast for the sisters and their friends. It turns out that Babette was a world-class French chef, and this is her chosen service to her benefactors.

Babette's Feast is a richly beautiful and profoundly intricate parable both of the glory of God that we experience through the foods He has made for us to enjoy and the glory of God revealed in the service required to subdue His creation into a lifegiving meal. As Babette replies when confronted with the fact that now she will always be poor, "An artist is never poor." Reviewer Jeffrey Overstreet observes: "[Babette] is revealing the glory of God to them through food. She shows them that food, like all of God's great gifts, is meant to be celebrated and shared with vigor, reverence, and gratitude."[10] And served with humility and sacrifice.

So how does this final goal of serving get expressed at your lifegiving table? That is for you to discover, not for us to define. The important quality to be gleaned from this final aspect of a lifegiving table is about attitudes, not just actions. The idea that "we give ourselves" in service begins not just with the acts of serving that create the table, but with the attitudes of humility that create the servant. The apostle Paul summarizes this beautifully: "Do nothing from selfishness or empty conceit, but with humility of mind regard one another as more important than yourselves" (Philippians 2:3, NASB).

And this applies to those who are served at table, not just those who serve. Our experience should never stop with just sitting around the table and enjoying the experience. The experience of being served at the table is meant to motivate our own acts of service—both at home and in the world.

For children, especially, the family table provides an ideal context for learning what service means. Little ones learn from having their own needs lovingly met, from observing the attitudes and actions of those who care for them, and from being specifically taught the skills of preparing food and nurturing relationships. A huge element of table discipleship is modeling and teaching what it means to be a servant.

There is no greater goal for the lifegiving table than for each of us to leave the table pondering how we might give ourselves in service to others, just as Jesus did: "For even the Son of Man did not come to be served, but to serve, and to give His life a ransom for many" (Mark 10:45, NASB).

The Table in You

This book is an exploration of some of the ways the Clarksons have attempted to create lifegiving tables for our family and friends, tables where we could disciple our children and encourage other disciples, one meal at a time. There are no prescriptive formulas here, only some descriptive examples drawn from our thirty-plus years of family "faith

by feasting" at hundreds of tables in eighteen homes on two conti-
nents and in four states. We've had lots of practice at figuring out what
worked best for us, and we want to share that.

Your table might not look like ours, however. The food you serve
and the dishes you use might be very different. Your family may have
different interests and different schedules. And that is fine. There is no
one right way to create a lifegiving table. But in order for your table to
be a lifegiving table, you must choose to do it. It will not happen by
accident. The more attention you give to the dynamics of gathering,
blessing, eating, sharing, and serving, the richer and more meaningful
your family table time will become. Combining faith and feasting will
become almost second nature.

And that, in the end, is the ultimate purpose of this book. The real
challenge is not just getting food on the table, but getting the table in
you. It is about giving you a vision and passion for the art of creating
and maintaining a lifegiving table—letting it influence how you think,
what stimulates your creativity, what delights your heart.

If the table is in you, then the table will be in your home.

If the table is in you, then your family will love gathering with you
to feast, and you'll grow disciples in the process.

CHAPTER 3

IF MY TABLE COULD TALK
Discovering a Vision for Table Discipleship

Love of beauty is taste. The creation of beauty is art.
RALPH WALDO EMERSON

Jesus replied, "I am the bread of life.
Whoever comes to me will never be hungry again.
Whoever believes in me will never be thirsty."
JOHN 6:35

Table-Discipleship Principle:

Creating an environment of beauty,
comfort, and acceptance cultivates hearts
that are open to your messages.

THE CHILL AIR OF a winter's day breathed on my face as I stepped out onto the sidewalk next to my contemporary stucco apartment building, which stood in striking contrast to the elaborate hundred-year-old buildings on either side. I glanced up at our fifth-floor window, still bare against a gray sky. Excitement bubbled up inside as I mentally reflected on the mission I was about to undertake.

Clay and I had just moved to Austria together to work for a year at the International Church of Vienna. Married just a year before, we were excited about our first international venture together and our new little apartment (three rooms plus a kitchen). But as was common in that part of Europe, the place was starkly empty—no curtains, no closets, no furniture, no kitchen cabinets, not much but empty rooms. (We considered ourselves blessed to have a kitchen sink and a small stove with an oven.) Our first few nights I had spread a small cloth over our steamer trunks and lit a candle; we had sat on the floor for our meals. So I had begun exploring secondhand shops, bargain basements, fabric stores, and the like to find what I needed make our empty rooms into a cozy home.

Today, armed with the Austrian equivalent of about a hundred dollars in my pocket, I was out to get a dining table—somehow I knew this would be the center of life in our home. I conjured up a picture of meals savored, cups of tea and coffee, hearty discussions, life-changing Bible studies, secrets shared—all over warm-tasty treats, comforting bowls of soup, satisfying slices of bread, melted butter and pungent cheese. I could just imagine the memories we would make over the table I would find. (At that point I couldn't even have imagined the parade of people who would eventually march through those humble rooms—diplomats from South Africa; refugees from Iran; an opera singer and her husband, who played in the Vienna Philharmonic; students eager for a home-cooked meal; many of our Austrian neighbors; and more.)

And so I boarded the squeaky tram, determined to bag my treasure but having no idea where I would find it. Two stops later I dismounted on foot and began perusing the shops along the street. A furniture store begged me to enter, but I left after five minutes, knowing I would need to set my sights lower. I couldn't afford even a chair in that lovely shop! I continued on my way, peering in every window shop and wandering down every crooked street, anxiously seeking the place where my table waited for me to find it.

Finally, after two hours of weary walking, my eyes lit on the dark, dusty window of a secondhand store. Through the glass I could see all sorts of knickknacks and odd pieces of furniture piled high throughout the crowded room. As I opened the creaky front door, bells jangled against the top of the door frame.

A stooped, wrinkled old man crept out from an even darker room at the back. *"Ja, bitte?"*

In my very limited German, I asked if I could look around to find some furniture to fill my apartment. He looked at me questioningly through thick, smudged spectacles and waved me in. My heart raced as I looked at stacks of chairs, bookshelves, dusty books, and miscellaneous items. Then, high up in a corner, I spotted four dark, round oval legs that looked like they were the base of some kind of a table.

"Was ist das?" I asked, hoping he would understand.

He then brought the legs down, went to the back room once again, and brought out a stained, mildly scarred tabletop to fit on top of the base. There it was! I just knew this could be my table.

"Wieviel kostet das?" ("How much does that cost?") I asked, hoping for the best. It was the equivalent of fifty dollars. I was ecstatic. Maybe I could even afford some chairs. I looked up and down the aisles between piles of stacked items. And there on top of each other, at the far end of the wall, were two charming carved-wood chairs, the seats covered in bronze vinyl that looked like leather. How much, I asked again. Only thirty-five dollars—again, in my budget. How surprised Clay would be to see that we could actually sit down in real chairs to eat dinner. And we could do it that very evening. I had a friend who had promised to help me pile my finds into her small station wagon.

I used my last fifteen dollars on the way home to buy one yard of colorful fabric, a candle, and a small bunch of flowers from the lady at the street market near my apartment. Looking back, I wonder if these small purchases, made in the spirit of great adventure and expectation, brought me more pleasure than all of my more expensive purchases in the years since.

Once home with my treasures, I worked hard to beautify that scarred old table. I poured lemon oil on its top and gently polished every inch of the surface. Gently folding my new piece of cloth as a centerpiece, I found a tiny vase from my suitcase and arranged what would be the first flowers and candles to welcome weary guests to my feasts.

When Clay and I sat at our very own table that evening, I was proud to have provided something so essential to the many memories we would make.

That same table has been moved seventeen times since then, and has anchored many different rooms. In our Colorado mountain home, it served as a chess table near the living room window. When we lived in Tennessee, it occupied a corner of an enclosed porch overlooking fields of trees and thousands of daffodils. Today, in another Colorado home, it sits in our little kitchen nook.

So much of our shared lives have happened around that old piece of wood. Our table has lived the history of Clarksons through every season, every move. In fact, I'm sitting at it now, waiting for the kettle to whistle so I can enjoy a cup of tea.

It's not the only table in our house, of course. There's also the big table in the dining room, which I saved for many years to buy. It seats eighteen when fully extended. And there's always room for one more, even if we need to drag in the folding chairs. This table, purchased many years ago now, has witnessed countless birthday celebrations and long evenings of sharing hearts at other family occasions.

Years ago, while I was rummaging through an antique mall in Texas, an old tea cart seemed to speak my name. The flaps lift up to make it more than a cart—a small table. When I open the tiny leaves, I have room for two place settings, a tiny vase of flowers, and a small candle. I keep it between two overstuffed chairs in my den for a private time with one other person. (Sometimes tables need to be small, to invite one-on-one confidences.)

Our coffee table has held countless bowls of popcorn and cups of hot cocoa. The coasters on our end tables invite confidences over warm drinks. Bedside tables in our rooms often hold cookies and tea during a private time. So do the little tables beside our rockers on the porch.

If my table—my tables!—could talk, I wonder what tales they would tell.

A Story of Vision and Commitment

Souls are shaped in the common moments of life, the daily stuff of memories.

If my table could talk, I know it would tell of moments like those— toddlers happily munching on bits of food and Cheerios scattered over plastic place mats. Birthday breakfasts with cinnamon rolls, mugs of hot tea, and morning presents companioned by words of love and appreciation. Warm soup and stories shared on cold winter nights. Sunday afternoon teatimes with James Herriott's animal stories read dramatically. Countless lively discussions about morality and worldview as we filled up growing teenage bodies with satisfying food.

But souls grow by season as well. As we celebrate the passage of time by establishing and commemorating joyful traditions, honoring milestones (however small), cultivating a taste for greatness through the stories shared, books read, memories made, and faith lived out, we also make a path for growth and development.

Godly legacies are built, in other words, when we bring the life of Christ to the table through the grace of loving relationships and intimacy shared moment by moment. This is the essence of table discipleship. But doing it well requires both vision and commitment.

What is my vision for my lifegiving table? I picture that I am nourishing souls and spirits with both physical food and the everlasting food of the Word of God. I am providing grace and peace through gently accepting whoever joins us at the table. I am speaking hope forward by articulating my confidence in God's love, faithfulness, and kindness for each person. I am establishing a spirit of graciousness by welcoming all who come as guests of the loving Host who serves all and makes us all whole.

I picture that I can be an instrument through which God brings life, beauty, and redemption to the limitations of my marriage and my family—because, in His spirit, I am filled with the life that always brings light to the dark places and redemption to the broken places.

Jesus said, "I am the bread of life. Whoever comes to me will never be hungry again. Whoever believes in me will never be thirsty" (John 6:35). And this knowledge, too, informs my vision for table discipleship.

As I serve those around my table, am I offering them the real Bread of Life that will satisfy their souls—my Jesus?

Am I satisfying the thirst they feel for a life that is meaningful in light of knowing their Creator?

Am I willing to give and even sacrifice until my home and table reflect the elegance of my Designer, the artistry of His hand, the loveliness of His presence?

These questions fuel my vision for the mission of table-based discipleship.

If my tables could talk, I think they would remind me that I have an important work, a strategic task to engage my heart. They would remind me that I can persevere in this work by His tender encouragement and my own commitment to celebrate each and every day, each person, each interruption, each mundane (or not so mundane) moment as He has given it to me.

Yet as the hostess of such a table, I have to prepare my heart to generously give in a way that brings life to the souls of others. Making my heart ready to serve when I sit down requires a daily choice of mind, heart, and commitment. The cultivation of the life of Christ at table doesn't just happen. It comes through planning and intentionality.

A Story of Comfort and Restoration

"Mama, I think I finally understand what it means to have a broken heart," one of my children whispered so no one else would hear.

That evening we sequestered ourselves in a private room over candlelight and a light meal. Sympathy was the need of the moment—

compassion and a word of love and understanding given as we sipped soup and munched on crusty bread together.

Relationship is at the heart of all influence, good and bad. When people feel loved and accepted, affirmed and believed in, they are more willing to receive the messages we feel are important to share.

The lifegiving table isn't really about furniture, after all. It's about making our homes centers of nourishing comfort and acceptance, places where we invite others to come, just as they are, and share life with us. It's about being willing to see all who come to our tables through the lens of how we might serve them.

Each person, like my old table, has a history and some scars and blemishes—physical, emotional, psychological. (Some of us have many!) But just as my table could be cleaned up and beautified with lemon oil, elbow grease, and a couple of fresh flowers, each life can be improved with a listening ear and a cup of tea.

That's not to say that what I offer at my table can cure all human brokenness. How well I know that isn't true! It is God who heals. He does it in His own time, in His own way. Yet He does work through us, through our lifegiving tables, to bring His redemptive presence into others' lives—to encourage, inspire, comfort, teach, love, and affirm.

And believe me, being an agent of healing isn't always easy, especially when the ones in need are the people I love best in all the world, these precious ones who create constant demands on my energy, my time, my very life.

One of my friends recently commented that she thinks everyone is either in a crisis, leaving a crisis, or entering into a crisis. In the landscape of contemporary culture, this does seem to be true for many. Certainly for our family, there is rarely a moment when one or more of us is not going through some difficulty, life challenge, illness, or broken relationship.

One of the issues that have brought tears and deep discouragement to my young-adult children is the loneliness they feel at times in a world that seems to be at odds with the foundations of their faith, their strong sense of virtue and idealistic morality. Holding fast to godly foundations as the barrage of spiritual battle rages around them takes its toll. But knowing they can come home for a dose of comfort (and comfort food) helps them keep fighting—or so they have told me.

I love that my grown children still have need of my lifegiving table. I have to admit, however, that this dynamic of serving and giving out can take a physical and emotional toll on me. Preparing my heart to be an agent of God's comfort and peace requires a daily commitment to lay aside my needs in order to be Christ's mercy and love to those He interrupts my own life with on a daily basis. Almost always, however, I am restored and blessed in the process—at least eventually. As I have practiced these values over the years, my serving muscle has grown stronger and my capacity to keep going has grown more resilient.

Not long ago, after ushering one grown child to the airport to fly back home to a faraway city, I found myself especially depleted. We had spent a lot of time alone together on this visit. (Clay was attending a conference in another state.) Candlelight, a favorite meal (spaghetti pie), and gentle music had set the stage for hour after endless hour of talking and opening deep-heart issues, unearthing hidden pain and scars from many difficult years.

And all that table time had clearly helped. By the time we reached the airport, the change in heart of this adult was palpable—heart restored, mind strengthened with truth, soul ready to engage once again in the battle of life. Waves of weary relief floated over my body and soul as I drove the silent hour back from the airport. Deeply gratified, I was also ready for a break.

But even then I knew that a break was not forthcoming—because another child was due to visit just two days later. I spent those days restocking the cupboards with favorite foods (different from the favorites of the previous child) and making the expected chocolate chip cookies. Then I lit the candles again and prepared to extend a heartfelt welcome.

Same scenario, different child. Yet home was the place where each had come to refuel in order to face the arduous clashes of contemporary life. The next afternoon, as the winter shadows crept in slowly, I served a warm apple crisp with cream and sat down next to this other battle-worn child. Tears spilled from the red-lidded eyes and shoulders sagged as the story of the recent few months poured out.

Another cup of tea, a string of fairy lights switched on to change the ambience, and gradually I saw those shoulders relax, their burden laid down. The easy flow of intimate conversation between us came from hundreds of such hours invested over many years. Breathing slowed, facial expression eased as though a magic wand was rubbing out each wrinkle of worry. My own weariness faded, and the shadows seemed to disappear from the room as God's light invaded both the atmosphere and our hearts.

Our coffee table, tea table, and dining table have each witnessed thousands of such transformative moments—so much restoration in a simple bowl of soup, a crust of bread, a fragrant dessert warm from the oven, one more cup of hot brew combined with acceptance and lifegiving words.

If my tables could talk, that's another part of the story they would tell—the power of simple fare, candlelight, and the offer of self as an agent of God's comfort and healing.

A Story of Beauty

Living most of my life within sight of some part of the Rocky Mountains has established a lifelong love of the high mountain terrain. Spring wildflowers begin with blues and purples, move to reds and whites as summer heats up, and finally end in fall with a flourish of yellows and golds. Stars sparkling in the night sky above our home at 7,300 feet in altitude call us to linger long in the evenings, stretched out on blankets, cuddling in the cool night air, and listening quietly to God's voice speaking to us in the overwhelming velvet sky. Shimmering crystal snow blankets our pines and wild grasses in the winter, reminding us of the purity and holiness of our God and His transcendent loveliness.

Even as God's beauty calls out to us in what He has created, beauty in our homes lifts the spirits of all who live or visit there. There is great joy in creating something for the table that pleases the eyes, delights the creative juices, and satisfies our created longing for aesthetic pleasure.

Why does beauty matter? Because our Creator cared enough to fill His world with color, form, design, sound, and tastes that would reflect a part of His personality as well as His skill as an artist—and because He created us humans both to respond to that beauty with pleasure and to find joy in our own creations. When we strive to bring beauty into our lives and our homes, we reflect the nature of the One who made us. Beauty and creativity are the melodies that wrap around our souls and sing to us of His amazing, infinite life.

That first table of mine wasn't necessarily beautiful in itself, but it became a place where beauty and life were displayed and celebrated. Even now, every changing season, I ponder how to make it a new place of life and memory, considering how I will adorn it to reflect color, tradition, meaning, and the life of the One in our midst. What we bring to the table will constitute its glory.

Years ago I was wandering through an open-air market in Oxford, England, and found a secondhand antique stall. An eighteen-inch-tall brass vase rounded with a copper ring was calling my name. I bought the old beauty for a mere seven dollars. Today it graces my big coffee table with a spray of burgundy roses (on sale at my grocery store this time of year). At other times it holds crimson carnations or white snowdrops.

At least four fresh pine wreaths garnish four tables throughout my home every December, some decked with dried red flowers, blue juniper berries, or pinecones picked from my yard to add a tiny bit of color. Candles in a variety of glass jars adorn all my rooms all the time because I personally love the flickering light. And when I light them at dinnertime, it calls all who sit at table to a sort of announcement that we are about to celebrate life together.

A Story of Who We Are

Personality, preferences, and appetite for life are the places we have opportunity to exercise our own imprint on the color and design of the

Creator reflected uniquely through us. Being made in the image of our creative God grants us agency and freedom to decide how we will craft our tables and our homes into places of art.

Sprinkled throughout my home and on my tables are objects that hold special meaning for me, that reflect a promise, a truth, a message of hope, or a touch of whimsy.

Birds, for example, appear throughout my house—glass birds, ceramic birds, fabric birds, pictures of birds—because they remind me of God's care for even the smallest creature. God reminded me early in life that "not a single sparrow can fall to the ground without your Father knowing it" (Matthew 10:29). And so I realized that God saw me as well—that He was with me at all times.

Candles and those strings of white fairy lights gleam warmly throughout my home and on my table to remind us that He is the light coming into our darkness every day.

Music plays from early morning to late evening as an offering of my grateful heart, reminding me to worship Him who is King over all of my days, even the dark ones.

Framed calligraphy of our favorite verses line the walls of our home, collected one at a time on anniversaries. Etchings and small paintings, obtained here and there in places we have lived and visited, provide personal reflections of the many cultures that have shaped us.

Even the dishes used to set our tables have special meaning—the delicate bone china cups and mugs that hold our tea, collected in thrift shops; the crystal milk jug and sugar bowl, bought in Poland and carefully guarded through the years; the chipped but cherished Austrian Gmundner Keramik pottery we always use for birthdays, purchased at the "seconds" tables; our rose-and-butterfly bedecked "best china" inherited from a grandmother. Even our everyday dishes have been carefully chosen to lend beauty as well as practicality to even the most mundane meals.

And then, of course, there is the food—the favorite meals and treats we have shared so often among ourselves and served to others. A delicious, fragrant chicken soup or vegetable-rich minestrone. Tender, fragrant muffins and breads. Special desserts that remind us of the places we have lived together and all the moments we have shared—English scones, Austrian cookies, all-American pizza. We've tweaked the recipes over time until they fit our tastes and our appetites. They, too, tell the story of us.

Our home reflects, in many ways, our family history through thirty-five years of living all over the United States and in other parts of the world, so if our tables could talk they might speak in several different languages and accents. Altogether, they would tell a story that is uniquely Clarkson.

The same could be said of every home and apartment, every table big and small—including yours. The more of *you* that goes into your surroundings—the more they reflect your personal taste and experience—the livelier and more lifegiving both your home and table will be.

A Story of Acceptance and Individual Attention

Now, in my midsixties, with children scattered over the world seeking their own purposes and ways in life, I love to revisit cherished memories we made around our tables.

Today I'm remembering the morning when Joy and I, in our jammies and crazy bed hair, sat close together on a couch, drinking hot tea from real china cups, munching buttered toast, and talking. We looked at articles together in a magazine we both loved, admired a book she had found at a secondhand bookstore, and felt totally at ease in the comfort of our safe and close friendship. Sipping our hot liquid gold, with candles lit, she and I giggled uncontrollably and shared our thoughts and ideas and dreams for almost an hour.

She found my computer and played me a favorite song that had special meaning for her, one she'd listened to at midnight the night before. She shared her devotional book with me since I couldn't find mine, and her inspiring reflections about a passage in Matthew caught my heart.

My sixty-plus-year-old self has learned to love the worlds of my children, and these times have given me a window to their hearts. I do not expect them to conform to me. I let them be who they are at this season of life, and I have adjusted my own expectations to enjoy and really delight in who they are at every stage. This has brought me much joy. But I had to give up a little of my selfish self to enter their world. (God had to give up something, too, when He became Jesus.)

I also had to adjust the way I approached each child to account for his or her individual needs. I had to study them all and observe carefully to find out what was in their heart—their individual personalities and temperaments, what spoke love to them, what put them off and what drew them near, and how to fill their heart's cup so that I could reach their heart with a love for Jesus. Mentoring and passing on faith is not about curriculum, church attendance, rules, or indoctrination, but always about reaching the heart.

Nathan was the one who taught me this lesson most powerfully. Even as a little tyke, my Nathan rarely sat still for long. He always had something to say and didn't mind creating conflict through his opinions. Sarah and Joel had been quieter, more compliant, and I had assumed that was because I was such a great mother! But clearly this child needed a completely different kind of mothering, and often I felt at a loss about how to do it. Studying Nathan's personality in order to understand how to reach him became one of my goals.

One night Clay took the older two to church and left five-year-old Nathan home with me because he had a cold. Exhausted from a busy day, I sat wearily in an overstuffed chair and said, "Hey, you want to climb into the chair with me?" He climbed up, snuggled in, and then began to talk . . . and talk. That child talked for almost an hour without stopping. All I had to do was keep saying, "Really?" or "Oh!" or "How funny!" When he was finally talked out, he said, "Love you, Mama," jumped out of the chair, and ran off to play happily.

I was pondering this event—my mystery child sitting still for so long and talking and talking and talking. Then suddenly it dawned on me: *He is an extrovert, and he needs people. He wants to talk and be heard. He doesn't want to be quiet or to compete for my attention amid a constant crowd of people.*

So I learned that the way to Nathan's heart was to acknowledge him and to *listen*—to his dreams, his thoughts, his ideas, his feelings. As long as I made time to do that, he would listen to me, too, and try to obey. If I neglected this deep need of his, I would see the consequences in his behavior.

The same was true, in a different sense, for Joy. As the baby of a rambunctious family, she sometimes felt lost in the crowd, and her response was to get louder, perform, call attention to herself. What she needed more than anything was personal, alone, focused time with me. If I went to her room or made a special teatime in my room just for her, she would settle down, and her heart would be open. She and Nathan were my extroverts who would not be ignored.

Sarah, as the oldest girl, had followed after me her whole life and enjoyed a "best friend" role in my life almost from the beginning. But I could always tell she needed some private time with me when she grew a little withdrawn and sensitive. Her heart melted when I quietly invited her into my room for a private teatime, to talk and read *Victoria* magazines together on Sunday afternoons. Alone time was her love language.

Now, Joel showed his need for me by withdrawing, becoming grumpy or agitated. He was rarely a "misbehaver." But if I arranged a quiet time for just the two of us, he would bubble over talking to me. He's an introvert, just like Sarah. Neither of those two would compete openly with the others for heart time, but I had to assume they needed it.

I had to learn to do the same with my husband, too, especially when our children were young. Another extreme introvert, he needed to know he wasn't competing with the kids, and we both needed private time to talk and share our hearts. Sharing tea and an oatmeal cookie alone in our bedroom helped. A date night could be a godsend. But if I failed to make this a priority, it would never happen, and our relationship would suffer and cool down, leaving me feeling alone. Making time to be just with him changed everything.

And that's not to mention time for friends and those I felt called to mentor. These also needed my attention, and I needed theirs. And so I practiced figuring out what each needed by the personality they exhibited and how to fit everyone in with short amounts of time.

And believe me, none of this was easy! Educating and training four children, traveling with Clay, and maintaining my speaking, writing, podcasting, and blogging career meant that all of my days were beyond busy. Frankly, I do not ever remember an "easy" season in our lives together. Often illness, company, outside activities, and commitments got in the way of living a quiet life. And often I felt stretched thin to the point of breaking.

But observing Jesus' influence on His disciples helped me get this all in perspective. I noted the way He spent time personally with them away from the crowds, the way He affirmed the unique personality of each disciple (John, the one who defined himself by being loved; Peter, the one He called "rock"; Thomas, the fiercely loyal but skeptical one). I realized that everyone needs to be treated according to his or her unique, God-given personality and needs.

So I began to make time alone with each child, with Clay, and with friends. When I planned my week, I would build in little "dates" when we could connect. I would also look for opportunities tucked in here and there among the busy hours—even with a pat on the head, a surprise kiss on the cheek, a tiny flurry of a back rub—to say, "I see you. I value you."

The habit of taking short fifteen-minute breaks through my busy days has provided sweet memories and a bit of restoration for me as well as for children and friends who, as a result, do not feel neglected. And almost always, these breaks were table based. My freezer always held balls of cookie dough and frozen muffins (easy to pop in the oven for a quick treat). My refrigerator and pantry were perpetually stocked with fruit, nuts, and cheese chunks. So when my radar told me someone was not doing well or was angry or having problems, I would find time for a quick, private, fifteen-minute "teatime" just to talk and take that person's emotional temperature.

When my older kids reached their teen years, because I had invested that "me" time with them, I was always the go-to person for them when they had secrets, fears, or problems. I learned to plan times for this as well. I would take each boy out by himself for breakfast every week or two, just to keep the channels of conversation going. For Sarah it was a Saturday morning walk and coffee at a French café—we did that weekly for almost eight years! And Joy and I enjoyed breakfast together in her room or mine, away from all the teens, at least once a week.

If my tables could talk, they would tell so many tales of confidences shared, of relationships nourished because they are a priority.

In the mundane moments and through the revolving seasons, the lifegiving table remains a constant—but only if we hold to the vision that each moment is packed with potential for life-changing conversations and relationships. This vision in turn will shape the vision of those who come to us for their whole lives.

And now I must be off to my day. The teakettle is whistling and calling my name. For this mundane and sacred moment I will celebrate a one-woman teatime and reflect on all the sweet memories made at my tables with those who have now become my cherished best friends.

And I'll give thanks for the blessing and the opportunity of the lifegiving table.

Something to Ponder

John 6:35

> Jesus replied, "I am the bread of life. Whoever comes to me will never be hungry again. Whoever believes in me will never be thirsty."

Jesus was speaking not only of what we need to sustain our bodies (bread), but also of what is necessary to sustain our spirits. When we serve others at our table and nourish relationships, we are also serving up Jesus, the Bread of Life.

- Why do you think Jesus used these eating and drinking pictures for the life He offers those who come to Him?

- How would the people hearing this have understood these words?

- What does this statement say to you about how you approach discipleship in your home?

Proverbs 9:2-5, NASB

[Wisdom] has prepared her food, she has mixed her wine;
She has also set her table;
She has sent out her maidens, she calls
From the tops of the heights of the city:
"Whoever is naive, let him turn in here!"
To him who lacks understanding she says,
"Come, eat of my food
And drink of the wine I have mixed."

These verses show a picture of a wise woman—wisdom personified—preparing her food and table.

- Whom, according to these verses, does the wise woman invite into her home to eat with her? Why do you think she specifically invites these people?

- What does she do to set a welcoming environment? How do these verses depict her lifegiving table?

- What words show her intention to use her table as a place to teach? How do her preparations make it more likely that her teaching will be effective?

Something to Try

- Write down three conversation starters that would draw your children or friends into an engaging discussion at your table.

- What are some practical ways you could set the tone of acceptance and encouragement so all at table will feel listened to and understood?

Recipes to Warm Your Table and Your Hearts

✖ The Clarkson Kids' Favorite Potpie Chicken Soup

Our family has lived either in Europe or the mountains of Colorado for most of our lives together, which means we have shared many a cold, dark winter evening. Consequently, when I ask what someone wants for dinner, often the answer will be soup and bread. This chicken soup is the favorite (with White Christmas Soup running a close second), so I had to share it with you! Be sure you take the time to linger over the luscious warmth.

2 cups diced red or russet potatoes

3 cups (12-ounce bag) frozen peas and carrots (If you can't find this frozen mix, you can substitute 1½ cups each frozen peas and fresh carrots. Or you can use a bag of frozen mixed vegetables, but check the ingredients—my family won't eat the kind with lima beans!)

4 cups water (You can add more later if needed.)

2 tablespoons olive oil or butter

1–2 teaspoons minced garlic or garlic paste

1 medium to large onion, chopped (We love lots of onion in almost everything.)

1 tablespoon dried thyme, parsley, and rosemary combined or to taste. (I like a lot, especially thyme. If you want to use fresh herbs, triple this amount.)

2–4 cups diced cooked chicken breast

2 tablespoons butter

1½ teaspoons condensed chicken bouillon or base (This is a kind of concentrated paste that comes in jars or plastic containers. I buy mine at health food markets or Sam's Club, but you can also find it in many grocery stores. If you use the dry powder, you'll need to adjust the amount to taste. Try to avoid the kind with MSG.)

⅓ cup unbleached all-purpose flour

2 cups milk

½ cup wine, optional (For this soup I usually use a white wine
     such as Riesling.)

1 teaspoon or more salt (I use sea salt of different varieties.)

½ teaspoon pepper

Sour cream and chives or fresh herbs to garnish, optional

Boil the potatoes and frozen veggies in the water until cooked
through, about 20–30 minutes. (I use a pressure cooker for
4–5 minutes and veggies and potatoes are done.) While veggies are
cooking, heat 2 tablespoons olive oil or butter in another pan; sauté
garlic, onion, and herbs until onion is translucent. Add onion mixture
and chicken to pot with the veggies and let soup simmer on low while
you make the sauce.

For the sauce, melt 2 tablespoons butter in another pan. Stir
in chicken bouillon. Whisk in flour and stir mixture constantly
over medium heat until all the lumps have disappeared. Add milk
and cook until mixture is thickened, then add the wine (if using).
Slowly add milk mixture to soup, stirring as it thickens. Taste and
season with salt and pepper as needed. If desired, add a dollop of
sour cream and a sprinkle of chives or herbs. We like to serve this
soup with croutons sprinkled on top and with toast and applesauce
on the side.

This is a really simple recipe that can be adjusted many ways.
For instance, you could use brown rice or noodles instead of
potatoes, fresh veggies or a different mix of frozen ones, or even
omit the milk mixture and just put the bouillon directly into the
soup. I use whatever I have on hand and whatever sounds good at
the time.

Serves 6–8, depending on size of serving.

✳ Sarahstrone

Another recipe I like to make when I'm in a hurry—one that seems to fill up the hungriest of my family—is a soup Sarah invented years ago on the spur of the moment. This was a great summer treat for us and definitely pleasing to my boys! Cornbread or muffins are a great addition to this satisfying meal.

2 links turkey sausage, sliced thin (We usually buy organic Italian sausages that are about the size of hot dogs and keep them in the freezer until needed. If you prefer smoked sausage or kielbasa, you'll need about 7–8 inches.)

1 onion, chopped

1 heaping teaspoon minced garlic or garlic paste

1–2 tablespoons olive oil

1 29-ounce can diced tomatoes

1 full can or a little more of water (Less water will yield a stronger tomato flavor.)

2–3 zucchini, thinly sliced

1 15-ounce can navy beans, drained and rinsed (We have also used other beans, such as pinto.)

1–2 teaspoons salt, to taste

1 heaping tablespoon dried Italian seasoning

Grated Parmesan cheese and sour cream to garnish

Sauté sausage, onions, and garlic in olive oil in a large soup pan until onions are soft and sausage is slightly browned. Add the tomatoes, water, and zucchini and simmer 20–30 minutes until zucchini is soft. Add beans, salt, and Italian seasoning. Simmer at least 15 minutes more. (I think it tastes better if you just leave it on to simmer while you are doing other things—the flavors blend together better.) When ready to serve, spoon soup into dishes. Sprinkle each serving with grated Parmesan cheese, add a small dollop of sour cream, and enjoy.

Serves 6–8, depending on size of serving.

CHAPTER 4

THIS IS WHO WE ARE
Shaping a Family Culture around the Table

❈

*That's something I've noticed about food: whenever there's a crisis
if you can get people to eating normally things get better.*

MADELEINE L'ENGLE

*They were continually devoting themselves to the apostles' teaching
and to fellowship, to the breaking of bread and to prayer.*

ACTS 2:42, NASB

Table-Discipleship Principle:
Practicing the rhythms of life regularly
with your loved ones creates a secure
feeling of belonging—of being welcomed
and able to share convictions and faith
with a community where one belongs.

Traveling is a sort of hobby for me and for our family. It is also part of our livelihood and our mission. Having our books published in numerous languages and managing a small-group ministry with an international focus keep us crossing borders and oceans on a regular basis. Every year I find myself on at least two international ministry trips. And that doesn't even include the trips to visit our children who live overseas.

However, when I have the rare privilege of *choosing* where to travel, using frequent flier miles saved from multiple mission trips, I go back to Austria. I lived there for almost seven years at a formative time of life, and my time there instilled a love for many things Austrian. I think of it as a sort of second home—a place that comforts me and soothes my soul. And one reason I love it is the way it has held on to its culture and values.

When I travel in many other countries, especially the big cities, I see signs of American culture all around me. McDonald's, Starbucks, KFC, Subway, and Apple Stores seem to be everywhere. Globalization is evident in that many of the products I see or use in America are now available in countries all over the world.

But not as much in Austria—especially not in Vienna. Although American influence is not completely absent there, Austria's distinct, centuries-old culture still prevails, particularly in Vienna's downtown first district and in the Austrian Alps.

Uniquely Austrian aesthetics seem to fill every corner: hearts carved on wood in homes and on doorways, women often wearing the colorful mountain costumes called dirndls, mountain chalets flanked by piles of wood for the wood-burning fireplaces and stoves, cobblestone streets lined with white stucco homes. Restaurants appointed with pristine white tablecloths and flowers in tiny vases appear in many neighborhoods, serving strong Austrian coffee in real porcelain cups, accompanied by a small glass of water. Delectable pastries abound, especially in the afternoons when most people pause for their daily *jause*—afternoon snack time with tea or coffee. All of these are evidence of a beautiful culture that has not changed for decades.

In Austria, most places of commerce operate with efficient, predictable order. The streets are clean. Service is dependably good. Beauty and graciousness are palpable. These robust, durable values provide a strong balm to my soul. I love that the Austrian culture has retained much of its unique character. Perhaps this is where I picked up some of my values and the habits that grace my table every day.

Not Conformed

Romans 12:2 admonishes us, "Do not be conformed to this world, but be transformed by the renewing of your mind, so that you may prove what the will of God is, that which is good and acceptable and perfect" (NASB).

I have pondered many times what it means to be transformed, changed, reshaped as an antidote to being conformed to the world. To be transformed means to become something other, to be changed into something different. And the idea of being transformed in order *not* to be conformed to the world applies so clearly to family culture.

The more we can do to instill a sense of "This is who we are," "This is why we believe," "This is what we stand for," the better chance we and our children will have of resisting the urge to conform to the world. A family culture that is distinct and grace-giving has the power to both change and protect us.

It won't happen by accident, however. Establishing and shaping a family culture requires intentionality, thoughtful planning, commitment, and sacrifice. But the result can be truly transformative.

Even as Austria has resisted being shaped by contemporary global culture because its own national culture is so strong and lively, so must we construct a strong, definitive, faith-giving, biblical family culture. Then those in our home will be better able to resist the compromising draw of the world because they will have been shaped and changed by the place where they spend the majority of their days. If they grow up steeped in Scripture and truth, beautiful and lifegiving practices, and the sacrificial example of love at home, chances are they will carry these virtues with them. In the absence of such foundational shaping, they will by default go the way of the world.

The culture of the world around us—the music, movies, moral values (or lack thereof)—call out to us and our children every day. It's hard to miss the messages: devaluation of family and home, sexual permissiveness, materialism, self-centered (as opposed to God-centered) philosophies, the temptation to follow whatever "feels good." Teenagers, especially, are bombarded by the world's cultural messages at a time when they are learning to own their lives and values and put their convictions in order. The cultural impact of smartphones and social media and the lure of the Internet add magnetism to the cultural values that would draw the hearts of both teens and adults away from the spiritual and moral underpinnings of home and family and church.

Let me make clear that our family members are all computer/smartphone users and are engaged online with our jobs and education every day. However, we've learned that we must intentionally set apart "device-free" times in our schedules every day in order to build the strong ties that are necessary to sharing ideals and building relationships. More important, we've worked hard to cultivate a home culture that is strong enough and attractive enough to counter the world's voices.

We must recognize that children, teens, and adults of every age have a natural, God-given desire to have friends and to belong. It is normal and good for all of us to be part of a community where we have a specific role to play, a way to contribute, where we feel needed and valued. This felt need is especially strong in children and teens.

When this longing is met within a home culture—where kids feel happy, loved, secure, needed, and valued—then this culture will have the greatest influence on the values those kids develop. Being involved in traditions and activities that engage their imagination better, shape their souls more powerfully, and provide more true satisfaction than that of the world culture will hopefully cause them to adopt the values of that home culture. Developing intimate, personal, defining relationships that say, "I love you. I know you. I validate you. I am listening to you, and I care for your thoughts and dreams" makes all the difference.

If we desire a different sort of leadership and morality that contrasts to the world around us and holds its own against the bombardment of outside voices, then it must be defined, practiced, and cultivated daily, from the early years of life. That is the lesson I learned in Austria. Even as the Austrian culture has maintained most of its cultural values and strength against the onslaught of many modern influences, so our children can retain our family cultures if we make our influence stronger than the world's influence.

Building a Family Culture through the Rhythms of Life

A family culture is created by nurturing habits, values, and traditions over time, by repetition. It develops through the rhythms of life—the practices and experiences, sights and sounds we repeat daily and weekly, monthly or yearly, or on special occasions until they became part of who we are as a family. Below are just a few that came to define the Clarksons. (Many of these are explained in more detail in a book that Sarah and I wrote together, *The Lifegiving Home*.)[1]

- family devotions every morning
- daily hot breakfasts with homemade bread and music
- a home-cooked dinner together by candlelight each evening (with television and phones banned from the table)
- book baskets and piles of magazines everywhere—with regular read-aloud sessions
- loud discussions on every possible topic nearly every day
- back scratches and verbalized blessings as a going-to-sleep ritual
- afternoon breaks with tea, coffee, or hot chocolate and a snack after the schoolwork or classes during the day
- all kinds of friends personally greeted and intentionally welcomed when coming through our doors
- Sunday morning feasts (see chapter 6)
- Saturday-night pizza and a movie every week (see chapter 7)
- game nights and treasure hunts at least monthly
- birthday breakfasts with cinnamon rolls and family affirmations (see chapter 9)
- a "Shepherds' Meal" on Christmas Eve (see chapter 12)

- a "friends and strangers" Thanksgiving feast
- fireworks, grilling out, and lake gatherings on the Fourth of July
- Family Day in August (see chapter 11)
- daily walks together during the warm seasons (when the snow isn't too deep)
- every-month-no-matter-what dinners with a special group of friends
- whole-family support for recitals, speech tournaments, awards ceremonies, sports activities
- a "rite of passage" teen dinner for each child at age thirteen
- a moving-to-adulthood ceremony and blessing for each one at age sixteen
- "girls' club" (Mom, Sarah, Joy) and "boys' night out" (Clay, Joel, Nathan) each week
- working side by side in national conferences for twenty-one years as a family project

And yes, I know it's a long list—but that's part of the point! We always had so much fun and activity going on in our home and so many invisible threads from our hearts to our children's that the pull of home and the deep connections and friendships we shared caused them to look to home for comfort, acceptance, and fulfillment.

Family culture is built from the time children are born (or adopted) into the home—or even before. It takes years (and some trial and error) to find the right mix. Some rhythms are best practiced when children are young. Other traditions come into play when teens are busy with life and activities and work and may be a challenge to work into the schedule, but they still make a powerful impact. But all help build strong roots, positive emotional expectations, and stable foundations.

This kind of culture takes a lot of work, the investment of time and emotional care, and all the creativity we can muster. It is a work of life art for the one who would weave beauty, love, and a grace-giving atmosphere into the very fiber of home, so that every day brings life to the hearts, minds, and souls of all who live there.

And the necessity of a strong family culture doesn't stop once the kids foray out into the world. If anything, it becomes more important. I certainly see this in my own children. Finding friends with similar values, strong faith, and compatible souls has been challenging for all of them, and all of them at times have wrestled with deep loneliness. Yet now we see them practicing their own relational rhythms—many of them the same as what we practiced at home—in other parts of the world with their roommates, spouse, and friends.

On top of that, they still have us—and they have each other! Because their relationships were shaped over thousands of meals together, over the same books and music and films, through hours of intense discussion and enthusiastic play, they have a lot in common and a deep love for one another. So they return home, to deep roots, whenever they can just to experience that kind of fellowship once again. The table that shaped their lives is now the table that renews and refreshes them when they are able to come home.

Creating family culture is so important in our increasingly busy and overcommitted society. A sense of isolation and a strong desire for community are both common threads on the Internet, yet personal relationships seem elusive for so many. People search for meaning and validation through frenzied lifestyles but still feel lost in a sea of relative meaninglessness. An intentionally developed family culture can provide a powerful alternative.

And family culture doesn't have to be just for families! When I was a single adult, my friends and I cultivated our own "family" culture by having regular dinners together, going out once a week for brunch, inviting friends for dinner together once a week, praying together at regular times. These rhythms are not just for traditional families, but for those who live in a variety of places where they want to have close relationships with those living together.

A Cultural Battle Plan

To ignore the pull and draw of the world is to ignore the battle strategy of Satan, who desires to confuse us and to steal away our hearts. So we must outwit him and be stronger in our own battle plan. Cultivating a family culture can be a powerful weapon in that effort. If we are to hold hearts faithful, we must aim intentionally, work diligently and wisely, and allow the Holy Spirit to use us to keep their hearts strong, protected, and sure.

Each child is different, of course, and not all will conform to the family culture without a special effort to establish a foundation of unconditional love. Engaging with and enjoying all persons in the family as they are, no matter what stage or age, is essential to build a healthy emotional atmosphere—listening to their fears, laughing at their jokes, seeking to understand their dreams, sympathizing with their fears and hurt feelings, and making sure they always know who they are in the family and in Christ.

This was always our goal in cultivating our family culture. But in reality we had many moments when we failed to be patient, to correct with a gentle voice, or to laugh at jokes that did not seem funny. But we did our best to do these things as often as possible, ask forgiveness when we failed, and then move on.

No family is perfect, and all of us are a messy work in process. Give yourself grace as you would give your quirky children grace. You usually have at least eighteen years to improve over time!

Creating a Table-Talk Culture

It was the lunch that changed my life.

Clay and I were working at the International Chapel of Vienna in those days, and we often invited people home for lunch after our church service. On one such day, our table included an opera singer and her musician husband; a refugee who had escaped under the barbed wire, running from guards in Iraq; a couple who worked as attachés in the South African embassy; and a businessman and his wife who worked in Russia. (Because Vienna is one of the four headquarters of the United Nations, on some Sundays we had as many as thirty-five countries represented in our English-speaking chapel.)

This particular day, I had put chicken and rice in my slow cooker in the morning and tossed a quick salad before everyone came knocking at my door. Throughout the meal, I heard riveting personal stories, stimulating discussions of books and music, knowledgeable debates about biblical ideas, and a fascinating sharing of customs.

I distinctly remember sitting there with a burning passion building in my heart. I longed to understand history better, to know more about these countries I did not know existed, to be familiar with composers and art and great writers and ideas. Though I had graduated from college and could speak four languages with varying degrees of fluency, I still felt terribly uneducated and underinformed.

Having been one of those students who had been bored most of my years in school, I had just passed from one year to the next by the seat of my pants. Yet in this environment I recognized a deep hunger to know, to understand, to be able to converse with these interesting friends—in short, to become more personally educated in these vast ideas that interested me so much.

Perhaps if all I was hearing around our table had been presented to me in lecture form, requiring me to sit still and listen for hours on end, I might still have been bored. But hearing stories from real, live human beings, laughing together and engaging in discussion over coffee and cake, kept me deeply absorbed. And a conviction began growing inside me. I decided that if Clay and I ever had children, we would present interesting topics at our own table. We would discuss stories, read books out loud together, listen to and evaluate music, critique movies, evaluate world view, and talk lots about faith and the Bible (we would later come to call this "talking Torah").

I understood for the first time that education is not merely about facts learned in a classroom, but about living ideas that can fill hearts, minds, and souls with intellectual food that satisfies. And for the first time in my life I got a vision for creating a truly lifegiving table, a feast for the whole person.

If there is one main idea I would like to communicate in this book, it would be to underline the profound importance of talking together, communicating, and discussing ideas at every mealtime gathering because the table is a very satisfying place to educate both children and adults.

In all our travels, I still find it rare to meet people who are widely read, who are bubbling over with convictions and ideas, who are driven by messages that have captured their imagination, whose lives are driven by ideals both biblical and wise. Yet I think these qualities in a person's life show emotional health, mental muscle (the ability to think well), a soul engagement with wisdom, and the ability to live a productive and focused life. They are what Clay and I purposed to develop in our children by creating a strong table-talk culture.

Often people ask us, "How did your children end up studying at Oxford, Cambridge, and other great schools? What did you do to prepare them for that?" Honestly, we just lived our table routines. Looking back, all of us think our table culture of talking and discussing every possible idea was profoundly educational and gave our kids a great vocabulary without even using a vocabulary list.

My kids pursued an education away from the table, too, of course. Yet the hour or so of time we spent talking together over meals—repeated thousands of times over many years—became its own kind of classroom, one we all enjoyed immensely. It was through this practice that we passed on a love for thinking, speaking, teaching, and sharing at our table. So our mealtimes became training grounds for all of our children to flourish in their adult lives.

Creating a Culture of Honor

Our dinners together were not always peaceful. Far from it! On many a night, quarrels ruled the time we shared. Misunderstandings seemed to sprout up from nowhere, even between Clay and me. Sometimes it seemed as if contention was hiding, waiting to spring upon us when our intentions were to make our table a place of grace. We had to spend more time than I like to admit correcting behavior and attitudes.

Yet it was in the context of these times that our children learned, over time and with a certain amount of duress, how to develop social skills that took into consideration the feelings of others. A hard-learned lesson was that it's possible to think something without saying it out loud—especially if saying it would hurt someone's feelings. Another lesson was the importance of not letting an issue go until the relationship was restored. We practiced (and enforced) asking for forgiveness and granting forgiveness. The law of love was the foundation for all we taught, and we revisited it again and again.

If necessary, we interrupted our time together to take a child away from the crowd to talk to him or correct her. (I have missed many a hot meal because I needed to sit with an errant child and talk to him or her until an apology was forthcoming.) Time after time we taught our children not to let anger fester, but to seek peace instead. But this training built an expectation in all our children that both people and relationships are to be given honor at all times.

Honor is an old virtue that recognizes the worth of a person and the need to behave in such a way as to show respect and esteem, to validate the person's worthiness through heartfelt gracious behavior. I often told my children that if they did not learn to honor Clay and me, they would never be able to honor God. When they learned to honor us by using eyes, voices, and attitudes to show their respect and esteem, they were learning what it would be like to bow their knee before the living God.

And what was the best way for them to learn to show honor? That's where manners came in.

From the time our family began, I was determined to make manners a built-in part of our family culture. It was something we taught and practiced again and again when our children were young (and repeated through their teen years). I wanted to ingrain in them habits of respect for the value of every human being.

Manners are simply tools that build bridges of strong relationships to others. They are the way we communicate an attitude of honor. When we look at people when they are talking instead of looking away or glancing at our phone, we are honoring them, communicating that what they have to say is of value. When we remember to say please and thank you, we are honoring the contribution others make in our lives. When we chew with mouths closed or ask someone to pass the salt instead of reaching across the table for it, we are honoring everyone at the table by helping create an ordered, comfortable environment.

Teaching manners is also a way to instill valuable habits. A child who is taught to wait for everyone to sit down and allow time for a mealtime blessing learns self-control as well as an awareness of the needs of others. A teenager who is trained to greet others graciously will find it easier to negotiate the world outside the home. So cultivating an honoring atmosphere at the table serves other areas of life as well.

When I was a child, my mother often told us that her goal for our family was to help us learn habits of civility so that we would be fit to eat with paupers (and have a sympathetic and thankful attitude for what we received) or with kings (and feel comfortable at any table). She wanted us to learn how to be flexible and appropriate in any situation.

Later in my life, I was so very thankful for my mom's lessons in becoming civilized in my behavior. I was invited into every imaginable situation when I lived overseas. I ate with refugees who lived in temporary tents until they could be moved to a more permanent home, and I dined with the well-to-do in opulent settings. (They all needed Jesus.) And because I had passed my mother's training on to my kids, they learned to conduct themselves admirably at the table and elsewhere.

Yes, kids will fidget. Yes, some discussions might be silly or even become argumentative. Yes, sometimes you'll think nothing is happening. But a family culture is being built even when progress is hard to see. Keep the conversation going and teach your children to work through those discussions. Most important, day by day, keep them coming back to the table. I promise it will be worth it.

Defining Your Family Culture

Defining your own special family culture will help you move in the direction of building it. What is it about your family that's unique and special? What do you enjoy? What do you value? What do you want to build?

Just as important, what do you *want* your family culture to be? What qualities and values do you care enough to instill in your children? Your answers to these questions will help you get a sense of how to shape your family culture, especially at your table.

Here's how I would define the Clarkson culture: We are a people of words, faith in God, and a love for God's Word, music, tea drinking, books, walking and hiking outdoors, international work, ministry, discipleship, reading, hospitality, and, of course, feasting.

Consequently—and intentionally—we talked about these subjects all the time, especially at the table. Reading a story, sharing something we read, playing a new piece of music—these kinds of activities were a part of literally thousands of meals. It is no wonder all of our children are writers and communicators today. Words and ideas were a part of almost every meal we ever shared.

You, of course, might define your family culture differently. Perhaps you come from a medical family or a region defined by its cuisine or its cultural values (growing up in the South or the Northwest, for instance). Perhaps you cook, build things, camp in the mountains, raise animals, do business, engage in crafts, love languages, have a heart for the homeless, enjoy neighborhood outreach, or have an academic orientation. There are countless ways to develop your family culture by sharing these interests at the dinner table and elsewhere.

But again, intention is the key. As with any great work of life, a plan must be made. Determine what messages you want your children to take away from your table and the rest of your life together. What skills or hobbies can you teach? What family activities would reinforce your family culture? What family stories could add a sense of history and heritage? Any of these can give children a sense of "This is who we are. These topics define our family. These values are what we practice." Approach your mealtime as a family legacy-building time and plan activities, questions, and ideas to share.

Sharing life together in this way is a habit that sometimes takes a while to develop. My husband, Clay, is an introvert and grew up in a family that did not talk much or even eat together at the dinner table very often. So it took a bit of planning together and practicing our determined values before family discussion became natural for us. But now you cannot keep the Clarksons quiet—even the introverts!

A Family Culture of Hospitality

Hospitality is a word that basically means to care for and about the needs of others. It also carries a specific connotation of welcoming others into our home and our lives. And it's a biblical commandment, not optional for Christians. Romans 12:13 says it directly, telling God's people, "Always be eager to practice hospitality."

Even though in some ways Clay and I are both introverts, our value system from the first included ministry to others, cherishing friends, and serving those in need. And gradually the conviction grew that we wanted to be stewards of our home and to use it to meet needs, encourage, teach, provide refuge, and celebrate life with those God brought our way. We wanted hospitality to be an important part of our family culture.

So we followed Paul's advice and "practiced" hospitality until it became almost second nature. Having guests was a regular activity in our home—friends, family, acquaintances, strangers. We threw baby showers and Christmas teas. We welcomed overnight guests. We hosted book clubs and Bible study groups. We hosted neighborhood cookouts. And in the process, we learned ways to make all our guests feel comfortable and at home—usually with a meal or at least a snack.

From the time they were little, our children were included in our hospitality efforts. When we were expecting guests, each child was given a task to complete to make our table ready. Setting the table, cutting flowers, lighting candles, putting on music, cooking, meeting guests at the door, and making them feel welcome in our home were standard responsibilities shared by us all. Because we wanted our children to learn conversation skills, each one was to think of one question to ask our guests. There were even times when they were asked to give up their room or their bed for someone who was staying with us—a great lesson in serving.

Another important way we taught hospitality to our children was encouraging them to invite their friends over as often as possible. We served juice and cookies to toddlers, lemonade and sandwiches to ten-year-olds, pizza and popcorn to teens, and enough chocolate chip cookies to fill a fleet of semis. We opened our rooms and our yard to study groups, kids' clubs, and lots and lots of games. In the process our kids learned even more about what it means to welcome and serve others.

Last month, I was speaking at a conference in London and eagerly took a bus to visit Sarah in Oxford afterward. When I walked through her door, I saw fresh flowers adorning tables and rooms. Her table was set with lovely linens, a candle flickered atop it, and the fragrance of chicken, wine, and herbs wafted through the house. She greeted me with a piece of chocolate and a cup of tea, "Just in case you're hungry."

I practically melted into her wonderful living room couch, feeling like a queen in her palace—the honored guest, for once, instead of the hostess. It was a moment of deep satisfaction, seeing the results of so much thought, so much planning, so much intentionality. Seeing my daughter's serving heart and her skill at ministering to another's need made all those years of careful planning and diligent training worth it.

These days I'm seeing the fruit of our family culture in so many different ways. Though sometimes it seemed as if none of our work was taking root in our children's hearts, now I stand in amazement when I see what has grown from it.

I see family traditions picked up and carried forward, and new ones established.

I see a deep love of learning and culture and young adults who can talk with almost anyone about anything.

I see loving hearts, strong relationships, habits of honor and service and hospitality, and countercultural faith.

And I love what I see. For me, it's the legacy of a lifetime.

Something to Ponder

Romans 12:1-2 (NASB)

Therefore I urge you . . . by the mercies of God, to present
your bodies a living and holy sacrifice, acceptable to God,
which is your spiritual service of worship. And do not be
conformed to this world, but be transformed by the renewing
of your mind, so that you may prove what the will of God is,
that which is good and acceptable and perfect.

- Paul urges his readers to offer themselves as "a living and holy sacrifice." How can that apply to parents trying to establish a family
  culture that is strong enough to resist the culture of the world
  around it? What kind of sacrifices do we have to make?

- How do you think a strong family culture works to help children
  "be transformed by the renewing of [their minds]"? Can it work
  for parents as well as for children?

Romans 12:9-13, 15-16

Don't just pretend to love others. Really love them. Hate what
is wrong. Hold tightly to what is good. Love each other with
genuine affection, and take delight in honoring each other.
Never be lazy, but work hard and serve the Lord enthusiastically.
Rejoice in our confident hope. Be patient in trouble, and keep
on praying. When God's people are in need, be ready to help
them. Always be eager to practice hospitality. . . . Be happy
with those who are happy, and weep with those who weep. Live
in harmony with each other. Don't be too proud to enjoy the
company of ordinary people. And don't think you know it all!

- What does this passage say about the attitudes we should practice toward one another in a family? Toward those outside the
  family?

- What elements in this passage do you recognize and appreciate in your family culture?

- What elements would you like to incorporate in your family culture? Where would you start doing this?

- Are there any elements in Paul's counsel that sound particularly challenging or difficult to you? Which ones? Why? What changes could you make in your life and home to make them a little easier?

Something to Try

- Write out your own definition of who you are as a family or what you would like your family definition to look like.

- What characteristics would you *like* to develop in your own family culture? Make a short list, then pick one and make a plan for something you can do in the next week to instill or reinforce that characteristic.

- Plan an occasion to invite someone to your home, considering his or her needs. Plan ahead of time the preparation you will make and the words you will use to encourage that person.

Our Family's Favorite Company Meal

In our house, food was always the frame that enhanced the picture of our shared days. I thought I would share with you a favorite family meal, starring my own roast pork concoction. I love making it because it's simple, satisfying, and impressive. Since the children were little, we have traditionally sipped sparkling white or red grape juice with this meal.

❈ Pork Roast à la Sally

This recipe is always a hit for crowds or for my kids, and so very easy to make. The meat is luscious and just falls apart. I have a great source for natural, organic pork, which I recommend if you can find it. We don't have this meal often, but when we do, it is a real treat.

1½–2 cups apple juice
1 tablespoon minced garlic or 1 teaspoon garlic paste
1 1-ounce envelope dry onion soup mix (from a 2-ounce box)
2 tablespoons Worcestershire sauce
1–2 pork loins or a pork roast (about 4 pounds total) to fit your
    slow cooker
4 apples, sliced thinly (Sometimes I peel them; sometimes I don't.)
2 onions, sliced thinly
½–¾ cup dried cherries, optional (Some don't like these in the recipe,
    but most of my family loves them.)
Sea salt and pepper to taste
¼ cup cornstarch or flour, optional
¼ cup cold water, optional

Stir apple juice, garlic, soup mix, and Worcestershire sauce together in a slow cooker. Place the pork loins (or roast) in the sauce. Cover the meat with apples and onions and sprinkle the dried cherries over the top. Put lid on and cook 6–8 hours on low. Salt and pepper to taste. Serve meat with vegetables and fruit. If you would like a gravy, strain the leftover liquid into a small saucepan, skim off any fat, and heat. Stir the cornstarch or flour and cold water together in a cup until all the lumps are dissolved, then whisk mixture into the pan juices. Stir constantly over medium heat until thickened.

Serves 6–8.

❋ Mashed Potatoes

I almost always use red potatoes these days because they have less sugar when cooked. I also use a pressure cooker and do them in four minutes. (See your pressure-cooker manual for instructions.) But you can also choose to cook them in a saucepan, as directed below. Adding chicken bouillon to the potatoes gives them a wonderfully rich taste and allows you to use less butter.

6–8 large red potatoes, cut into 1-inch pieces (We don't peel ours, but you can if you want to.)
Water to cover
1–2 teaspoons condensed chicken bouillon or base (See note in chapter 3.)
2 tablespoons butter, or to taste
½–1 cup milk (or cream for richness), to taste
Sea salt and pepper to taste

Cover cubed potatoes with water in a large saucepan. Bring water to boil over high heat. Cover, reduce heat, and cook 15–20 minutes, until potato chunks are soft. Drain water from the potatoes. Add the chicken bouillon and butter. Mash with a hand masher or whip with a handheld mixer, stirring in milk or cream a little at a time as you mash. They will absorb the liquid, so add whatever amount you need to make the potatoes the desired consistency. Salt and pepper to taste.

Serves 6–8.

❊ Steamed Green Beans

Even folks who hate vegetables have been known to enjoy these. I love to use fresh beans whenever possible, but whole frozen ones will also work. And the very same cooking technique will work for asparagus!

1½–2 pounds fresh, whole green beans or approximately 24 ounces
      frozen ones (2 12-ounce or 1½ 16-ounce packages)
Fresh or dried herbs (rosemary, thyme, summer savory, dill, or
      whatever you like)
1–2 tablespoons extra-virgin olive oil or to taste
Sea salt to taste
Thinly sliced raw almonds, optional

If using fresh green beans, snap off the ends and pull off any strings. Rinse and place in a steamer basket over boiling water. Sprinkle with herbs, then cover and steam until just tender. Toss them in olive oil and sprinkle lightly with sea salt. If desired, sprinkle the sliced raw almonds on top of the dish before serving.

Serves 6–8.

CHAPTER 5

TABLE TALK
The Gift of Dinnertime Conversation

The most influential of all educational factors is the conversation in a child's home.

WILLIAM TEMPLE

They were talking with each other about all these things which had taken place. While they were talking and discussing, Jesus Himself approached and began traveling with them.

LUKE 24:14-15, NASB

Table-Discipleship Principle:

Shaping the mind and heart through
repeated discussions about truth, beauty, and
righteousness and engaging in these ideas
regularly shapes convictions that last a lifetime.

"HERE'S WHAT I THINK . . ."

It was a night just like any other, which is to say it was another evening of rousing discussion. Soup spoons suspended in midair, quizzical brows, the thumping of a printed-out article on the table. The article in question had been the source of that evening's discussion. I can't recall the exact topic of debate, but it likely had something to do with a current event, a book, an important idea or theological point, or some aspect of music or art or culture. And everybody—everybody!—had an opinion about it.

Once a learning exercise that Clay and I established and encouraged, dinnertime discussions grew to be the pulsing heartbeat of the Clarkson table. It seemed dinner had two purposes—to eat and to discuss.

In the beginning, I hosted these conversations. When our kids were very young, I would ask each of them to tell Clay the most interesting thing they had learned that day, share where we had gone on a field trip, or talk about what they had done with their friends. Their simple but enthusiastic sentences would tumble over each other as they shared the new facts they had picked up and adventures they'd had. In those days the dinner table was a place to practice manners and especially the arts of listening and asking. The goal was to honor the extroverts with a listening ear and gift the introverts with space enough for their words to be heard.

As they grew older, sometimes Clay would bring a book or article, read or summarize part of it, and then ask their opinions. We made a family policy that no idea was considered unworthy of our discussion and that no one, regardless of age or background, would be chastised or ridiculed for sharing an opinion. We sought to validate the thinking process in order to strengthen the muscle of thinking and engaging in ideas.

These days, when everyone is home, we still enjoy the ease of conversation and sharing that became so precious to us—along with the lively discussion that feels so familiar.

It is no wonder that Joy grew up to be a debater. Breathing in the oxygen of our table talk each evening prepared her brain to express her mind and back up her opinions.

I believe that fostering mealtime discussion has been vital to the spiritual, social, and emotional growth of all the individuals at our table. I hear tales that there are families who sit quietly at dinner, speaking not a word. And I must admit that at moments I wish we could practice that more often—especially when there are just boys at home. I am quite convinced that the glory of a man, at least a Clarkson man, is to *win* a discussion.

And yet I believe that our lively dinnertime discussions are one of the things that most positively shaped my and my children's lives. Establishing the dinner table as a place of discussion fosters an environment where truth is sought through dialogue, graciousness is taught and upheld, and convictions are formed.

Thought and will are two of the greatest gifts God has given us through His image in our hearts. In His great wisdom and love, God designed us not to be automatons who respond with thoughtless obedience, but to be thinking, willing participants in His will. Though it is hard to fathom, God has made a place for us at His table, and He invites us there to pray, to ask, to wrestle, because He values our responses to Him. He wants us to relate to Him out of love and conviction.

True discipleship must reflect the fact that God values our voice, thought, and will. Dinnertime discussions reflect and enact this value, making a place where everyone can be heard, be exposed to truth, and have the space to develop convictions in the context of community. Through dinnertime discussions, convictions can be formed, confidence can be gained, conversation can be practiced, and consideration can be taught.

Forging Convictions
God is all about the heart. That is the gist of Psalm 51:6, which addresses God by saying, "You desire truth in the innermost being" (NASB). What the psalmist meant is that God desires for His love and truth to have so formed us that they are tucked away in the deepest, truest parts of ourselves. Really following God can never just be a matter of memorizing a list of rules and doing our best to follow them, but must rather be

a deep-seated part of our identity. Knowledge of God is of no ultimate good unless it sinks into our heart and changes the way we view and interact with the world.

When discipling our children, we can easily become obsessed with teaching the right things (indoctrination). And teaching is definitely important! But the true difference is made when truth becomes a part of the disciple's life (conviction). Indoctrination is from the outside in; convictions are from the inside out. We must all reach a point where our knowledge of God goes from intellectual assent to holding a truth in our "innermost being." That's when knowledge becomes conviction.

But what does all this have to do with dinnertime discussions?

Convictions aren't memorized; they are digested. A sense of individual voice is essential to developing convictions because it is through articulating what we personally believe that we are able to own and live by our convictions. Dinnertime discussions were the time when I hoped to encourage this process in my children, to encourage them to use their voices to develop their own convictions. By asking their opinions about various topics, I sought to show them that their voices mattered, that they had the ability to think well, and that their convictions would shape the way they lived. Just as God said to Isaiah, "Come now, and let us reason together" (Isaiah 1:18, NASB), I wanted to prepare a table for my children to exercise their conviction capabilities.

Because we always welcomed and encouraged their opinions, our children thought discussing was as natural as breathing in oxygen. We did not seek to indoctrinate them through force, but rather asked questions and listened to their thoughts and opinions, as outlandish as they were at times. Each one was encouraged to make his or her own observations about news and life events, and we did our best to respond thoughtfully to their reflections.

Communities of discussion foster the deepening of convictions. A perfect example of this is the Inklings, the group of writers, artists, and academics who met weekly in the 1930s and 1940s to discuss ideas and projects. Perhaps the best-known members of this weekly discussion and reading group were C. S. Lewis, J. R. R. Tolkien, and Charles

Williams. Each week they would bring new writing or an idea they had encountered and discuss it over plate of hot, crispy fish and chips. The creative output of that group is almost mind-boggling, and many people believe the foundation for that prolific output was the friendship they shared. They sharpened each other's thinking, critiqued each other's ideas, made each other better.

I wanted my dinner table to be a place to develop my own little Inklings—a place where my children could practice stretching their minds, engaging with new ideas, building each other up—making each other better. And I think this effort was successful. In fact, one of my grown kids recently texted, "Mama, I have started an Inklings group in my apartment every week to discuss books and movies over hummus and chips. So fun to see my community of friends enjoying great discussions." I know exactly how that feels!

I love to think of the conversations Jesus and His disciples must have had around a meal. (At least two are described in the Gospels, but of course there were many more.) The disciples clearly felt free to ask Jesus deep, sometimes silly, even offensive questions. And Jesus asked His disciples what they thought as well—perhaps because He, too, knew that convictions so often come to us once we've articulated our ideas for the first time.

Jesus set the model of dialogue with His disciples and showed us that there is no substitute for personal conviction. And so too should we cultivate spaces where our children can learn to voice their beliefs, question and understand ideas, and articulate their developing convictions.

The Art of Conversation

In his letter to the Colossians, Paul instructs the church by saying, "Let your conversation be gracious and attractive so that you will have the right response for everyone" (Colossians 4:6). Isn't it interesting that with a limited amount of writing material and an urgency to communicate only the most important truths, Paul included the topic of good conversation in his letter? Perhaps it was because Paul understood the importance, the difficulty, and even sometimes the awkwardness of having important conversations about our faith, our convictions, our lives, and our differences.

Why is conversation so important? Because it's the most personal and immediate way we have to share our faith, hear the stories of others, and learn to listen and speak boldly.

I'm not the first person to observe that conversation is becoming a lost art in this age of cell phones, instant messaging, and social media. Technology makes it so easy to communicate that we become accustomed to lazy forms of messaging. Instead of meeting a friend for tea, we send a text. Instead of dropping into an office to ask a question, we hide our request behind an e-mail. Instead of meeting over lunch, we hold a teleconference and talk to screens. Instead of working out a disagreement with a friend, we write an anonymous rant in a blog comment.

While digital communication, social media, and even snail mail are helpful in connecting us with others, especially those far away, they lack the personal, satisfying, impacting effect of a face-to-face conversation complete with questions, answers, smiles, laughter, tears, and even touch.

This is a great loss. One of the essential parts of being human is our capacity for connection. We are made in the image of a triune God, which is to say a relational God. To reflect His image is to live in communion with and response to our fellow image bearers. Texts and e-mails and even videoconferencing can bring us only so close to that kind of relationship. Sooner or later we need to have a direct connection. An actual, in-person conversation.

And conversation is essential to discipleship. In fact, discipleship can be thought of as a long conversation about the things of Jesus over a lifetime. If we are to live into God's fullness for us and be skilled disciplers, we must pursue the art of conversation.

Fortunately, like any art, conversation can be practiced and improved upon. I saw dinnertime discussions as opportunities to teach my children good conversational skills. I wanted to help them practice letting their conversation be "gracious and attractive."

When we were expecting company for dinner, I would often ask each of my kids to think of one or two questions to ask our guests. During the meal, I would invite them to chip in on the conversation. I would ask them what they thought about whatever topic we were discussing, and I would encourage them to ask a question that pertained to the topic. We even talked about conversation as being like a game of tennis: One person hits the ball (a question) to another, the second person responds, and then the first person smoothly returns an answer and another question as if returning the ball.

Through all this patient conversation training with my very different children, I learned that people of all personalities are capable of being excellent conversationalists. While conversation may come more naturally to some, it is something we can all grow into.

Conversation is essential when it comes to sharing our faith. In my lifetime, the most impactful experiences I've had with people, the times I most naturally shared my faith, involved meaningful conversations. While forced sharing puts people on the defensive, warm and thoughtful conversation opens hearts. Through learning and practicing the art of conversation, we not only grow in social skills, but open the possibility of sharing our faith more honestly and openly.

Teaching Consideration

I don't think my children could be more different from one another. The bouquet of our family includes a bold verbal processor, a sensitive-souled introvert, a passionate and emotive extrovert, and a methodical dreamer . . . and I love them all! These differences are beautiful, but it would be incorrect to say that they did not cause moments of friction. A recurring theme in our family, in fact, was the effort to learn graciousness toward each other, to cherish our differences and cheer our similarities. The dinner table was our stage for rehearsal in this endeavor.

Much of life involves navigating awkward relationships with grace—and family is an ideal place for developing these skills. Quirky personalities, differing levels of maturity, moodiness, exhaustion, even offensive behavior pop up in every family. Families are like cross sections of culture—all sorts of people and personalities gathering together in one place, seeking to find harmony and community. Learning to be kind and forgiving at home prepares a child to engage in friendships at church, at school, at work, and out in the world. Learning to be gracious to others, to make room for personal differences, to listen, and to uplift will shape the pattern of that child's whole life.

How does this happen effectively? By patient and persistent teaching. By repeating the instruction over and over and over again and consistently reinforcing the lessons. ("Train up a child in the way he should go, and when he is old he will not depart from it" Proverbs 22:6, NKJV.) And again, by studying each child to determine what approach will fit best with his or her personality and temperament.

I think most people fall somewhere along a continuum when it comes to learning to speak and learning to listen.

For some, speaking comes naturally. For enthusiastic extroverts, the world is a place teeming with ideas, connections, and jokes. When they find themselves at a table, words come easily, and the dance of conversation pulses like a rhythmic beat in their hearts. But sometimes, these personalities find it hard to really listen. They have so many interesting thoughts to share that they inadvertently rush over the quiet speakers whose words come more slowly.

And then there are the quiet souls to whom listening comes naturally. They find themselves the observers of the world, taking in their surroundings. They notice the deeper meanings of conversations; they see the patterns of interaction between people; they hold their convictions quietly. But when it comes time to speak, they find it difficult. They certainly have something worth saying, but in the rush of fast-paced conversation they tend to retreat into themselves; they'd rather not enter the fray. What a shame it is when that happens. Their voices could add such wisdom to the discussion.

When I think of Jesus' followers in the Bible, I know that similar dynamics must have been at play. Peter must have been the extrovert, jumping to conclusions and rushing into action, afire with stormy conviction. Thomas was quiet but obstinate, loyal and courageous, but cherishing questions and doubts in his heart he didn't dare say until the very last moment. John the deep feeler with a poet's heart. Mary the passionate. Martha the efficient. Even in the sparse descriptions the Bible gives us of these people, we get a picture painted in many colors.

I'm sure that even in the godly ranks of these early followers of Jesus, there were clashes of personality, hurt feelings, and petty arguments; the Gospels even record some! (For example, see Mark 10:35-45.) And yet all of these were invited and made unified at the table of Jesus, where they were loved and saved. Through the lives of those disciples in the New Testament, we can take a beautiful picture of diverse personalities learning to relate to each other with patience.

The dinner table is a perfect place to practice consideration and graciousness. At our table, I pictured myself as the conductor of an orchestra and sought to make our table a place of harmony. Clay and I were intentional about helping the kids learn to listen to each other before speaking, to let the quieter, slower speakers have a chance, to praise someone who made a good point.

I will admit that at moments I felt more like a referee than a conductor. But just like practiced musicians, the more we rehearsed graciousness, the more it became a part of our family culture. Guiding your family in graciousness can be exhausting and can sometimes feel useless. But I always encourage mothers to keep going. You cannot always see the difference it is making day by day, but the fruit of years is always rich. When I look at the adults my children have become, I do not regret a single ounce of the effort I put into shaping our family dynamics.

Learn to be the conductor of your table. Set the rhythm and the rules of your conversation. Make sure the quiet are heard, make sure the talkative are loved. Through your example, teach your children to be "quick to listen, slow to speak, and slow to get angry (James 1:19). Let your table be the training grounds for graciousness and consideration.

As I have shared before, once when Joy was nearing her teens (and many times after that), her big brown eyes found mine, and she heaved a quiet but heavily meaningful sigh.

"Are we going to have another deep discussion at dinner tonight? Can't you just tell the teenagers to be quiet for one night?"

I laughed and gave her a hug, expressing my sympathy.

Today, of course, Joy is right in the thick of our dinnertime talk. And after all those years of fostering discussions, I find that my children create them on their own. I just finished fifteen days of having five adult children at home for the holidays (one was a new son-in-law). After just the first night, I was exhausted by their rambunctious dialogue and even arguments about complicated theological subjects. Were they going to make it through the two weeks and still be friends?

Yet by the second night, I was watching and listening with my heart. It was as though the Lord said, "Just look! You have five young adults sitting at your table—all of them passionate about their faith, loving God with all their hearts, and caring greatly about the Bible—close friends passionately sharing stories, discussing books, and swapping funny stories with all the energy they can muster. This is a gift. Enjoy and make more food!"

This had been my goal as a young mama—that they would fall in love with Scripture, learn to think profoundly about what really mattered, listen to the wisdom of Scripture as they made their choices, and invest their lives in God's Kingdom work. I wanted them to love learning and become creative communicators of all they were learning. And while the process of getting there has sometimes been wearying, the impact on all their lives has been profound.

I saw Joy, night after night, engage her heart and mind in conversations beyond her years, forming her own convictions behind her quietly determined eyes.

I saw my thoughtful and introverted Joel develop a voice and an ability to articulate his thoughts with grace. This eventually turned him into a writer and composer.

I saw outspoken Nathan learn to temper his passion and arguments, at least some of the time, to make conversation productive and winsome. In the process, he fell in love with stories and became a story-teller through the medium of film.

I saw Sarah learn to enjoy bringing her own love of beauty and literature to each conversation we had. This led to her writing blogs and books and obtaining a degree in literature from Oxford University.

Our dinner table became what I had dreamed it would be—a place of sharing and of growing. As I look back, I know that this has been one of the most formative parts of my parenting and discipling and my life in general—watching Jesus, the Word made flesh, bring life to all of us through the gift of words.

Something to Ponder

Colossians 4:6

> Let your conversation be gracious and attractive so that you
> will have the right response for everyone.

Establishing ground rules for appropriate engaging conversation is helpful so that an atmosphere of acceptance and affirmation becomes the standard of talking together.

- Define what you think gracious conversation is. What about attractive conversation?

- What attitude must be developed in order to have a "right response for everyone"?

Proverbs 15:1, NASB

> A gentle answer turns away wrath,
> But a harsh word stirs up anger.

I have used this verse many times to help my children understand that they can help guide a conversation toward peacefulness or they can become agitators of arguments that heat up.

- How potentially powerful does this verse indicate a gentle answer can be?

- What is a gentle word?

- What is a harsh word?

Something to Try

- Write down three phrases that create unity or affirmation in a conversation. (Examples: "I understand what you mean." "That makes sense to me.") Write down phrases that could stir up strife. (Examples: "You're wrong!" "That's stupid.") Have a table discussion about how to create influence in a conversation by practicing speaking wisely.

- Tell your children early in the day to think of one question they're going to ask the others at the dinner table. While you're eating, go around and take turns asking questions.

Recipes to Talk About

Little Italy Spaghetti Pie

Many years ago, I was speaking at a conference in Ohio. A gentle, sweet, smiling woman shyly approached me after my talk and said, "I have a gift for you that I hope you will use for many years." She handed me a little book. "It's collected recipes from my family and friends." In the storm of the moment, with people begging for my attention and gathering in a long line, I thanked her distractedly and shifted my glance to the next person in line. But I never forgot that sweet and very personal expression of friendship. Many recipes from this collection became family favorites for us, and they always tasted better knowing they came from generations of great cooks. Spaghetti pie has become our "Welcome Home" meal, and now it is expected.

This recipe begs to be doubled or even tripled! It is a quick and easy way to make a dinner that tastes like mom's homemade lasagna, although it takes a fraction of the time to assemble and cook. Another option I love is to make lunch-size spaghetti pies using a muffin tin. This yields twelve great after-school snacks or a great addition to your salad at lunch! Cook, cool, wrap up in plastic, and place them all in a gallon-size zippered bag in the refrigerator.

Wowing your family with a delicious meal doesn't have to be time consuming or difficult. Turn your home into your favorite Italian restaurant tonight. Light candles, put down your favorite red tablecloth, and you can even tune in to the "Little Italy 1930" radio station from Pandora for free. It is such fun and really creates the Italian ambience!

½ cup diced onion
2 teaspoons olive oil
½ cup diced mushrooms, optional (We usually do without them.)
1 clove garlic, minced

1 pound ground beef (or ½ pound Italian sausage and ½ pound
    ground beef)
1 24-ounce jar of your favorite marinara sauce
1 teaspoon dried oregano or Italian seasoning
1 teaspoon dried basil
Salt and pepper to taste
Olive oil or cooking spray to grease pan
6–8 ounces uncooked spaghetti (or your favorite pasta)
1 teaspoon salt
1 tablespoon olive oil
2 tablespoons butter
¾ cup grated Parmesan cheese
2 eggs, well beaten
1 cup cottage cheese, any kind
1–2 cups fresh mozzarella cheese, shredded
Pinch of Italian seasoning to finish, optional

Sauté onions in olive oil over medium-high heat until translucent.
Add mushrooms (if using) and sauté until cooked through. Add garlic
and stir mixture for 1 minute. Add ground beef to the skillet and stir
until completely cooked. Carefully drain off any excess fat and return
meat mixture to medium heat. Add marinara sauce, oregano, basil,
salt, and pepper. Stir, turn off heat, and set aside. This will make a
chunky, rustic-style sauce.

To make the pie, preheat oven to 350°F and grease a 10-inch
pie pan. Cook pasta per package instructions with 1 teaspoon salt
and 1 tablespoon olive oil. Drain, then stir in the butter, Parmesan,
and eggs. Pour warm pasta mixture into the pie pan and press
against bottom and sides to form a "piecrust." Spread cottage cheese
on top of the crust. Add meat-sauce mixture. Bake uncovered
for 20 minutes, then remove from oven and top with shredded
mozzarella and, if desired, a sprinkle of Italian seasoning. Return
to oven for 5 minutes longer, until cheese is bubbly.

Serves 6–8, depending on how you cut the pie.

✖ Boys' Favorite Blueberry Crumble Muffins

Carbs sometimes get a bad rap in our culture today. We do watch our carbs and have added lots of salad, fresh veggies, and protein to our diet over the years, but some breads beg to be made and devoured—like these wonderful blueberry muffins. I love summer fruit, and of course blueberries, they say, are rich in antioxidants. They also help strengthen the brain—which I really need these days!

Having muffins like these in the freezer opened many a talk with my boys when they were teens. (In the middle of a growth spurt, sometimes a cookie just isn't enough.) I've found that warm breads and a hot drink just have a way of easing conversation. Want to search someone's heart and foster friendship? Serve these muffins with tea or cocoa and some encouraging words.

Oil or cooking spray for greasing muffin cups
1½ cups freshly ground whole-wheat flour (We use a flour mill
        to grind our own flour—it's surprisingly easy to do. But if
        you don't have a mill or access to the whole grains, you can
        substitute unbleached all-purpose flour. As always, organic
        is preferable.)
¾ cup brown sugar
½ teaspoon salt
2 teaspoons non-aluminum baking powder
⅓ cup vegetable oil
⅓ cup vanilla yogurt
1 egg
Milk, as needed
1 cup fresh or frozen blueberries (If frozen, don't thaw before using.)
½ cup granulated sugar (I use organic cane sugar whenever possible.)
⅓ cup unbleached all-purpose flour
¼ cup butter, cubed
1½ teaspoons ground cinnamon (very important!)

Preheat oven to 400°F. Grease 12 muffin cups or line with muffin liners.

Combine the flour with brown sugar, salt, and baking powder. Pour vegetable oil into a 1-cup measuring cup; add yogurt and egg, then enough milk to reach the 1-cup mark. Add this to flour mixture and mix until all flour is incorporated. (Don't overmix.) Fold in blueberries. Fill muffin cups right to the top.

To make crumb topping, mix together granulated sugar, all-purpose flour, butter cubes, and cinnamon. Mix with a fork or pastry cutter until mixture resembles coarse crumbs. Sprinkle over muffins before baking. Bake muffins 20–25 minutes until tops spring back when pressed or a toothpick inserted in center comes out clean.

These muffins freeze well. To reheat, wrap in foil and warm in a 350°F oven for 10–15 minutes, until just hot enough to melt a butter pat inside.

Makes 12 medium muffins.

CHAPTER 6

AN ANCHOR FOR YOUR WEEK
Starting Your Sundays Right

❈

All true friendliness begins with fire and food and drink and the recognition of rain or frost. . . . Each human soul has in a sense to enact for itself the gigantic humility of the Incarnation. Every man must descend into the flesh to meet mankind.

G. K. CHESTERTON

Nehemiah continued, "Go and celebrate with a feast of rich foods and sweet drinks, and share gifts of food with people who have nothing prepared. This is a sacred day before our Lord. Don't be dejected and sad, for the joy of the LORD is your strength!"

NEHEMIAH 8:10

Table-Discipleship Principle:
We must be intentional to guide, discuss, and celebrate the dependable rhythms of life.

I SLIP A LACY fold-over sock onto Joy's delicate foot and glance at my watch. Forty-five minutes until takeoff. I straighten her hair bow and kiss her head.

"Do you want to help Mommy set the table?"

"Yes, Mama! And I want to tell you something."

Joy patters behind me in her Sunday best, regaling me with every thought and feeling she's experienced in the last twenty-four hours. While she happily chatters, I flip pancakes and murmur "mm-hmm" to each important point she makes.

I hand her six forks and six napkins to fold. I glance again at the clock—thirty-seven minutes to go! I hurriedly drop pecans and chocolate chips into the bubbling piles of golden batter. Pulling out our old faithful teapot, I flick on the electric kettle and go to rally the forces.

The hurricane of bustle it takes to get six people into a car and on their way to church never ceases to amuse and exasperate me. On the very day we all feel compelled to be spiritual, focused, and thoughtful, we are usually rushed, urgent, and—dare we admit it?—a slight bit annoyed.

The more years I've lived, the more I've come to think that it is better not to fight mornings like these. It is better to resign oneself to the bustle and make room for meaning and delight in the midst of it. Accepting this reality helps soothe my mood, even if it means being five minutes late to church.

There will come a day when we arrive on time, I think, *but today is probably not that day.* So I take a deep breath and flip another pancake.

"Breakfast in five minutes!" I shout up the stairs, "Be ready for church!"

Within a few minutes I hear the hurried flutter of feet upstairs, followed by pounding on the stairs—a familiar sound to me. Nathan arrives, combing damp hair behind his ears. My two oldest amble in shortly thereafter, looking slightly more ready. Then comes Clay, who was dressed before any of us.

Clay's "amen" has barely reached our ears before we descend on the pancakes with gusto. Joy likes the chocolate chip, while Sarah is partial to pecan. Soon not a single pancake is left. With mugs full of tea and mouths full of scrumptiousness (if I do say so myself), we listen while Clay reads aloud a psalm that has captured his imagination this morning. Joy wiggles a little as he reads. But I can see on her attentive face that she is chewing on the words Clay reads out in rich baritone.

Clay thumps the book closed and removes his reading glasses.

"What do you all think?" he asks, surveying the breakfast table. This week's Scripture focuses on holiness—a lofty topic for preteens.

"I think that if God gave everything to make us His, then we should live our lives set apart for Him. It's how we should respond to His kindness."

These words come from Joel, who until this moment has been sleepily consuming chocolate chip *and* pecan pancakes, leftover from Sarah's plate. I am reminded once again that it's hard to know when children's hearts are deeply engaged. They can be paying attention even when they don't look it. (Never stop teaching, training, and pouring into your children because you think they aren't listening. Patience reveals investment.)

Everyone else chips in their thoughts, even little Joy, who was destined from a young age to hear many conversations beyond her years. Then Clay leads us in a prayer, and everyone rushes their dishes to the sink. I decide we'll finish washing up later and leave them to soak. After a mad dash of socks, shoes, and unevenly tied shoelaces, somehow we all end up in the car. And I don't even think we'll be late.

What a miracle!

An Anchor in the Week

We did that every Sunday morning while our children were growing up—a sit-down breakfast with a special treat like pancakes or French toast, a family devotional, and time for us to reflect together on what we had read. In fact, we still do it with whoever happens to be home at the moment.

Why is it so important to us? Why did I go to the extra trouble of yet another special meal on yet another morning—especially when church offered doughnuts?

I know that some might see traditions like our long-loved Sunday morning feasts as frivolous or simply impractical—lace on life that can only be accomplished by a particularly put-together stay-at-home mom with nothing better to do. But I strongly believe that we *need* traditions like these because they give us necessary anchors in our lives—our days and weeks and months and years.

Anchors are the moments when, no matter what, you stop, breathe, enjoy, rest, and check in with the Lord. They are moments of pause that lend significance to the everyday hustle and bustle. And just as we have holidays throughout the year to remind us of the story of our faith and to foster contemplation, we should have small anchors in our daily and weekly lives that remind us to stop and draw close to the Lord.

From the beginning, I wanted to set aside Sunday mornings as one of those significant moments in my home. The world may fall to pieces, but Sunday breakfast is something my family can always count on.

In practice, Sunday morning feasts are neither complicated nor overwhelming. All they require of me is to make breakfast, perhaps a dish we wouldn't normally have on weekdays. And all it requires of everyone else is to be ready in time.

There have been years when this was more difficult than others, but I've found that in almost all the stages of my life it's been manageable. Food, discussion, prayer—I can almost always do that.

And the effort is so worth it! Over the years I've seen three consistent benefits of our Sunday breakfasts. They provided us with times to celebrate, to converse, and to navigate the world of church and faith.

Sunday Morning Celebration

It is so easy to think being a Christian is a somber affair—church clothes, silence, never-ending prayers. Haven't we all had a moment when we couldn't wait for lunch and laughter after a boring service? When we felt like we would crawl out of our skin if we had to sit for two more minutes listening to the droning baritone of the preacher? When we were struck with the insatiable desire to giggle at an inopportune moment?

This mama most certainly has felt like that at times. (It's possible—no, probable—that I have a touch of ADD.)

But Jesus was the best celebrator!

John's Gospel tells us that His first miracle was turning water into wine. The God of the universe chose to begin His revelation of Himself to the world at a great, delightful wedding feast. And Jesus did not provide inferior wine when they ran out—oh, no. He provided the very best, showing Himself to be a generous and exuberant celebrator of all that God has called good.

And God, the creator of all that is good and beautiful in the world, is the ultimate Celebrator. He made puppy dogs, daisies, sunsets, chocolate, and first loves. Since He has given us the generous gift of His creation, it would be thumbing our nose at God not to revel in it and thank Him with every breath we have.

In his book *Orthodoxy*, G. K. Chesterton describes the celebratory nature of God's character in an unforgettable way:

> Because children have abounding vitality, because they are in spirit fierce and free, therefore they want things repeated and unchanged. They always say, "Do it again"; and the grown-up person does it again until he is nearly dead. For grown-up people are not strong enough to exult in monotony. But perhaps God is strong enough to exult in monotony. It is possible that God says every morning, "Do it again" to the sun; and every evening, "Do it again" to the moon. It may not be automatic necessity that makes all daisies alike; it may be that God makes every daisy separately, but has never got tired of making them. It may be that He has the eternal appetite of infancy; for we have sinned and grown old, and our Father is younger than we.[1]

How often do we forget this exuberant and celebratory nature of God? Why do we walk around with dour faces at church as though our displeasure will somehow please God more than being His hopeful, cheerful, grateful children?

And let's not delude ourselves: This grim attitude will teach our children to regard faith with a resigned endurance instead of a delighted enthusiasm. When we model to our children that pleasure, delight, laughter, and food are not God's afterthoughts, but His generous gifts to us all, we do them a great favor. For the good of our souls and the souls of our children, we must learn to celebrate to the glory of God.

This is yet another reason why our Sunday morning feasts have been so important to me. Through them I impressed upon my children a simple truth: A life with God is one worth celebrating.

The psalmist said it so beautifully:

Taste and see that the LORD is good.
Oh, the joys of those who take refuge in him!
PSALM 34:8

This command is not only metaphorical. I believe that God intended us to experience the full range of beauty in the world as a testament to His generous love for us. To neglect delight, feasting, and celebration is to neglect worshiping God in the way He intended us to. Our Sunday breakfasts also helped establish a positive attitude toward church.

Once, when asked why she was still a Christian, my daughter Sarah said, "Because of pecan French toast with butter and syrup." People chuckled, but I think she was sincere. In the midst of a difficult life and an unstable world, we consistently celebrated God's goodness, kindness, and generosity. And that helped make our lives worth living.

Sometimes, in our weary and broken world, celebration almost seems wrong. When we look at our news feeds and TV screens, we see a profoundly fractured world. And even in our own homes and hearts, there are wounds, losses, and difficulties. Can celebration, feasting, and joy possibly be an appropriate response?

Yes!

Jesus was born into a world just as broken as our own, and the definitive first move of His ministry was to add His personal touch to a profoundly important celebration—a wedding feast. Later, even when faced with crucifixion, Jesus gave His disciples reason to celebrate: "When everything is ready, I will come and get you, so that you will always be with me where I am" (John 14:3). The Gospels are focused toward a good ending—another wedding feast and a home to belong in. In celebration we declare that God is not done with us yet. Ultimately, evil does not have the final word. We celebrate in thanksgiving for what God has done, and we celebrate in expectation of His final victory.

And so it is good to have French toast on Sundays.

Sunday Morning Conversation

I always wanted my children to come to us with their most earnest questions. Because of this, I established the dining table as a space for discussion and conversation. Sundays were consecrated days for us to discuss what we were learning about the Lord and to open up space for questions.

In Joshua 1:8, Joshua describes how the Israelites were to keep the laws of God. He says, "Study this Book of Instruction continually. Meditate on it day and night so you will be sure to obey everything written in it. Only then will you prosper and succeed in all you do." Essentially, Joshua was saying that the way the Israelites were to stay faithful to the law was by making it a topic of conversation, something the whole family discussed, thought upon, and had convictions about. This is what we hoped to establish with our Sunday breakfasts.

Most children spend almost one thousand Sundays at home before setting out into the world. It is a significant investment in their future to establish a habit of going together before the throne of God on Sunday mornings. Doing this together before church teaches them to prepare their hearts, minds, and souls for worship.

We discussed matters of our faith on other days, of course, but Sunday was the day we held holy for such conversations. Sometimes these conversations manifested themselves through the natural progression of our children's thoughts. Sometimes I came to the table with a question, a passage that I had been reading, perhaps one that pertained to preparing our hearts and minds for church. Sometimes Clay prepared a small Bible reading to stimulate our conversations. Whatever the method or mode, I was intentional about creating a space for spiritual conversations on Sunday mornings.

This was also a time for Clay to shine. Since I was the one who was most often home and with the kids, I had many opportunities to guide conversations and connections with them. Hardworking and busy, Clay had less opportunity. I know from many women I have had conversations with that this is a common problem among couples—wives who want their husbands to be involved in spiritual conversations and husbands who are too busy, overwhelmed, or confused about how to start. For us, Sunday mornings were a low-pressure time when Clay could, if he wished, guide the conversation and be the master of ceremonies. Armed with a brief reading and a few questions, he could have a space to invest in our familial spiritual conversations without a sense of overwhelming expectation.

Clay wasn't the only leader in these devotional times, however. Sometimes I would lead, perhaps sharing a passage from a book I had been reading. We partnered together to bring about our Sunday morning table talk and worked in harmony with our ultimate family goals.

I saw these Sunday morning conversations not just as a duty to be fulfilled, but as an important opportunity for my children. They were able to ask questions that bothered them, be exposed to the ideas and thoughts of their siblings, learn to listen, and learn to articulate their own opinions. This turned the responsibility of discipleship back to my children, allowing them to shape their own convictions instead of having me constantly teach them. It didn't always happen that way. Sometimes they were just sleepy. But we knew it mattered to keep our rhythms going, so we persevered.

Sunday Morning Preparation

Another benefit that emerged from our Sunday morning breakfasts is that they helped us as a family set an intentional tone toward church and our relationships with God.

In the whirling and frantic urgency of life, it is easy to lose touch with our own hearts. On no day is this so evident to me as Sunday. It's a day when our hearts should be centered, quiet, and focused on the Lord, but so often we find ourselves seated in church feeling depleted and disconnected. Since this is so often the case, it is vital to one's spiritual health to approach church and Sundays with a heart of expectation and preparation, stillness and consideration.

But church is not always an easy thing. In my experience, it is rare to meet someone whose story with the church doesn't involve at least a little bit of struggle, frustration, conflict, or pain. To me this seems only natural. We are fallen people in a fallen world, and the pursuit of God, love, and a righteous character in the context of other sinful, fallen people is bound to be fraught at times.

People—good people—find themselves blindsided by their inability to see eye to eye. Secretly cruel or wounded people sow seeds of gossip and dissension and end up breaking up a church. Unanswerable questions lead to doubts that are difficult to manage—or rigid suppression by those who cannot handle doubt. People who move to a new city or state may have trouble settling into community and find themselves deeply lonely, without a kindred spirit in sight.

These struggles are not new, of course. They've been around for centuries. But that doesn't make them any easier to navigate.

Not surprisingly, sentiments toward church and Sundays are as diverse as the people who hold them. Our personal histories profoundly impact our experience and outlook. Some of us look forward to church every week as a place to enjoy community and joyous praise. Some dismiss church attendance as a legalistic practice designed to produce guilt. For some, church is a confusing place full of unanswered questions and suppressed doubts, while for others it is a place for growth and delight and depth. For still others, church represents the feeling of isolation, of never fitting in.

I have at various times and in various ways experienced all of those feelings toward church. Knowing in my heart that such difficulties were inevitable, I always desired to prepare my children for them. I wanted to make a safe space where they could work out such tensions in the safety of our home, at the comfort of our breakfast table.

Some parents are understandably afraid of these moments of tension arising in their children's lives, especially where faith is concerned, and as a result they seek to avoid conversations that might raise questions. I understand this fear, and yet I think giving in to it can only result in damage.

It is almost inevitable that when children reach their teen years, they will push against some of the beliefs and values they have grown up with. They may become acutely aware of the seeming hypocrisy of believers, even in the family itself. This is actually a good thing. Spiritual muscle is built by testing faith in order to build personal convictions and make that faith their own. But growth often involves growing pains, and these may include uncomfortable feelings and attitudes about both God and church.

Better than avoiding such difficult moments in life is to prepare your heart for them. And I've found that setting aside a special time *before* church helps with that. It gives my family and me time to center ourselves and ask, *How are we going to approach church, rest, and God this week? What is bubbling in our hearts today?*

Jesus did not come to save us into isolation, but to save us into community. We are called to live out our discipleship in the context of other believers with whom we worship, eat, pray, and grieve: church. But in a fractured world where church is not easy, we should be thoughtful about how we approach it. I wanted my children to have the opportunity to prepare for this reality and to explore it. What better time could there be than right before we headed to church ourselves?

I have often been struck by Jesus' patience with His disciples. For the most part, He did not reprimand His disciples for their questions, but patiently redirected them again and again to the Scriptures and to truth. He prepared them for what was to come, be it good or bad. I want my heart to be shaped by Jesus in such a way that I lead my children in the same way, guiding them through difficult questions and seasons, preparing them for the storms of life and celebrating the beauty of life. And as I attempt to do that, I ask God for the grace to guard my own heart for all the seasons that come.

In setting the table every Sunday for a feast, I hope to create in them a sense of belonging—not only to the Clarksons, but also to the family of God. In the midst of questions or frustrations, I want them to know there is always a place for them. Just as Sunday morning feasts are anchors in the week, I hope that our table can be an anchor in their hearts. That through pecan pancakes and hot tea they might know they will never face a struggle alone.

Looking Back and Forward

Much to the ache of my mama heart, Joy no longer needs me to slip on her lacy Sunday socks. My children have grown into beautiful adults, and I often miss those days of familial unity and familiarity. Yet even now, when my children are home, I see the closeness those years wove. Individually and communally, our family has weathered our share of storms and celebrated more than our share of gladness.

And when, on those cherished occasions, we join hands to pray around a table filled with pecan pancakes, I am deeply thankful for the ways our hearts have been knit together in pursuit of God and love of each other. And I can say with thorough enthusiasm that each flipped pancake was worth it.

Something to Ponder

John 21:12-13

> "Now come and have some breakfast!" Jesus said. None of the disciples dared to ask him, "Who are you?" They knew it was the Lord. Then Jesus served them the bread and the fish.

I have always loved that one of Jesus' last actions on earth was to make breakfast for His friends.

- Why would Jesus do this?

- How did preparing breakfast for His friends prepare them to listen to His message?

• Why was this His last action before sending His disciples out into a difficult world?

John 21:15-19

After breakfast Jesus asked Simon Peter, "Simon son of John, do you love me more than these?"

"Yes, Lord," Peter replied, "you know I love you."

"Then feed my lambs," Jesus told him.

Jesus repeated the question: "Simon son of John, do you love me?"

"Yes, Lord," Peter said, "you know I love you."

"Then take care of my sheep," Jesus said.

A third time he asked him, "Simon son of John, do you love me?"

Peter was hurt that Jesus asked the question a third time. He said, "Lord, you know everything. You know that I love you."

Jesus said, "Then feed my sheep.

"I tell you the truth, when you were young, you were able to do as you liked; you dressed yourself and went wherever you wanted to go. But when you are old, you will stretch out your hands, and others will dress you and take you where you don't want to go." Jesus said this to let him know by what kind of death he would glorify God. Then Jesus told him, "Follow me."

• What kind of message did Jesus give to Peter after he was fed and full?

• In light of this verse, what kind of messages might you be called to give over your meals?

• How did Jesus prepare Peter for what would come in his life? How did feasting play into Jesus' discipleship in this moment?

John 21:9, NASB

When they got out on the land, they saw a charcoal fire already laid and fish placed on it, and bread.

- How does this verse model Jesus, the Creator of all things (including food), preparing the setting for an important conversation to take place?

- Jesus had planned the meal He knew would be pleasant to the disciples. How can that be a model for our lives?

Something to Try

- If you don't have one already, consider establishing an anchor in your family's schedule. What would work for your family?

- When you have something personal and possibly difficult to discuss with a friend or family member, set the table of friendship by meeting their physical and emotional needs and thus assuring them of your commitment before sharing the message. A message given in gentleness and in an atmosphere of serving is more easily received.

A Sunday Breakfast Feast

✳ **Make 'Em Smile Pancakes**

This breakfast staple can also be a delightful spur-of-the-moment dinner. If you are new to making pancakes, be patient and remember that practice makes perfect. Don't worry if every pancake doesn't turn out flawlessly. Keep trying and keep flipping—and remember that pancakes don't need to be perfect to be delicious.

2 cups freshly ground whole-wheat flour or unbleached all-purpose
    flour
2 teaspoons non-aluminum baking powder
1 teaspoon baking soda
½ teaspoon salt
¼ cup raw sugar or maple syrup, or to taste
2 eggs
1 cup plain or vanilla yogurt (Greek or not—buttermilk can also
    be substituted)
1 cup milk
¼ cup vegetable oil
½–1 cup peeled, grated apple
2 tablespoons melted butter for greasing the griddle
Buttered pecans (see recipe below), chopped, or chocolate chips,
    optional
Your favorite pancake toppings—butter, syrup, jam, whipped cream
Cinnamon sugar, optional (Clay's tried-and-tested mix is found in
    chapter 10.)

Grab a big bowl and add the flour, baking powder, baking soda, salt, and sugar. (If you prefer to use maple syrup, wait and add it to the wet ingredients.) Whisk together until blended. Set aside.

In another bowl combine eggs, yogurt, milk, and oil (and maple syrup if desired). Whisk together until mixture looks smooth.

Whisk the wet mixture into the dry ingredients and stir the two together until just barely mixed. You want any visible loose flour to be completely stirred in, but the batter should still be lumpy. Stir in grated apple.

If the batter seems too stiff, add more milk a tablespoon at a time. (The consistency will vary according to factors such as altitude.) Batter should be thick but easily pourable.

Preheat your skillet or griddle to 375°F. If you're not using an electric griddle, turn the burners to medium-high and heat until a drop of water skitters across the surface. (Don't be afraid to adjust the heat if pancakes cook too quickly or slowly.) Grease the griddle with melted butter. Add small scoops of pancake batter (they should spread out to about 3–4 inches). After the pancakes are on the griddle, sprinkle chocolate chips or buttered pecans over the top of each cake, according to individual preference.

Cook until the edges look dry and little bubbles form on the surface. Slip a spatula underneath a cake to see if the bottom is browning. If so, flip it with your spatula and cook for a minute or two on the other side. When another peek underneath reveals that the bottom is golden brown, remove cake from the griddle and serve with your favorite toppings. We like to sprinkle ours with cinnamon sugar for special occasions.

Serves 6–8, depending on the size of the pancake.

❈ French Toast Frenzy

French toast is always a hit in our household because it is easy, satisfying, and delicious. It seems like I can never make enough of it, so stock up on bread and eggs!

Eggs—1 per serving, plus 1 more
Melted butter to grease pan
Thick slices of bread—one per serving (I usually use my own fresh
      homemade bread, but brioche is a great alternative.)

Confectioner's sugar
Buttered pecans (recipe below), chopped
Real maple syrup, warmed

Whisk eggs while heating butter in a griddle or pan. Dip one
slice of bread at a time into the eggs. Turn slice over to soak both
sides. Place into hot skillet. When toast is browned to your taste
on the underside, flip it. (We prefer our French toast to be crisp
and crunchy.) After removing slices to plates, sprinkle each with
confectioner's sugar. Add chopped toasted pecans and then smother
with warmed-up real maple syrup.

❋ **Buttered Pecans (or Other Nuts)**

*When I was growing up in Texas, we were fortunate to have pecan trees
growing in our yard. Every year we would have a gigantic bowl of pecans
in a wooden bowl in our den. I thought it a fun task to crack the fresh nuts,
pull the nutmeats out of the shell, and munch on them. Later, when I had a
home of my own, I learned to roast the pecans in butter and keep them out
on the counter as snacks. They seemed to disappear into thin air!*

*Though nuts can be caloric and should be enjoyed in small quantities,
they provide all sorts of health benefits. They contribute to cardiovascular
fitness and brain health, provide important minerals, and are high in fiber.
Nuts can also be expensive, so I buy mine in bulk and am always on the
lookout for sales.*

*I have toasted pecans, walnuts, almonds, and pumpkin seeds, but I use
pecans and walnuts the most. I like to chop them up to sprinkle on our
pancakes or French toast. They're also delicious in green salads or chicken
salad, on ice cream, stirred into Greek yogurt, or incorporated into your
favorite cookie recipes.*

1 pound (or more!) pecans or other nuts
2–3 tablespoons butter per pound of nuts, melted
Sea salt to taste

Preheat oven to 325°F. Place nuts into a bowl. Pour melted butter over the nuts and toss until nuts are thoroughly coated. Spread to cover two 9 × 13 pans in a single layer. (Don't put too many in the same pan or they won't roast evenly.) Sprinkle sea salt over nuts, then place pan in oven to roast. This usually takes about 15 minutes, but ovens do vary, so set the timer to check at about 12 minutes. Roast nuts until they are a dark, rich brown but not turning black. Take pan from the oven and let cool. Nuts will become crisper if left outside the oven at room temperature.

CHAPTER 7

FUN, FAITH, AND FEASTING
Celebrating Everyday Discipleship

Make space in your life for the things that matter, for family and friends, love and generosity, fun and joy. Without this, you will burn out in mid-career and wonder where your life went.

JONATHAN SACKS

Eat your food with joy,
and drink your wine with a happy heart,
for God approves of this!

ECCLESIASTES 9:7

Table-Discipleship Principle:

Discipleship happens at every moment along the way—morning, noon, night, and every time in between.

"Hey, Dude Mama."

The gravelly voice came from a curly haired almost-man ambling into my kitchen with four more of his kind following. These scraggly headed teens were Nathan's friends, and "Dude Mama" was the name they'd given me. Far from being disrespectful, it was a term of endearment, a sign I had won their angsty teenage trust. It was a moniker I embraced with pride.

"Hi, there." I smiled. "How are you? How about some pizza?"

The crowd of teenagers gathered hungrily around as I pulled two jumbo pizzas out of the oven, the cheese bubbling deliciously on top. It was a paper-plates night, with glass bottles of root beer. When entertaining teenagers, sometimes the goal of eating healthy must be suspended in favor of winning the food-centered hearts of sixteen-year-old boys. I spent my children's younger years carefully feeding them carrots, salads, and whole grains. When the teenage years hit, I shamelessly bribed them with grease, cheese, and ice cream.

The crew piled slices of pizza and grapes (my one attempt at healthful food for the evening) on their plates and bungled out to the back porch. I sat with them for a bit, asking them questions about school, sports, dreams, and even venturing momentarily into their romantic lives. I then left them to their own teenage devices, only popping out later with chocolate chip cookies.

I was always a bit amazed when the friends of my teenage kids opened up to me. It felt like an honor to win the trust of these burgeoning adults. Through our occasional weekend visits and back-porch talks, I realized they *wanted* to be talked to and inquired about. This made me think of my teenage years and the inevitable angst I had felt in growing awkwardly into young adulthood. I knew how I had longed for grace, for someone to help me piece together my half-grown heart without criticism or judgment. And I wanted to relate to these kids in a way that spoke grace to them.

Teen years can stretch a parent's heart. These kids are at the edge of adulthood—straining for more independent friendships, yet not fully developed in maturity or discretion. I wanted my children to have free-dom, but also safety.

The answer to this conundrum to me was obvious—to make our home the best place to be. The most comfortable place to relax and ask questions (any subject fair game). The most fun hangout. And I got them there by tempting them with an unending stream of delicious food and irresistible treats.

Sometimes I think that grace is best experienced through greasy pizza and gentle curiosity.

To me, this strategy was not only a home philosophy, but a disciple-ship principle put in action—perhaps the most important one of all: Discipleship happens at every moment along the way—morning, noon, night, and every time in between.

Even in the ordinary moments.

Even in the not-so-serious moments.

Discipleship happens through relationships that are cultivated by lis-tening to the needs of the moment and moving to meet those needs—even when those needs involve laughing and having fun.

Pizza nights were also movie nights when our family was younger. Feasting on pizza was usually followed by a movie and popcorn. We used to have an air popper, and then we moved to popping our own organic corn in a pan on the stove. No matter how it's made, popcorn has always been a big hit with us, and our family has eaten bowls and bowls of it over the years. Afterward there were always tiny kernels everywhere, but we had a little hand vacuum that ate them up quickly.

The movies were always specially chosen to be heart-filling, mind-shaping, discussion-cultivating ones. Many nights found us staying up into the midnight hours because of the fun discussions that took place. (If the popcorn ran out, there were always chocolate chip cookies or brownies.)

Movies are the stories that move our culture today. They shape val-ues and establish worldviews. When carefully chosen, they provide a more interesting way to examine world issues, discuss the consequences of choices, and explore human motivations and desires.

Often movies allowed us to open up spiritual conversations with the many non-Christians who were welcomed into our home on a regular basis. But they also brought us together as a family. We enjoyed watching great hero tales, historical epics, and adventure dramas—and we solved a million-zillion mysteries along with a variety of sleuths. Some of them we watched over and over again, learning to love the characters together.

Movies coupled with food and great conversation helped shaped our souls. We even made it a habit to join our teens at midnight openings of some of their favorite films.

I've known people in my time—and I have sometimes been this person!—who think that nothing can be of spiritual value that is not serious, thoughtful, and prayerful. But I have learned that this is an incomplete way of thinking about God, and it can actually impede discipleship. Our Christian culture can focus so much on the logic and truth and philosophy of faith that we forget there are other ways to encounter God—through creation, in stories, in relationships, in prayer—and also, I've come to believe, in enjoyment and pleasure.

Fun and delight are two key elements in the life of our home. Creating an atmosphere of comfort, laughter, and enjoyment helps people feel at ease, embraced, and accepted for who they are. In this atmosphere of tranquility and safety, a foundation of connection is built so that people feel able to ask deeper questions.

Fun is often overlooked in the intentional life. The ability to play—to laugh and enjoy little things in life—is reflective of the image of God in our lives. It reminds us that we are not here as cogs in the universal system, but as children of a loving Father who loves to watch His children laugh. I firmly believe a life without fun, friendships, and pizza nights is a life not fully lived as God intended it to be.

But can we develop a culture of godly fun in our homes? How do we begin to create these bonds? Why is fun important, and how do we cultivate it? What does it mean to embrace the discipleship principle of fun? Let's look a little closer—and hopefully have some fun doing it.

Discipleship in the Midst of Life

People have often commented that my books make it sound like all my family does is sit around having serious theological discussions and drinking too much tea. This is more true than we sometimes like to admit. We are definitely a verbal family, we like to go deep in our conversations, and we definitely like our tea. Some families like sports or playing games; mine likes to wax eloquent while sipping caffeinated beverages—though we also pontificate when playing Monopoly, hiking, driving, or playing tennis. (And then we break for tea.)

But we also brush our teeth. We also take out the garbage and throw balls for the dog. We watch videos and read e-mails and read novels and eat lunch. In other words, most of our lives, our ministry, and our work consist of ordinary day-to-day moments. Even for us, not every moment can contain a deep conversation about God's work in our lives.

I do not say this to discourage "meaty" conversations, but simply to be realistic. When you have toddlers, five minutes at the dinner table without someone dropping food or wailing over the fact they don't like peas is a sought-after dream. A discipleship that cannot make room for the ordinary is unrealistic. A realistic discipleship model makes space for pizza and popcorn, movie nights and messes, for doing chores and relaxing together, for deep conversation and delighted laughter, and even for people cratering into arguments and emotional messes.

Christians sometimes feel a pressure to be "spiritual" all the time. But to separate the spiritual from the ordinary is to say that Jesus is not King over those everyday moments in life. We should learn from Jesus to embrace the mundane moments—even the silly, fun ones—and find God's fingerprints of grace within them. If we can do this, we will learn to see God in a fuller dimension.

Jesus didn't come just to save our souls; He came to redeem every part of our lives. When we give our whole lives to Him—food, drink, work, play, body, spirit, and family—we glorify God by living into the beauty He meant for us.

And Jesus' ministry modeled this. He didn't just preach to the five thousand; He fed them! He didn't just give a homily at the wedding;

He gave the guests wine and made the party even better! He conducted His everyday business amid the daily activities of life—fishing, drawing water, collecting and paying taxes. And eating—definitely eating. If you ever needed assurance that Jesus thought positively about food, look to the Gospel of Luke, which records no fewer than ten scenes in which the main concern of all present was to eat.

I like to picture these feasts in my imagination. In the time Jesus lived, meals were not nice, orderly things. I imagine dusty garments, loud arguments, pungent spices, and stinky feet. (Come to think of it, this doesn't sound all that different from my table at dinner, especially when my children were teens.) Jesus' ministry not only allowed for these meals; it took place in the context of them.

Not all holy moments are somber and serious. If Jesus discipled His apostles in the midst of food, drink, laughter, and mundane moments, I believe we should too. Instead of viewing them as spiritual "downtime," we should see them as the times when God is most likely to work.

Our laughter can glorify God as much as our thoughtful meditation.

Our cheerful performance of mundane tasks like vacuuming can honor God as much as our faithful church attendance.

Serving pizza to a houseful of teenagers can strike spiritual gold.

We must learn to cherish *all* the moments of our lives and to call them holy.

Fun Lays Foundations of Connection

Are we going to pray . . . again?

This was the comment I would get on occasion as my children grew older and felt they had outgrown our morning times or had other things to do. Adjustments have to be made for maturity, with an assumption that the routines of all the years have made an impact. There is a mysterious time when our children need wings and freedom to create their own priorities and schedules. There is no formula for following through on this, just freedom in the Spirit to discover what is best for each one and how to set each free to flourish in adult life with our blessing.

Too much overspiritualizing can actually make all of us feel a bit uncomfortable at times. Our family often experienced this when we found ourselves attending yet another dinner at the Johnsons' (not their real name!). They were actually close friends, but our whole family harbored a silent dread each time we visited. Why? Because of the earnest lectures and long prayers that accompanied even the most casual occasion.

The members of this family genuinely loved the Lord and others. I truly believe their prayer times came from a sincere heart. But every social gathering in their home inevitably led to a time of extended religious contemplation. As a result, I never felt comfortable to be myself there. I felt condemned for laughing at their comical little dog or dropping salad in my lap. I eventually found out that Clay and the children felt uncomfortable in the same way. And we suspect the same was true for other guests.

I would never presume to say that the Johnsons' efforts at discipleship were ineffective. (God does move in mysterious ways.) But in my experience, deep conversations bloom more naturally from comfortable conversations. No one likes to feel forced to talk about anything, particularly the gospel and spiritual matters. I know I certainly don't. And yet so many well-intentioned Christians end up driving people away from possible connection because of pressured conversations.

One of my professors in college used to say, "Laughter is the first form of acceptance." To laugh is a vulnerable thing, so allowing a space where people can laugh creates vulnerability that leads to spiritual and personal conversations. Setting a tone of friendly ease rather than the creeping feeling that the whole endeavor is leading to a foregone conclusion allows people to be their real selves. Simple questions and genuine interest draw people into conversation instead of driving them away.

A helpful way to think of this is the idea of the difference between *phatic* and *emphatic* communication. The dictionary defines *phatic* as "denoting or relating to language used for general purposes of social interaction, rather than to convey information or ask questions."[1] *Emphatic* is defined as "showing or giving emphasis; expressing something forcibly and clearly."[2]

We communicate with both phatic and emphatic communication

all the time. If we erred on either side too heavily, our relationships would either be strained or shallow. If we only had phatic communication (lighthearted and social), our relationships would never achieve any depth. But if our conversations are always driven by an agenda, there is no space to simply enjoy the presence of others and build a friendship based on interest in each other.

We need both phatic and emphatic communication for strong connections with our spouses, friends, coworkers, and children, and anyone else we hope to disciple. So do not be afraid to let the pendulum swing. Enjoy depth and serious matters, but also enjoy just being together in friendship.

Food and fun are sure ways to cultivate this sort of balance. I learned this in my time working for campus ministries. Our leaders always told us that if we were going to have an outreach event, there needed to be both food and icebreakers. For most events my ministry partners and I would need to get dozens of boxes of pizza and multiple bags of chips, and we'd plan games that would make people laugh and feel comfortable with each other.

As a naturally mission-minded but introverted person who harbored a conflicted relationship with small talk, this often went against the grain for me. It seemed somehow frivolous. Why couldn't we just get down to the important business of winning hearts for Jesus?

But I came to realize that the games and eating and conversation were key to opening people's hearts. For lonely college students, having a space to laugh, meet people, and feel accepted was a profound answer to the deep longings of their hearts. Like Jesus, we were attending to their emotional, physical, and social needs as well as their spiritual needs and presenting the gospel as a personal appeal, not an agenda. As a single woman, I had many opportunities to talk to students about God's love in the context of food, fun, and identifying with their student lifestyles. As a result, I saw many embrace a lifelong commitment to Christ.

The most effective discipleship, I learned, flows from genuine and deep connection, and such connection often begins in an atmosphere of fun, friendship, and both noticing and meeting needs.

I carried this lesson with me when I started a family of my own. It was always my goal that our home be the place our children and their friends loved to be. I wanted our walls to be a haven in a weary world, a place where people could come and know they would find love and laughter and perhaps some spare chocolate chip cookies. In the process, I hoped, they would also come to know Jesus.

To my children, especially, home was best. Even now, in their adult years, their heartstrings are tied to home because it is a place where they know they will be cared for and known. A web of connection and love knits us together from the many fun times we have had as well as from our shared and growing faith.

Fun Is Valuable in Itself

God didn't make us to use us. Have you ever thought about that?

God is completely sufficient in Himself. He needs nothing. No one can "help" God.

The opening chapters of Genesis show clearly that God didn't create us because He wanted little slaves, but because He wanted new sons and daughters. He set Adam and Eve in a lavish garden full of vibrant colors, lush pastures, rich fruits, and glorious sunsets. Then He essentially said, "Go! Enjoy! Taste. Touch. Eat. Garden. Love."

He didn't create us because He needed some creatures to work for Him.

He created us because He wanted someone like Him—His own image bearers—to love and share His beautiful new world with.

And yet so often I think we perform in our lives as though our primary goal in life is to be useful to God. We hustle, bustle, and fret, wondering if we are doing enough for God—as if we could *ever* do enough. We see every moment that is not occupied with something "productive" or "devotional" as wasted and a bit shameful.

Isn't this contrary to God's original design for us in Genesis?

Often delight and pleasure are overlooked in the Christian life because they do not appear useful, functional, helpful, or practical. Christians sometimes fall into a utilitarian mind-set, pushing things aside that are not "effective" or "spiritual."

There are two problems with this mind-set. First it assumes—falsely—that the goal of our walk with the Lord is to be useful.

Of course we are called to be instruments of His peace, to live righteous lives, and to care for others. But ultimately, our calling is to bring glory to God and to let Him perfect us into the image bearers He always meant us to be. I think sometimes we can bring much more glory to God by being cheerful and delighting in the world and people He has given us than by living a "useful" life where we trot grimly around with a martyr complex that annoys everyone we encounter.

The second problem with the utilitarian mind-set is the assumption that fun is not meaningful. But fun and delight have the power to knit our hearts together in community. They create the basis for a relationship that can go deeper when the moment is right.

I've come to believe, in fact, that thoroughly enjoying life is one of the things that can bring the most glory to God.

Do movies and friendship open hearts to talk about true and deep things?

Absolutely.

Do jokes and games and food create a strong foundation for good relationships and effective discipling?

Yes.

But aside from all of these benefits, enjoyable activity is valuable in its own right because it naturally draws us to worship. When I put aside all of my busywork and take a day off to relax, I am amazed at how much my heart is restored and opens to the Lord.

As I take a walk, my eyes are opened up to all the beautiful flowers, the mountain sunsets—what a creative God we have! The rigorous exercise makes my body feel good.

I bring iced tea to the front yard, where my adult children are throwing balls for our silly little golden retriever, Darcy Dog.

What a gift family is! How fabulous that God made dogs for us to love.

In the evening I stretch out on a blanket in the grass and marvel at the sparkling stars, with children and dog surrounding me.

What a miracle that the same God who made the stars made us!

When we enjoy the world, we come back to the truest realization: that everything in life is a gift from God that we should enjoy and be thankful for.

Once Nathan said to me, "Mama, I'm so glad we worship a God who made jalapeño peppers and puppy dogs and Celtic music to dance to and jokes to laugh at." Nathan saw God's love in all of those things, and so do I. God has given us this old world as a gift. Just like someone handing over a carefully and thoughtfully chosen present to a loved one, God has given us this beautiful planet full of things for us to taste, see, smell, hear, and love. We deny His love when we refuse to enjoy this perfect gift and to thank Him for it.

Fun is valuable in itself because it requires us to be present to the graces and delights God has given us freely as gifts. It draws us into worship. It fills us with thankfulness.

Isn't that worthwhile? In fact, isn't that wonderful?

Sometimes Pleasant Diversion Is the Solution

She sat misty eyed on my couch with a heavy heart. A young adult emerging into our unstable world, Joy was having a natural reaction to the brokenness she saw. And there I was, wanting to give her a thousand answers that I didn't quite have.

Should I pray?

Should I pull all of the apologetics books off the shelf?

Should I join her in this existential crisis?

I found myself in this situation so many times with my dear and deep children. In trying to help them, I would carry around their sadness. The sadness and questions multiplied, and I would feel like a failure.

I finally realized that questions and sorrow will always be present in this broken world. They will not disappear. So how could I build a bridge to my dear ones' aching and doubting hearts?

The first step was to come along beside them, identifying with their worries, anxiety, and disappointment, offering my sympathy and my presence.

Second was verbalizing that I believed God would answer them faithfully in their doubts. Great people have doubted faithfully through all the years. Wanting to believe God but needing to find His satisfying answers and faithful character is a part of becoming mature.

And third was finding a way to lighten the load. My children must wrestle through things with the Lord, but sometimes my role is to remind them of the beauty and delight left in the world. So instead of fretting and trying to explain away the issues of the universe, I would take my anxious teens to get ice cream at our local lakefront, where we licked our cones and meandered the path around the lake. Or we would take a hike on our mountain trails with a small snack to enjoy along the way. Or paint toenails as an act of love.

There should always be space for questions and weeping, but I was always amazed at how much more likely my children were to believe in God, goodness, and hope after a trip to their favorite coffee shop or a back rub accompanied with a warm cup of spiced cider.

Reason to Celebrate

It has been one of the greatest delights to see those scraggly teenagers who used to eat pizza on our porch grow into handsome and capable adults, getting married and setting out into the world. I love to hear from them from time to time, to celebrate the milestones of their lives: college, jobs, marriage, and someday even children of their own. The fruit of those pizza evenings and movie nights is sweet.

Sometimes celebrating, enjoying, and laughing seem almost inappropriate in a world as broken as ours. We look around and see panic on the faces of everyone we see. Tragedies become ordinary. How, in good conscience, can we laugh and celebrate and eat pizza?

I believe we *must* celebrate—because celebration is one of the most effective weapons we have against the darkness of our day. The real grief of the state of our world is the pervasive fear that settles in our hearts.

Did not Paul say to Timothy, "For God has not given us a spirit of fear and timidity, but of power, love, and self-discipline" (2 Timothy 1:7)? When we give in to fear and silence, we give in to the dark powers of our day. When we celebrate, however, we proclaim the fact that there is still good in the world because God is still faithful. Though dark and scary events may take place, our homes and communities can still be bastions of celebration, laughter, worship, thankfulness, and fun. Our love, our friendship, our sympathy can be lifegiving instruments of hope.

We celebrate God's work in the ordinary.

We create foundations of connection and relationship.

We worship God for the gift He has given us of the world.

Take it from a Dude Mama—nothing could be more lifegiving than that!

Something to Ponder

Luke 5:33-35

> One day some people said to Jesus, "John the Baptist's disciples fast and pray regularly, and so do the disciples of the Pharisees. Why are your disciples always eating and drinking?"
>
> Jesus responded, "Do wedding guests fast while celebrating with the groom? Of course not. But someday the groom will be taken away from them, and then they will fast."

Matthew 11:19

> The Son of Man, on the other hand, feasts and drinks, and you say, "He's a glutton and a drunkard, and a friend of tax collectors and other sinners!" But wisdom is shown to be right by its results.

- What did people accuse Jesus of in these two passages? How did this show their disdain for the joy and fellowship of eating and drinking together? What does Jesus' response tell you?

- Do you tend to see mealtimes and fun as meaningful and important, or do you find yourself pushing them aside as unspiritual activities? Under what circumstances are you most likely to do this?

- Have you ever felt uncomfortable with the pressure to have a spiritual conversation? What happened, and what was your response?

- How do you think you can foster a space of comfort and connection in your home?

Psalm 104

O LORD my God, how great you are! . . .
You stretch out the starry curtain of the heavens;
    you lay out the rafters of your home in the rain clouds.
You make the clouds your chariot;
    you ride upon the wings of the wind. . . .
You send rain on the mountains from your heavenly home,
    and you fill the earth with the fruit of your labor.
You cause grass to grow for the livestock
    and plants for people to use.
You allow them to produce food from the earth—
    wine to make them glad,
olive oil to soothe their skin,
    and bread to give them strength.

PSALM 104:1-3, 13-15

What a picture this passage paints! It is full of beautiful poetry describing the wonderful works of God's hand in creation. Read the entire psalm and consider.

- What verses stand out to you? Why?

- Before God communicates to us with commands or truth, God communicates to us with wordless delight and glory. Are you enjoying that delight? If not, why not? What would it take to enjoy God's creation more?

Something to Try

- Plan a fun evening for your friends or family with the purpose of enjoying them. Game nights have given us some hilarious evenings with people we did not know well, but who became sweet friends through the laughter and fun shared. Invite someone over for a time of connection.

- Stop your cycle of busyness for at least fifteen minutes today and do something purely for the sake of enjoying it. Go for a walk in a lovely place, get a cup of coffee and people watch, stargaze at night. How does your heart feel after such a time?

A Pizza Feast for Teens and More

❋ **Much-Better-than-Delivery Homemade Pizza**
(For a Crowd)

Our homemade pizzas are so much better than the ones we buy at the fast-food places. Every inch can be covered with yummy toppings. My family prefers the whole-wheat crust—though you can use unbleached white flour too. We like to let each friend or family member make his or her own slices. That way, everyone can be satisfied. We cut in an inch or so at the edges before cooking to delineate the individual pieces. (Make sure to cut all the way through the crust to keep the pieces separate during cooking.) This recipe makes a lot, but you can easily halve it if you want only one pizza.

Your favorite pizza toppings: onions, green or red peppers, pepperoni,
    mushrooms, pineapple, Canadian bacon, ham, cooked
    sausage, or hamburger
1 large bag (16 ounces) shredded mozzarella cheese (or shred your
    own—about 4 cups)
1½ cups very warm water (around 110°F)
1 tablespoon instant yeast
1 teaspoon sugar
¼ cup olive oil
4 cups freshly ground whole-wheat flour or unbleached all-purpose
    flour
2 teaspoons sea salt
1 15-ounce jar pizza sauce (I usually use a good organic brand from
    the grocery store, but there are many good recipes available
    online.)

Cut up your topping ingredients and set aside to use as soon as the
dough is ready. Grate the cheese if you don't buy it already grated.

To make the dough, put warm water into a large glass measuring cup or glass bowl. Sprinkle the yeast into the water and whisk it in. Sprinkle the sugar over this mixture and stir it in to help yeast grow more quickly. Let it sit for five minutes to be sure yeast is active. (Old yeast won't grow.) If the mixture turns creamy and bubbly, you're good to go. If not, get more yeast and try again.

Pour yeast mixture and olive oil into the bowl of a stand mixer fitted with a dough hook. I have a strong-motor Bosch mixer that has a lifetime warranty and can easily mix six loaves of bread without burning out the motor. Don't worry if you don't have a mixer, though. You can also do this by hand with a little bit of elbow grease.

Start the mixer (or start stirring!) and pour in flour a little at a time until the dough comes clean from the sides of the mixing bowl. (You may not have to use all the flour.) Keep mixing for several minutes. Add the salt near the end of mixing time.

Spread a little more oil on your counter or spray it with cooking spray to keep dough from sticking. Pour dough out onto oiled countertop and knead for 5–10 minutes, until dough is soft and elastic. Be sure to get all the bubbles out when you knead the dough, or you will have a hole in your pizza crust. Let it stand for at least 10 minutes and it will become easier to roll out. Divide dough into two pieces and then roll out each piece to fit the size of your pizza pans. (Mine are about 16 inches in diameter and do not need to be greased.) Move the rolled-out dough to the pans and, if necessary, stretch it to fit. (I usually have someone help me with this step because the large circle of dough can be unwieldy to transport.) Let the dough rise while you preheat oven to 425°F.

Spread pizza sauce over your dough. (I find that one can or jar of ready-made sauce will usually spread over two crusts.) Cover with your favorite toppings, sprinkle generously with mozzarella cheese, and place in your hot oven for 15–18 minutes. (Baking may take longer if pizzas are large.) Take out when cheese is bubbling and crust is the color you like it. We like our cheese crispy, so we let

them cook until the cheese is golden and a little crisp on top. Let
pizzas sit a few minutes, then cut and serve.

Makes 2 large pizzas (about 16 inches in diameter).

❄ Clarkson Snowballs (Russian Tea Cakes)

*I grew up with these delicate treats, but our family really fell in love with
them in Austria. Every year at the wonderful outdoor Christmas markets
there would be a baker making these little treasures. We would eat them hot
out of the oven, smothered in powdered sugar and piled high in a brown
paper cone. Even today they are my family's very favorite cookie—a perfect
surprise treat on the first day of snow or a cold winter's day.*

1 cup salted butter, softened
½ cup confectioner's sugar, plus extra for rolling
2 teaspoons vanilla extract
2½ cups unbleached all-purpose flour
1 cup finely chopped pecans
¼ teaspoon sea salt

Preheat oven to 375°F.

Cream together butter, confectioner's sugar, and vanilla extract
with a mixer or by hand. Mix together flour, nuts, and salt, then add
to butter mixture and stir just until dough holds together. You can
add a couple of pats of softened butter if dough seems too stiff.

Shape dough into 1-inch balls (bigger ones are also fun for
Christmas). Place close together on ungreased cookie sheet without
letting them touch. (They do not spread.) Bake 12–13 minutes
(longer for bigger cookies) until cookies are firm but not brown. Cool
on a wire rack, and they will become even firmer. When cookies are
cool enough to touch, roll in confectioner's sugar to cover completely.

Makes 4 dozen small cookies or 3 dozen large ones.

CHAPTER 8

LIVING OUT GRACE
Possibilities for Easy Feasting

It is better to light a candle than curse the darkness.
AUTHOR UNKNOWN

Then Jesus said, "Let's go off by ourselves to a quiet place and rest awhile." He said this because there were so many people coming and going that Jesus and his apostles didn't even have time to eat.
MARK 6:31

Table-Discipleship Principle:

A wise discipler must make space for
rest and beauty in the midst of life.

THEY WANT TO EAT AGAIN!

This thought flashed into my mind as my stomach clenched in a mix of exasperation and exhaustion.

Mealtimes occur at startlingly regular intervals, don't they? It often seems that I have only just finished cleaning up lunch dishes when I must begin thinking about what to make for dinner. Another meal, another dish, another counter to clean. And then, after sleepily tidying up the kitchen at the end of the night, I realize: *It all starts again tomorrow!* In my tired moments, it seems like such an injustice. How can my family expect food three times a day, every day? And I don't even get weekends off!

But that one particular night, it was more than the usual monotonous routine that caused my stomach to clench. I was weary. Soul weary. Physically weary. Emotionally weary. Heart, mind, and body weary. Life was hurling fastballs at me, one after another, and I was almost to the point of dropping the bat and running away.

I had just returned from a speaking engagement, and all I wanted to do was sleep and then curl up with a book, and indulge in endless cups of tea, coffee, or other, more mature sips. But alas, I had three children still at home with busy schedules, hormonal mood swings, and heartbreaks, along with my own personal and professional responsibilities that were unmoved by my desire to hibernate.

I carried around an achy soul with me but had no time to tend to it or be gentle with myself. And my young-adult children, even my sweet friends who came regularly to my home for meals or tea, either didn't notice or were so caught up in their own issues they couldn't see my need.

Joy was in the full throes of tournament season for speech and debate. Joel was working diligently at a retail job, returning emotionally drained and physically exhausted every day. Sarah was at an in-between point in life, walking through disappointment and, for the moment, drifting, struggling with the full frustration that is young adulthood. Nathan was in Hollywood, but called and wanted to talk multiple times a week. Clay and I were neck deep in trying to catch up on work after a busy conference season. And I hosted a regular Bible study in my home with sixty to a hundred people attending each meeting.

Every moment of my day was filled to the brim—driving Joy to appointments, supporting Clay, reaching out to friends, working on writing projects in snatched moments in between, and sharing the frustrations of my struggling children. And did I mention helping our two elderly moms, both senile and in need of attention? It seemed that all of life had conspired to ensure my physical, emotional, and spiritual exhaustion.

And everyone still wanted to eat again.

I heaved a meaningful sigh that no one was there to hear and sank into the faded cushions of my reading chair. A few minutes later, I spied Sarah's gently treading feet descending the stairs, closely followed by Joy's gangly legs bounding down two stairs at a time.

"What's for dinner, Mama?" Joy asked, blissfully unaware of my deep weariness.

"Oh my goodness," I sighed. "I'm not sure yet."

In that moment a decision presented itself to me. I could give in to the overwhelming, gray exhaustion I felt. Or I could create an environment of rest and beauty for my beloved family and, in so doing, create a space of rest for my own soul.

It was a habit of mine to take the clouds in my head and seek to blow them away with simplicity, moving toward gratefulness. In that moment, that habit saved me.

"I'm pretty exhausted tonight," I admitted to my girls. "But let's rest and enjoy this evening. How about a snack meal on the porch? It's beautiful out tonight. I'll cut some cheese slices. Can you all put something together for our snack feast?"

"I'll slice some fruit!" offered Sarah.

"I will do buttered toast and toasted nuts," said Joy.

In characteristic fashion, Joel poked his head in late in the conversation. I wasted no time.

"We're putting together a snack meal, Joel. What will your contribution be?"

"How about popcorn?"

This was a well-liked and very familiar idea. So we bustled briefly about the kitchen, toted our fare to the back porch, lit a candle, played soothing music from my portable speaker, and enjoyed our sumptuous snack dinner. As we munched on popcorn and each created our favorite combination of toast, cheese, nuts, and fruit, I breathed a sigh of relief. What could have been an evening of another tired meal, piles of dishes, and short tempers turned into an evening of rest and beauty. Our covered porch became a sanctuary for our tired hearts, and the mountain air and waving pines that bordered the porch provided the beauty we needed.

Such times have occurred throughout my life—for instance, the time when three of my children had chicken pox, followed by pneumonia and then encephalitis. Our house was a wreck of dishes, blankets all over the house, toys, and a pile of laundry as high as the sky. I don't think I slept for six weeks straight.

At times like this, comfort food means so much—especially comfort food that requires no cooking and minimal cleanup.

Just this week, I am helping Joy pack for Scotland to finish her master's degree, launching a book in three days, and preparing for a week of television and podcasts that will culminate in five national conferences. I have two single friends who each need private talk time with me. And everyone *still* wants to eat!

How grateful I am that a Qdoba Mexican fast-food restaurant just moved into our small town—and that the food my kids all miss when they study overseas is Mexican and Chick-fil-A. I'm thrilled to be able to fulfill their desires this week because it meets my need not to cook.

And as much as I treasure the benefits of home cooking and healthy meals, I have learned we can still have great table discussions over fast food on rare occasions. Just this week, while enjoying burritos and chicken sandwiches, we have enjoyed great conversations about incarnational living, the meaning of virtue, the presidential inauguration, a new movie in town, and the theses both Joel and Joy are considering for their PhDs—if they get into the schools they want for next year.

Life can be exhausting. Whether it be a season of busyness, a tragedy that strikes, a newborn, a new job, tax season (!), mental or emotional issues, a move, or just the ordinary hustle and bustle of life, there come times for all of us when cooking another meal and washing another dish feels like a burden too great to bear. Even getting food on the table seems like a stretch, much less using mealtimes for intentional discipleship.

Good, homemade, healthy food is a great goal to shoot for, especially on a regular basis. Yet making exceptions and enjoying the freedom that each of us has to rule over our own kitchen brings freedom and grace to this ever-repeating work of life.

For this reason I've come to believe in the profound importance of snack meals—meals that are easy, nourishing, and restful. They can absolutely save your sanity during those crazy times. But here's another benefit: When you bring beauty and rest into the occasional chaos of your life, you are teaching your children how to prepare for the storms of life and live well through them.

The rubber meets the road when we work out the question of *how* to bring beauty and rest to life in the midst of storms. For me, this boils down to three ideas.

First, that bringing grace to the busy moments of your life is not about performance or perfection, but sustainability.

Second, that bringing peace and beauty amid the whirlwind necessitates preparation.

And finally, that a little bit of beauty goes a long way to make things better.

Think Sustainability

Has this book made you feel guilty yet? Perhaps you read these chapters and are overwhelmed by all of the recipes and ideas and activities. Maybe you feel like your life is too full of toddlers, teens, chores, and responsibilities for all of this frivolous feasting! Perhaps, like me, your family needs you to earn money, and that, too, can be a regular drain of your physical and mental energy.

I want you to know that I completely understand and empathize with you. I've had my overwhelming seasons; in fact, they might even have made up a majority of my life.

People frequently say to me, "It's nice that you have ideals, but it's all been easy for you." But this is just not true. Through the years our family has encountered all the usual issues and quite a few unusual ones—deaths in the family, chronic health issues, job layoffs, money issues, mental illness, seventeen moves, multiple miscarriages, church splits, church plants, and more.

So my ideals did not develop out of ease, but out of difficulty.

Learning to create beauty and peace in everyday moments was what kept me going in the middle of it all. Food, feasting, and traditions are not frivolous, but ways to make life work, to make it sustainable. Predictable peace, comfort, and fellowship are something every home should provide—at least most of the time.

This provision is not about looking like a 1950s housewife, complete with pearls and heels. It's definitely not about doing everything perfectly or holding yourself to impossible ideals. It's about sustainability—discovering ways to sustain ourselves when life becomes challenging and developing techniques for tending to the physical, emotional, and spiritual needs of our household along the way. It's about learning to flex in the moment when life is interrupted without losing overall rhythms and without condemning yourself for failing. Unless we can make a plan that fits our needs, pressures, and seasons of life, we will constantly feel inadequate to keep our goals intact. Without a focus on sustainability, none of us will be able to do what God has called us to.

Keep in mind that there's a difference between a sustainability mind-set and a survival mind-set. Survival thinking is a kind of desperation, grabbing at whatever we can find to get us through the day or night. But though we may survive on ramen noodles and takeout for a while, we won't be able to sustain our energy or effectiveness on this for long. Living in survival mode will eventually erode the health of our bodies and our souls.

Sustainability thinking, however, takes a longer view. It's more thoughtful and strategic—realistically assessing needs and schedules, and planning ways to address both in a way that we can realistically keep. It asks, *What needs to happen for me to maintain my physical energy, my emotional balance, and my spiritual well-being even when I'm not able to do everything I want to do? And how can I provide for my family's needs in the process?*

Consider the verse at the beginning of this chapter:

Then Jesus said, "Let's go off by ourselves to a quiet place and rest awhile." He said this because there were so many people coming and going that Jesus and his apostles didn't even have time to eat. MARK 6:31

Even Jesus, the incarnate Son of God, made space in His life for rest when things got hectic. He knew what He and His disciples needed in order for His ministry to continue.

I love that this verse says they "didn't even have time to eat." Haven't you felt like this? Doesn't this capture the feeling we have all had in times of extreme busyness? In the midst of life—discipleship, family, work, and ministry—there will be times where it will be difficult even to fit a meal into the schedule. In these times, Jesus, through the example of His own life, calls us not to give in to chaos, but to think sustainability—to create a space of rest and to tend to our needs and the needs of our family. When we do that, we are modeling for our children how to live well and take care of ourselves as well as others.

As humans, we are essentially needy; we have needs that, if ignored, will lead to severe consequences. If we do not eat, we will eventually starve. If we do not drink, we will eventually die of thirst. If we do not sleep, we will become psychotic and eventually die as well. And long before these eventualities come about, we will become depleted and unable to attend to our responsibilities. It is impossible for us to tackle the day and life before us if our basic needs are not attended to.

Our basic needs are not only physical, of course. We have souls as well as bodies, and so we also have soul needs—for friendship, beauty, peace, and communion with God. Just as we must plan meals and snacks to feed physical bodies, we must plan ways to feed souls, including our own.

Consider Elijah. After having his most dramatic encounter with Ahab and Jezebel, Elijah found himself fleeing for his life in the desert (see 1 Kings 19). He was so weary that he lay down on the ground in the wilderness and asked God to let him die. Rather than rebuking him or letting him die, God sent an angel to minister to him. The angel made him sleep, then touched him and gave him food and drink. After that, God came to him in the still small whisper. God knew that before Elijah could continue his ministry, he needed his emotional, physical, and spiritual needs to be tended to. This teaches us that if we are to weather the storms of life, conquer the difficult times with grace, and bravely live out God's call on our lives, we must take time to tend to our needs. And again, this is not about perfectionism or performance, but about making life sustainable.

One last thought about sustainability. I would urge you to avoid legalism when it comes to eating. I have a goal of cooking organic, natural, homemade, and generally healthy, with as few added chemicals as possible. Yet I also know that in the irregular times of life, when we still need to eat, I have freedom to do something different to meet my family's need to eat so that I don't burn out.

Remember, there is great disagreement about what healthy eating means. And I have lived long enough to see many "healthy" fads come and go. Several years ago I spent a week at a health retreat center to rest, fast, and renew after a very wearying season. (Yes, I have done all the "healthy" things in my many years.) Attending with me were people who ate vegan, vegetarian, paleo, gluten-free, dairy-free, grain-free, grain based—you name it. Each opinionated idealist was quite sure that the others had it all wrong. I had never heard so many warnings and rules about eating in my life, so many choices of how to do diet well. It was a little overwhelming to me.

After a lot of thought, years of life, and experimentation, I have decided that (1) I am free to make my own choices for my family and

(2) getting it right 70 to 75 percent of the time with the things I consider healthy for us is good enough for our particular family. I do try to limit those foods that I know are less nutritious or possibly harmful in large amounts—sugars, fried food, fast food, chemically altered food. But I also give myself permission to make choices of freedom during a holiday season or on a birthday, in times of great stress when ease of eating trumps adding even more stress, or especially when I am in someone else's home.

I travel all over the world for both ministry and pleasure and eat in many diverse cultures and many different homes where diets vary greatly. Often I think it far more important to enjoy the meal and the company of those who serve me than to separate myself from them because of personal choices. I don't want to be "that picky American." So I make a choice to sacrifice my usual preferences in favor of graciousness and relationship, trusting that my long-term sustainable approach will keep me going.

In this area, as in others of my life, I will never be perfect, but I am always moving toward more understanding and more balance and maturity. And that's what sustainability thinking is all about. I commend it to you. Grace to your table and diet!

Be Prepared
We know that storms will come, so we ought to bring umbrellas. That's a philosophy that has served me well when it comes to my life and my table.

When I was a dewy-eyed new wife, I was surprised every time a difficulty came into my path. I was astonished at all the ways my life did not go as I intended it to. But I quickly learned that I could not fall to pieces each time a difficulty came. I needed a strategy.

Having a realistic view of life means that you anticipate difficulties, make a plan for meeting them, and seek to make life beautiful in the midst of them. As a wise ruler of your life and home, be intentional about making advance preparations that will bring you nourishment and enjoyment in difficult moments of life.

One of the most important elements of being prepared is providing for the most basic needs you and your family may have. Though we sometimes live as though it is not true, we have bodies that need to be taken care of or they will conk out . . . and at the most inconvenient time.

Abraham Maslow, a twentieth-century psychologist, theorized that before we can cope with social, professional, and emotional elements of our lives, we must have our basic physiological needs met. (This theory is commonly called the "hierarchy of needs."[1]) How can you make it through a night with a screaming baby if you are on the point of fainting with hunger? This is true of our spiritual health as well. How often have I sat down with every intention of praying deeply for the betterment of my family and the world, only to find myself dozing off or wondering what I'm going to make for breakfast?

But Jesus does not scorn us for our physical needs. He made us this way! Jesus calls Himself the Bread of Life, acknowledging the fact that we all need both physical and spiritual food to survive.

Taking care of your children's basic physical needs through feeding them nourishing food opens their hearts to your instruction. In seasons of difficulty, planning ahead and nourishing yourself and your family not only meets their hunger needs, but also instills a soul-deep trust that God will also provide for them and that they, too, can learn to be strong and prepare for difficult seasons.

I have several strategies when it comes to preparing for the basic needs of nourishment for my family in busy times.

My first strategy is packing my freezer with food I can take out and cook at a moment's notice with almost no work. I often make a big batch of any kind of soup or chili and freeze meal-sized portions in zippered freezer bags. (Freeze them lying flat and they will take up little space in the freezer.) Another handy trick is to make or buy several loaves of bread and then freeze them until you need them. This way, when an overwhelming night comes, all you need to do is take out the frozen soup and bread, thaw it, and you have a meal at your fingertips with no trouble at all.

I also use my pressure cooker to cook several packages of chicken when it is on sale. I cut it into bite-sized pieces, then freeze it so it's ready to add to pasta, rice, soups, or salads. This strategy works with any meat—hamburger, ground turkey, chicken, or stew meat—as well as rice, noodles, and even fruit. Keeping frozen bags of store-bought veggies and cans of broth on hand means I always have what I need for a quick soup.

Another favorite strategy of mine, as described in the beginning of this chapter, is snack meals. Snack meals are just what they sound like— a gathering of whatever healthy, yummy snacks we have on hand. The staples of this meal are simple:

- sliced cheese (cheddar, Swiss, Gouda, whatever you like)
- some kind of cold or leftover meat (rolled-up slices of chicken or turkey, ham, even pepperoni)
- fruit (apples, oranges, grapes, strawberries, bananas)
- raw veggies (carrots, celery, cauliflower, broccoli, green onions, bell peppers)
- bread (sliced, pita, naan, or tortillas) or crackers
- nuts (raw or roasted)
- popcorn (if you like!)
- some kind of sweet treat (cookie bars, muffins, individual chocolates—dark salted almond or dark caramel are my favorites—or something from the bakery)

These basics are just the beginning, of course. Other possibilities include spreads like hummus or pimento cheese, dips and organic chips, or condiments such as salty olives, roasted red peppers, pickles, jalapeños, or even flavored olive oils. It just depends on what you like and have on hand. Anything you can put together without a great deal of fuss or preparation will work just fine. We love cereal nights and grilled cheese sandwiches with tomato soup!

Snack meals are great because they are the easiest thing to put together but also oddly satisfying. Sometimes they can feel like a special treat. I was delighted the first time I realized that meals I organized in the moments I was most overwhelmed had actually become a reason to celebrate for my company and to my kids. This taught me that the specifics of the meal matter far less than the attitude with which it is served. If you present your meal as a feast, others will go along. So if you know a busy week is coming, why not stock up on components for an enjoyable snack meal for your family . . . and for you?

In addition to stocking my pantry, fridge, and freezer with the components of future meals, I've learned to plan ahead to give myself some delight in the duty. In moments of difficulty, I've found that chocolate chip cookies can make a critical difference. When one is exhausted in mind and body, a little treat can go a long way. For these moments, I always keep frozen cookie dough balls on hand that can be baked and served as a salve to the weary spirit in a few short minutes. There have been many times a chocolate chip cookie has renewed my faith—or a friend's faith—in humanity.

Another fun treat that does not take much work is popcorn. Popcorn stores easily, is quick to prepare, and if you stay away from the microwavable kind, it's not unhealthy. For us it's a pantry staple, perfect for quick snacks.

Preparing for difficult and busy seasons will soften the blow that life can sometimes deal. As you provide nourishment for your family, you live in faith that all seasons can be redeemed and that God will always be the provider of your daily bread . . . or popcorn!

A Little Beauty Goes a Long Way

In times of exhaustion, grief, or trial, holding on to a sense of order and loveliness is essential. Though many trials of life cannot be easily fixed with a pat answer, the difficulty of walking through them is often eased if it can be experienced in a lovely environment. Beauty has anchored my own soul so many times through many years.

In her wonderful book *Walking on Water*, Madeleine L'Engle speaks about art (and artful living) in terms of bringing cosmos from chaos.[2]

This idea stems from being made in the image of a creative God. Just as God looked into the void and created our orderly, lovely, magnificent universe—the cosmos—so we are able to look into the messiness of our lives and create spaces of meaning and beauty. We all feel the weight of the world and its ability to dissolve into chaos. A simple way to combat chaos is to focus on creating small spaces of beauty.

Lighting a candle or setting a vase of fragrant flowers on a surface will do it. Creating a little vignette on a corner table—a framed photo, a carefully arranged stack of books, a bird figurine—will help. Setting a place at the table with beautiful dishes or an interesting centerpiece will do it. Any of these little acts—or hundreds more—can soothe a soul overwhelmed with life.

Framed photos of special memories adorn the small tables and shelves in my own home. Candlesticks and candles appear in almost every area where there is a chair. Framed calligraphy of favorite quotations and verses adorn our walls, and at least three water pitchers full of flowers stand in our sitting areas. (I'm always looking for interesting "vases" at Goodwill and outdoor fairs.) Interesting and beautiful magazines and books are piled high in baskets and bins in every room. I rarely put curtains on our windows because I prefer seeing outside views. (We live at the end of a cul-de-sac, so neighbors cannot see inside.) I position chairs next to windows so it's easy to sit and gaze outdoors.

Keep in mind that beautiful spaces don't always have to be created; sometimes they can just be noticed. Try eating outdoors to take in the freshness of the outside world. (Our second-floor deck, surrounded by pine trees, is a favorite place for our meals.) Or maybe read an exquisite poem or visit an art museum. The essential thing is to give your soul a breath of beauty and not let it be stifled by the busyness of life.

And don't forget music as a source of calm or pleasure. Our kids often joke that I come with my own soundtrack. Several years ago Clay gave me a little portable speaker so that wherever I go, my music can go too. It is one of the best gifts I have received. I have my favorite channels on Pandora, great playlists from my kids, and a favorite film score or two stored on my phone, and I listen all day. Music heartens me on the gloomiest of days. My life would be so much poorer without it.

Again, adding a little beauty to your life is not about perfection; it is about creating a vestige of peace when our lives are fraught. Beauty reminds me that there is a pattern and shape to events of my life. By intentionally creating spaces of beauty, even if only tiny ones, we combat chaos, despair, ugliness, and exhaustion. When life is too much for you, light a candle, put on music, pour yourself a cup of tea, and take a deep breath.

Living Well in the Midst of Life

Many of the days in my life have been like that fateful snack-meal evening, and I anticipate many more to come. I learned some time ago to stop waiting for the moment life slows down. It's been thirty years since I started thinking that, and my life is still going full speed ahead. If anything, it's moving faster than ever.

I now know that those overwhelmed moments of life are the warp and woof of memories. Rather than putting my head down and trying to rush through them toward the elusive "someday" when things will be better and calmer, I have learned to find or create beauty and meaning in the moments that present themselves to me.

If I had spent my life waiting for the "right moment" to be idealistic, I would never have enjoyed the delight of idealistic seeds sown during trials. In fact, I developed most of my ideals in faith—creating beauty when I didn't know if it would make a difference, lighting one more candle in hope of a more hopeful day, cooking one more meal in anticipation of God's provision. These offerings are intentional acts of faith. And most often it is in those moments of weariness that I'm most likely to see God's gentle hand at work.

One of the great works of life is to learn to create an inner quietness that shapes our experience no matter what happens. If we tell ourselves, "I can't develop beauty for my children during this season; there is just too much going on!" we will never begin. Start to see your seasons of exhaustion as places to engage with God, create islands of peace (because heaven knows they won't create themselves!), and teach your children how to be good stewards of their God-given souls and bodies, attentive to their physical and spiritual needs.

When you choose to view life this way, you will be surprised how many graces God provides along the way. Even if grace comes in the form of cheese, turkey rolls, grapes, and popcorn.

Something to Ponder

Isaiah 30:1, 12-13, 15

"What sorrow awaits my rebellious children,"
   says the LORD.
"You make plans that are contrary to mine.
   You make alliances not directed by my Spirit. . . .
Because you despise what I tell you
   and trust instead in oppression and lies,
calamity will come upon you suddenly—
   like a bulging wall that bursts and falls. . . ."
This is what the Sovereign LORD,
   the Holy One of Israel, says:
"Only in returning to me
   and resting in me will you be saved.
In quietness and confidence is your strength.
   But you would have none of it."

The prophet Isaiah was speaking to a troubled and rebellious nation about the consequences of trying to cope with life's demands without God's help and guidance.

- Have there ever been times when you were weary and depleted mostly because of your own stubbornness and lack of faith? What happened?

- How can you tell the difference between this kind of weariness and the weariness that comes from what God is calling you to do?

- What answer for difficult times does Isaiah suggest in this chapter? How can it help you live sustainably in a busy or pressured season of your life?

Matthew 6:28-33

And why worry about your clothing? Look at the lilies of the field and how they grow. They don't work or make their clothing, yet Solomon in all his glory was not dressed as beautifully as they are. And if God cares so wonderfully for wildflowers that are here today and thrown into the fire tomorrow, he will certainly care for you. Why do you have so little faith?

So don't worry about these things, saying, "What will we eat? What will we drink? What will we wear?" These things dominate the thoughts of unbelievers, but your heavenly Father already knows all your needs. Seek the Kingdom of God above all else, and live righteously, and he will give you everything you need.

- Looking back, can you see ways that God has provided for you in the past? What happened? How can remembering His past providence help you navigate your stressful times?

- How can you make plans to meet the needs of others and yourself and yet follow Jesus' advice to not worry about what you will eat or drink or wear? How do you strike a balance between reasonable self-care and trust in God's provision?

Ecclesiastes 3:1-8, 11

For everything there is a season,
     a time for every activity under heaven.
A time to be born and a time to die.
     A time to plant and a time to harvest.

A time to kill and a time to heal.
A time to tear down and a time to build up.
A time to cry and a time to laugh.
A time to grieve and a time to dance.
A time to scatter stones and a time to gather stones.
A time to embrace and a time to turn away.
A time to search and a time to quit searching.
A time to keep and a time to throw away.
A time to tear and a time to mend.
A time to be quiet and a time to speak.
A time to love and a time to hate.
A time for war and a time for peace. . . .

God has made everything beautiful for its own time. He has planted eternity in the human heart, but even so, people cannot see the whole scope of God's work from beginning to end.

- How have you prepared for your current season of life? Have you been modeling healthy self-care to your children? Have you been tending to your physical needs (eating, sleeping, drinking) and spiritual needs (prayer, fellowship, beauty)?

- What wisdom can you take from this passage about navigating the stressful seasons of your life?

- What single specific step can you take right now to reduce your stress or make your schedule more reasonable?

- How can noticing the beauty God has set around you give you perspective for difficult times?

Something to Try

- Make a list of some ways you can create spaces of peace and beauty in your life. For example, could you: (1) call someone who fills your soul and have a conversation, (2) carve out some time for a hot beverage and a few pages of your favorite book, or (3) light a candle and enjoy an impromptu teatime with your kids? What will you try?

· Use your favorite drop cookie recipe to make your own frozen cookie dough balls. Make the cookies as usual, but scoop them onto a sheet of waxed paper or parchment on a cookie sheet and place the sheet in the freezer until the dough balls are firm. Transfer to zippered freezer bags (I use small bags and store the cookie balls in rows of four—sixteen to a bag.) Label the bags and stash in your freezer. When you want to bake the cookies, just pull out as many as you like, place on a baking sheet, and bake as usual, allowing a few more minutes than you normally would.

Some Great Recipes for Easy Meals

❋ **Heavenly Oatmeal Muffins**

These moist, mild muffins are wonderful with butter, jam, applesauce, or honey. They're our favorite staple muffins, and I could make a whole meal out of them! Like the blueberry muffins in chapter 5, they are easy to make ahead and freeze for stress-free eating at a later date.

Oil or cooking spray to grease muffin tin
2 cups rolled oats (Quick or old-fashioned both work.)
1 cup vanilla yogurt or buttermilk
1 cup milk
2 eggs, beaten
1 cup dark brown sugar, packed
1 cup vegetable oil
2 cups unbleached all-purpose flour
2 teaspoons non-aluminum baking powder
1 teaspoon finely ground sea salt
1 teaspoon baking soda

Preheat oven to 400°F. Use cooking spay or vegetable oil to grease a 12-cup muffin tin—or line with paper liners.

Combine oats, yogurt or buttermilk, and milk in a bowl and soak for at least 30 minutes. (This step is optional, but it will make the finished muffins more tender.) Whip eggs into batter, then add brown sugar. Stir in oil.

In another bowl, stir together flour, baking powder, sea salt, and baking soda. Add to the oatmeal mixture and stir just until flour is incorporated. (If you stir too much, the muffins will be rubbery.) Batter will be thick.

Fill muffin cups about two-thirds full. Bake in the preheated oven for 15–18 minutes or until they look golden and spring back when pressed. Do not overbake—they dry out easily.

Makes 12 muffins.

❈ **Easy-Peasy Chicken and Rice**

I have become a fan of cast-iron cooking and especially with Dutch ovens that work on the stovetop or in the oven. I use mine for this recipe, which is one of my favorite crowd-pleasing meals. It takes only 5–10 minutes to prep and then bakes quietly in the background, filling the house with fragrance while you take care of other things. People will think you have been slaving over a hot stove all day.

1½ cups uncooked basmati rice (brown or white)
3 cups water
1 cup half-and-half, milk, or a combination
4 tablespoons melted butter or olive oil
1 cup white wine (I usually use Riesling.)
1 teaspoon black pepper
1 teaspoon salt
2 pounds boneless, skinless chicken breast, thighs, or a combination
      of the two
1 tablespoon herbes de Provence or thyme (You can buy herbes de
      Provence as a commercial mix or make your own from one
      of the many online recipes.)

Heat oven to 325°F. Place dry rice in the bottom of a large ovenproof pot with a lid. In a mixing bowl, combine water, half-and-half or milk, butter or olive oil, wine, pepper, and salt. Stir half of this mixture into the rice. Bring to a low boil, cover, and let it bubble for 5–10 minutes. Remove lid from pot and place the chicken on top of the rice. Pour the rest of the sauce mixture on top of the chicken and spread it evenly. Sprinkle herbes de Provence over the top.

Cover pot. Bake for 1 hour without removing the lid, and then check to be sure the rice has not gotten too dry. Add more water—½ cup or so—only if it is getting too dry, then leave it to cook slowly for 1–2 hours. (It becomes more tender as it cooks.)

Serves 6–8, depending on size of serving.

CHAPTER 9

BLESSING FEASTS
Making the Most of Milestones

✥

If more of us valued food and cheer and song above
hoarded gold, it would be a merrier world.

J. R. R. TOLKIEN

The LORD bless you, and keep you;
The LORD make His face shine on you;
And be gracious to you;
The LORD lift up His countenance on you,
And give you peace.

NUMBERS 6:24-26, NASB

Table-Discipleship Principle:

Love and affirmation given generously provide
the foundation for opening a heart to influence.

"MAMA, WILL YOU SQUISH into my bed with me so we can talk just for a little while tonight?" my young-adult child begged with wistful eyes.

"How can I resist time with one of my best friends in all the world? What's on your heart, Tookies?" I asked as I scooted her over to sit close to her on the small single bed. Tookies was a nickname that had somehow evolved during her early years and could certainly be used on her birthday after she had been duly celebrated.

"You know, I didn't even know how emotionally empty I was. It seems there are battlegrounds everywhere in my life—at college, at work, with friends, every place. My values are questioned. My moral underpinnings are challenged. I feel alone and sometimes battle with doubt—you know me! And sometimes I don't feel like I belong to my world.

"But today, when everyone told me what they appreciated about my life, how glad they were that I was their sister, and when you and Daddy invested your words of faith in who I am, the woman I have become, my heart just soaked it in. It was like water to thirsty ground. All day I've been reviewing in my mind all the things that were said. And I've thought about the round-table prayers for my life, and it all seems sweeter to me than ever before. It's as though the love poured into me on my birthday is an anchor that keeps pulling me back to what we all believe together, our unity of commitment to stay faithful to God's call on our lives as a family."

This eloquent bedtime speech had been twenty years in the making. And it was sweet to my mama heart.

Sometimes when my children were growing up, I didn't know if they were listening or paying attention. Yet today I'm beginning to see the fruits of our years deliberately speaking forward into their lives. Reminding them that they are uniquely special to God, that His fingerprints are on their lives and on the story they will tell through their own days, has shaped the persons they're becoming.

Cultivating a lifegiving table is all about helping those who gather around it to know the love of God and to understand His truths, laying foundations of faith that will serve them years after they go out into the world. Intentionally crafting words and messages to share along with the food we serve and the conversations we enjoy is a part of my role as hostess and as mama. Table talks are where lightbulbs come on, where ideas are fully embraced as they are discussed, where love is received as it is generously poured out.

And birthdays are the place where our feasting table becomes a blessing table. They are the times when we intentionally speak words of encouragement and affirmation we hope will sink deep into their minds and hearts. They are also times when we remember that God has specifically created each one with a history, a unique personality, and a story only he or she can fulfill in His own story in our world.

Early in my marriage, I learned that this process was deeply biblical. It goes all the way back to the very first chapter of Genesis, when God finished creating Adam and Eve in His image, then immediately "blessed them" (verse 28). A traditional Jewish blessing, sometimes called the Aaronic blessing (because it was first given to Moses' brother, Aaron), became a mainstay of Hebrew culture. It was spoken over and over and written in many places, personal and public, as a proclamation that God desired to be with His people and surround them with favor and protection. And the Bible contains many other examples of verbal blessings that speak affirmation, encouragement, reassurance, and promise to those being blessed.

Clay and I decided we wanted to incorporate such blessings into our ministry and parenting plan, to plant them as seeds that would bear fruit over a lifetime. And we chose the once-a-year birthday table as the place to enact our plan. We did the same celebration every year for each of our children. We did the same for friends who happened to be staying with us when their birthdays rolled around and for friends in town who had no family around to help them celebrate. And every birthday celebration culminated in a blessing.

I will explain the elements of the blessing below, but first I want to describe the special celebration that set the stage for it. Through all the years, our birthday traditions developed into a set of expected practices, and we took great joy in repeating them every year. This particular story I will share was captured in my personal journal several years ago, after

Joy's fourteenth birthday, when all of my kids were still at home. I find it so sweet to look back and remember . . .

A Birthday in the Life of the Clarksons

The darkness of night slowly ebbs away, and the night shadows fade from the carpet as morning dawns. A deep breath, accompanied by a long sigh, unconsciously escapes my lips before I even leave my warm bed. After nigh on one hundred birthday celebrations in our home, I know the routines well, but as I grow older, I find I have to work a little harder at preparing our special mornings.

Despite my weariness, I feel a thrill of excitement. Today, once again, love and words will be strategically aimed at my child's heart, personal messages stored anew in the treasure chest of her heart for her to draw from in years to come.

As on each birthday morning, this morning the birthday girl will awaken to a tray with a tiny candle and a mug of something steaming hot—tea, coffee, or hot chocolate—to sip in her bedroom while anticipating the familiar celebration. Not allowed downstairs until all is ready, she will wait patiently for the other siblings to come and escort her to the breakfast table.

Meanwhile, I have put my whole-wheat cinnamon rolls—the expected favorites—in the oven and am working on the Cheesy Eggs, which always accompany the hot, sweet offerings. Every year the menu is more or less the same, and our palates rejoice in the familiar tastes.

Strong Austrian coffee drips through the filter while the whole family pitches in to prepare for the celebration. One of us sets the table with the special ceramic tea set traditionally used for birthdays. (The set was bought over several years at a secondhand shop in Austria. By now several of the dishes are chipped or cracked. But we cannot buy any more here in the States, so we are just glad that none of them is broken.)

Most often, presents are wrapped and cards written at the very last minute. Another child throws the presents into very familiar gift bags, many of which we have kept for years. In fact, the kids have all discussed which bags are their favorites—the ones depicting Winnie-the-Pooh and a pre-Raphaelite painting tied for first place—and warned me never, ever to let them leave the house with a present for someone else.

Every gift, however small, gets its own gift bag. Even if something was purchased for a song at Goodwill or the dollar store, it gets a full gift-wrap treatment. (Once a child received a set of ballpoint pens—each pen in its own bag!) The huge pile of gifts makes it look as though the birthday girl is getting a zillion presents, even though the ultimate value may not be much at all. It's all part of the sparkle and fun of the morning.

Preparations fly by in a flurry as time grows short. One person lights the candle and puts out cream and sugar. Another organizes presents. Still another picks music to give grace to the setting. I pull the hot cinnamon rolls out of the oven and start frosting them, while Clay, the official photographer, looks everywhere for the camera and batteries. (In just a few years, our phones would become the new standard for commemorative photography, so this part of the annual frenzy would disappear.)

Finally at least a couple of the kids go upstairs to fetch the birthday girl. When everyone was little, the birthday child was always blindfolded to prevent peeking, and even now my children often revert to the blindfold. What a funny sight to see six-foot-five Joel and six-foot-three Nathan still willingly participating—leading fourteen-year-old Joy down the steps for the big reveal!

Though the table essentially looks the same every year, we all treat it as a big surprise and sit down in a spirit of great expectation. It seems the conversation never varies from year to year—"I think your cinnamon rolls are the best, Mom." "Yeah, we've never tasted any that even compare." (Of course, they say this so I will keep making them from year to year. And yes, it does encourage me to keep up the work—even the fifth time this month!)

After breakfast is appropriately enjoyed, the birthday child begins opening gifts one at a time—each to be marveled at, commented on, and appreciated. Next come the cards. Everyone in the family usually creates one with a message for the birthday child to read and save in a special box.

Laughter always adorns every birthday meal we share, and something funny always seems to happen. Once our energetic golden retriever puppy nearly knocked down the table to get to the leftover eggs. And on Joy's most recent birthday, just as I was reading a Jane Austen quote out loud from a card she had received—"It is much easier to kill realities than phantoms!"—the front door mysteriously blew open. We all looked for the phantoms that must have entered precisely on time for a great effect. (Maybe you had to be there, but the timing was perfect and cracked us all up!)

The Ceremony of the Blessing

Finally, the pinnacle of the morning is the ceremony of the blessing. This is when all of us at the table share a verbal blessing with the birthday child, telling her specifically what she has meant to us and how we appreciate her and how she has grown. I am still astounded that my children take this ritual so seriously. When they were little and we had just begun the custom, I thought they would surely giggle and make sarcastic comments and find it difficult to finish the time. I am truly amazed that they have vested so much love and thoughtfulness into these times over the years. Each birthday, I can practically see the heart of the birthday child being watered and refreshed.

Nathan starts this year. "I have been amazed at how confidently and professionally you have been performing—through your Youth Performing Arts choir and through the musicals you were in. You have quite a voice, and you are so poised and confident. At the last concert, I got my whole row of friends to yell your name. They all said they wished they had a sister like you. I prayed you into the world, and I am very proud to have you as my sister!"

After Nathan's generous comments come Joel's, Sarah's, Clay's, and mine.

"You have really grown in your commitment to the Lord this year, and you have such intelligent things to say in our discussions."

"You have really developed in your personality this year. The way you decorate your room is amazing, your writing is very expressive, you're learning to read music so well on the piano, and you are passing all of us up in your many abilities! Your fun and loving heart is a gift from God to us to celebrate joy in life every day."

"You have been a real friend to me and continue to encourage me when I feel discouraged. And you always have such interesting things to say in the car when I pick you up from classes. It is obvious that you are reading and learning a lot, because you articulate your thoughts so well. I know God is going to use you in this world. You have also been a lot of fun for me."

And on it goes.

I see before me these children who have learned to love each other in spite of the personality differences, the various immature and hormonal and argumentative stages they have gone through. Flawed, contentious, imperfect in so many ways, our family has had to grow into maturity of relationships over many years of practice. But Clay's and my insistence that we would always speak well of each other and graciously to each other and, if there were quarrels, would make peace with one another at the end of every day bore fruit. Our table has grown in depth of shared love because we set this standard to practice.

I am amazed and grateful. How did this happen? These children threatened to undo me from time to time with their whining, their silly fusses, their selfishness and immaturity. Yet, here they are, enjoying each other, laughing at each other's jokes, discussing issues loudly, and participating in family bonding—willingly, generously.

What a gift to me, Lord, to see this picture.

What a blessing indeed!

Words of God's Commitment

Creating a blessing that will follow our children wherever they go begins with taking initiative and making the commitment to verbalize that blessing on a regular basis. In Numbers 6:22-26, God hands down the directive to speak blessing to the people, just as God would have us speak His blessing to our children. God ends the passage by saying, "So they shall put My name on the children of Israel, and I will bless them" (Numbers 6:27, NKJV).

But what *kinds* of words should a blessing contain?

The starting place for aiming our words at our children's hearts is to show them the sure anchor they have in God through all the days of their lives. He is the solid rock upon which they can stand and rest in all the circumstances they will encounter.

In studying the meaning and context of the Aaronic blessing and other "blessing" passages, I've come to understand that the foundation of all blessing comes from a knowledge that God is the ultimate source of all grace, favor, and strength. This is spelled out three different ways in the foundational Aaronic blessing, the one He gave to Moses and desired the Israelites to understand. Out of His heart of deep fatherly love and His kindness toward His chosen ones, God wanted them to have the security of knowing He was with them at every moment and would surround them with His love and protection every step. So He commanded Aaron to bless the people in His name:

> The LORD bless you, and keep you;
> The LORD make His face shine on you,
> And be gracious to you;
> The LORD lift up His countenance on you,
> And give you peace.
> NUMBERS 6:24-26, NASB

The simple message from God in this blessing was, "I really want you to know that My heart is to surround you with love, grace, guidance, and protection, to see that you have everything you need, because you are My beloved child."

He is the source of the grace and favor that empower us, make us productive, cause us to prosper. And He desires to be the main authority above His children, to provide for them and care for them, to be the one who companions them through a set-apart life.

Words of Promise for Hard Times

Jesus knew that His own disciples would face trials beyond their imagination, and so He wanted to give them words that would hold them fast through the storms of their lives. His words of blessing to His own inner circle, spoken at the table of the Last Supper, give us another model for what our own words can accomplish: "I have told you all this so that you may have peace in me. Here on earth you will have many trials and sorrows. But take heart, because I have overcome the world" (John 16:33).

As I review the landscape of my life, I realize there have been many more times of testing than I ever knew would be scattered along the pathways of my days. I encountered so many relational difficulties and heartbreaks that tempted me to doubt God's concern and presence in my life. Financial strain, marital challenges, long passages of loneliness, conflict and fears from the instability of the world—these are all factors that sometimes took me to dark passages deep in my hidden heart. And I know our children will face similar life obstacles.

And yet, at each juncture of my road, Jesus has been my strong defense against despair. The knowledge that He was with me, that He would sustain me, gave me the strength to take one more step, one more day. Similar words of encouragement and promise that I have repeated to my children have held them many times.

Here is another passage that God spoke through Moses to urge His people to take courage against any enemies they would confront: "So be strong and courageous! Do not be afraid and do not panic before them. For the LORD your God will personally go ahead of you. He will neither fail you nor abandon you" (Deuteronomy 31:6).

Children come to believe more easily in the constant strong and present commitment of God in every circumstance, no matter what, when they have a family who is there for them, parents they can come to with any trial or trouble on their heart. The unity of the family table, the commitment to change plans in order to celebrate our special mornings with one another, the decision to speak blessing—all these create a rhythm in which our children get a sense of God's commitment to them because they have tasted of our own active, constant, committed love in our home and at our table.

Words of Love and Appreciation

Because all of us are fraught with the fragility of a sinful nature, all of us will fail, falling short of our own expectations of who we think we should be. Realizing our own shortcomings is a gift that comes with maturity.

When we feel inadequate or insecure from not living up to the world's false standards of what we should be—in physical appearance, in intellect, in personality or outward performance—we long for the assurance that we are still loved.

One of the greatest strengths of a family table comes from the knowledge that no matter what we do, no matter how we fail, we have a place to belong, a place where we will be forgiven and where we will still be loved and welcomed.

Consequently, another emphasis we chose for blessing our children was to speak unconditional love and appreciation for who they are, warts and all. The knowledge that someone knows them and still loves them gives the emotional security they need to face the drain of life with confidence.

Paul reminds us in Romans 8:38-39,

> I am convinced that nothing can ever separate us from God's love. Neither death nor life, neither angels nor demons, neither our fears for today nor our worries about tomorrow—not even the powers of hell can separate us from God's love. No power in the sky above or in the earth below—indeed, nothing in all creation will ever be able to separate us from the love of God that is revealed in Christ Jesus our Lord.

We speak this love—God's love and our love—over and over again in our words of blessing. Love must be accompanied with forgiveness, patience, kindness, and time invested over days and years for our children to internalize the words they hear at our table. But the words themselves have power. A blessing shared at the family table and in countless other moments of life has kept many a child and adult strong during temptation and trials. The sure and steady belief that they are loved helps keep them confident and brave. The accountability of loving words can hold them fast when they might otherwise have strayed.

Many times my own boys have told me, partly in jest but also in complete seriousness, "Mama, wherever I go, I hear your voice in my head, and I can't get away from your words. It's like you are with me everywhere I go."

That's exactly what I want for my words of blessing. I want to speak words of love and grace that stay in their heads forever and influence the person they become.

Words of Affirmation and Purpose

God created each of us to have a special role in His story through history. He could have chosen to shape and influence His world through some sort of power play or authoritarian rule. Instead, His choice was to empower His children to be His love, His virtue, His truth, His purposes in our world through our individual personalities and skill sets, all put to use for His glory. His method for reaching the world was to send His people out to do the work they were created to do.

As Psalm 139:13-16 so eloquently depicts, He knows each one of us intimately, values us immensely, and created us for a purpose:

> You made all the delicate, inner parts of my body
>   and knit me together in my mother's womb.
> Thank you for making me so wonderfully complex!
>   Your workmanship is marvelous—how well I know it.
> You watched me as I was being formed in utter seclusion,
>   as I was woven together in the dark of the womb.
> You saw me before I was born.
>   Every day of my life was recorded in your book.

Every moment was laid out
before a single day had passed.

In the deepest recesses of our souls, we all long to live into what we were created to be. We want to be a part of something bigger than ourselves, to feel confident that we have worth and our lives have meaning. So that's another theme that all of us try to incorporate in our birthday blessings on our children. We deliberately set out to affirm both their inherent value (to us, to God, and to the world)—and the reality that God has a purpose for their lives.

Strong inner confidence is what gives any of us freedom to live into our God-given potential. Self-actualization comes from an internalization of our personal value and worth. A child who grows up feeling unworthy might well spend the rest of his or her life trying desperately to find that sense of worth by looking for the approval of others. This kind of living to please other people is unstable and elusive because other people are fickle, unpredictable, and usually struggling with their own issues.

Only God can grant the kind of loving acceptance and affirmation we all need to live by faith, to take risks, to understand the agency of making decisions and exercising one's will to work hard and to pursue a place in the world. But other people can become agents of that acceptance and affirmation by imitating God's love and acceptance and intentionally conveying it to others. And that's where the blessing comes in.

When parents thoughtfully (and repeatedly) speak words that affirm their children's worth, confirm lifelong commitment to them, and speak forward into their futures, they soothe their children's longing for affirmation and give wings to their dreams for life.

The apostle Paul reminds us that "we are God's masterpiece. He has created us anew in Christ Jesus, so we can do the good things He planned for us long ago" (Ephesians 2:10). The words of blessing we speak at our birthday tables are aimed at unearthing the God-given beauty of each child's personality, convincing them that they, too, are "God's masterpiece," fully capable, with God's help, of doing the "good things he planned" for them:

- "Your music is sweet to my ears."
- "You are so dependable in helping me get all of my work finished. I couldn't do without your help."
- "Your compassion and patience with people will touch people wherever you go."

We speak forward into the future lives of our children by seeing them for the potential God gave them and then holding this vision before their eyes so that they will store up messages to hear in their minds when they are far from home.

Birthday feasts, served up with intentional blessings, hold deep spiritual influence when we aim our words at our children's hearts to empower them to live into God's call on their lives. But it's important that we parents remember we are talking about *their* lives and not our own. We must seek to be sensitive to what they care about, what their unique dreams are—not pressuring them to live up to our expectations, but encouraging them to live into their unique design and the drives that God has built into their lives. This means we must give our children freedom to pursue God's course for them, while not seeking to tell them what they should do. The purpose of the birthday blessing is to empower and release, not to control and manipulate.

The Power of Belonging

Even as Jesus chose His inner circle to live with and learn from Him, so those of us who live in families have a premade inner circle—those who sit at our table every day and every night. Precious to each of us Clarksons is the knowledge that we have a team, our own "pack," so to speak, each of whom believes in us and in our potential to make a positive impact on our world.

We cheer each other on.

We have each other's backs.

We are here for each other, whatever life holds.

And when we share our carefully chosen words of promise and commitment, love and appreciation, affirmation and purpose, we remind each other that not only do we belong to one another, but ultimately we all belong to God.

Each of my adult children has now forayed into the wide world—working, studying, establishing new homes. And as I look at their lives, I can see the fruit of all those years of gathering together, communicating love, offering prayers and blessings to one another over birthday tables and other important milestones. All those words spoken with hope and intention have laid foundations of emotional, mental, and spiritual health that still serve to stabilize and encourage us when we are far apart.

The consistent message that I have heard from each one, in the privacy of a one-on-one teatime, is this: "Life can be discouraging at this time of history. But knowing I belong to a people, 'the Clarksons,' has given me the grace to keep holding fast to my spiritual ideals in a world that disdains what I believe. I know I will always have a home to come to when I need a place to fall apart or to belong. I know that wherever I go or whatever I do, I will have a place to come back to, a place where I know I'm welcome and have a role to play. And because I have that, I know I can persevere in whatever the Lord calls me to do."

As for me, what a joy it is to see that all my effort and cooking and washing of dishes and wrapping of presents and coming up with blessings did matter. They provided the frame around which love and confidence was painted on the souls of each of my precious children.

Okay, move over—I'll finish the dishes later!

Something to Ponder

Three Scriptural Blessings

Oh, the joys of those who . . .
delight in the law of the LORD. . . .
They are like trees planted along the riverbank,
    bearing fruit each season.
Their leaves never wither,
    and they prosper in all they do.

PSALM 1:1-3

God is able to bless you abundantly, so that in all things at
all times, having all that you need, you will abound in every
good work.

2 CORINTHIANS 9:8, NIV

Then you will experience God's peace, which exceeds anything
we can understand. His peace will guard your hearts and minds
as you live in Christ Jesus.

PHILIPPIANS 4:7

What elements of a blessing (as described in this chapter) can you
find in these three Scripture passages?

- Reword each passage so that it becomes a blessing you could speak
  into the life of someone you care about.

- Can you think of any other Scriptures that lend themselves to
  being adapted into a blessing?

Romans 15:13

I pray that God, the source of hope, will fill you completely
with joy and peace because you trust in him. Then you will
overflow with confident hope through the power of the
Holy Spirit.

God's desire as a loving Father is for us to experience the amazing joy
of knowing His love.

Read this verse and write out what it means to you, your children,
your friends.

- How can you convey this kind of love and joy to your family every
  day and especially on their birthdays?

- Memorize this verse and review it every day for a week to have it
  firmly impressed in your mind.

Something to Try

Plan two ways you can celebrate and convey a blessing to a friend or loved one. Here are some possibilities: (1) A tea party on your porch with a card of encouragement; (2) a picnic on the front lawn with a cupcake for everyone and a little message on a card that says something like "I am so thankful for you"; (3) A little box left on a desk with a single chocolate and an encouraging note.

- Write out a special blessing for someone you love, memorize it, and find an occasion to speak it out loud to that person.

- Even better, pick an occasion for regularly speaking forward into the lives of those you love.

A Birthday Celebration à la Clarkson

❊ Sally's Birthday Cinnamon Rolls

Baking bread, in my opinion, is one of the most gratifying ways to spend time in the kitchen. Once you get the hang of it, it is easy and quite the crowd pleaser. This is especially true of my special cinnamon rolls. This is one of the recipes I have made so often, I can do it in my sleep, so I generally go by feel and experience to know just how much flour to add and how much to knead the dough. I also live at high altitude, which affects baking results. I encourage you to take the basics of my recipe and adapt it to your circumstances. One last thing about the roll recipe—I also use my basic whole-wheat bread dough recipe to make cinnamon rolls, and it works fine. So if you have a recipe you like, try it out for cinnamon rolls!

2 ¼-ounce packages active dry yeast or about 2 tablespoons bulk yeast
     (I buy bulk yeast at Sam's Club.)
1¾ cups very warm water (about 110°F)
1 tablespoon sugar
½ cup honey or ⅓ cup maple syrup
1 teaspoon sea salt
⅓ cup butter, melted and cooled
1 egg, beaten
2¼ cups freshly ground whole-wheat flour or unbleached all-purpose
     flour
Approximately 2½ cups unbleached all-purpose flour
Vegetable oil to grease bowl; more vegetable oil or nonstick spray to
     grease pan
½ cup (1 stick) softened butter for spreading
½ cup dark brown sugar
¼ cup cinnamon-sugar mixture, or to taste (See recipe in chapter 10.)
½ cup (1 stick) softened butter for frosting

2 cups confectioner's sugar
1½ teaspoons vanilla extract
1–2 tablespoons milk
Cinnamon or red sprinkles to garnish, optional

In a large bowl, dissolve yeast in warm water and stir in the
tablespoon of sugar to help the yeast grow more quickly. Let stand
until mixture is creamy and bubbly, about 10 minutes. Mix honey
or syrup, salt, melted butter, beaten egg, and 2¼ cups freshly ground
whole-wheat flour or unbleached all-purpose flour into yeast mixture.
Add additional all-purpose flour ½ cup at a time until dough pulls
away from the sides of the bowl. Turn dough out onto a well-floured
surface and knead until smooth and elastic, about 8 minutes. (I just
put the dough hooks on my Bosch mixer and let the dough mix
for 5 minutes.) Lightly oil a large bowl, place dough in bowl, and
turn to coat. Cover with a damp cloth and let rise in a warm place
until doubled in volume, about 1 hour. While dough is rising, use
vegetable oil or nonstick spray to grease a 9 × 13 inch baking pan or
jelly-roll pan. Set aside.

When dough has risen, punch it down, turn it out onto a lightly
floured surface, and roll it out into a long rectangle about a half an
inch thick and approximately 9 × 18 inches. (It should be at least
twice as long as it is deep.) Spread softened butter over the rectangle,
then sprinkle evenly with dark brown sugar and the cinnamon-sugar
mixture. Use as much or as little of each as you like. We prefer our
rolls with a rich cinnamon flavor, so I use a lot!

Beginning at the long side, roll the rectangle of dough as tightly as
possible into a long log. Using a sharp serrated knife, a strong thread,
or a length of unflavored dental floss, cut the log into 1- to 1½-inch
slices and place slices cut side up in the prepared pan. Rolls can touch
each other at the sides. Set in a warm place and allow them to rise.
While rolls are rising, preheat oven to 350°F.

When rolls have risen to about double in size (30–40 minutes),
place in preheated oven and bake 15–18 minutes, or until slightly

brown. (Time will differ according to your altitude or the efficiency of your oven. Just watch the rolls and don't let them get too brown.)

While rolls are baking, make the frosting. Cream ½ cup (1 stick) softened butter. Add confectioner's sugar a little at a time. Stir in vanilla, then add milk a little at a time until frosting is thick but spreadable. When the rolls come out of the oven, frost them while they're hot and sprinkle with either a little cinnamon or red sprinkles to make them prettier.

Makes 12–15 rolls, depending on how large you make them.

Clarksons' Special Cheesy Eggs

1–2 tablespoons butter
10 eggs, cracked into a bowl and lightly beaten
½–¾ cup or more grated cheese of your choice (Swiss cheese adds a slightly sweet taste that I love, but cheddar is the boys' favorite.)
⅔ cup sour cream (the secret ingredient that creates a rich taste)
Salt and pepper to taste
Real bacon bits, sautéed onions or mushrooms, sliced avocado, or chopped tomatoes, optional
Chopped fresh herbs, optional

Melt butter in a hot skillet. Add eggs to pan and stir to keep eggs soft and mixed up. Don't allow them to stick to the bottom. When eggs begin to coagulate but are still runny (about two-thirds cooked), add cheese and sour cream and stir lightly together. Season with salt and pepper to taste and stir until eggs are cooked through but not overly dry. If desired, stir in bacon bits, mushrooms, avocado, or tomatoes.

Serve eggs onto each plate and then sprinkle a tiny bit of extra cheese for a more artistic presentation. Sometimes I sprinkle each serving lightly with chopped fresh herbs to add a little color.

Serves 6–8.

CHAPTER 10

TEATIME DISCIPLESHIP
The Power of One-on-One

"I don't feel very much like Pooh today," said Pooh.
"There, there," said Piglet. "I'll bring you tea and honey until you do."

A. A. MILNE

So encourage each other and build each other up, just as you are already doing.

1 THESSALONIANS 5:11

Table-Discipleship Principle:

Deep friendships and connected relationships happen best when intentional encouragement is planned and given on a regular basis.

Butterflies flittered in my stomach as I peered anxiously out the window of the red-and-white Austrian tram, which was slowing to a stop. I could just see the façade of a grand, ornate white-marble building behind the elaborate park of its tree-lined entrance.

Quickly I looked out to the other side of the street and spotted another imposing structure with a sign in front that read Volksoper. That was the clue I was looking for, the landmark my friend had described when she told me where to meet her.

I pushed the button to exit and was caught in the crowds of boot-wearing, wool-coated, and scarved people pushing their way in and out of the door. Frigid weather outside caused our breath to swirl in steamy curls as each of us rushed to our own destination.

Crossing the street with cars whizzing by and trams going in two directions on the unfamiliar street triggered a rush of adrenaline. But then, right in front of me as I made it safely across the street, I saw my destination—Café Landtmann, one of the oldest coffee houses in Vienna.

I entered and glanced around, getting my bearings, and was confronted by a waiter dressed formally in black, who spoke to me in German. Not knowing what he had said, I shook my head and put my hands up in total incomprehension. He then spoke loudly, too loudly for my comfort, and pointed to a coatroom. Quickly I understood that I was not allowed to take my coat into the café area. I walked over and handed my heavy navy-blue coat and scarf to a small woman who hung it up and gave me a number in return.

Everything I was doing was completely foreign to me. I had no prior expectations about how to do life in formal Vienna in the late 1970s. But I just kept muddling through and looked around until I found the entrance door to the room where people regularly met for afternoon coffee.

It was a magnificent space. Green and brown velveteen cushioned seats, dark wood ceiling beams and inlays, and a formal crystal chandelier gracing the center of the room gave the café a grand old-world elegant atmosphere. I was drawn in to the warmth of friends talking, leaning forward, sipping drinks in intimate groups. But I couldn't help feeling a little out of place until I saw my friend Gwen waving at me from a small window table toward the back that looked out at the magnificent building I had seen from the tram.

We greeted each other, and finally I was able to breathe out my last bit of anxiety. Now I was with a companion who could speak my language and who delighted in my company. Her arms of friendship embraced me, giving warmth and energy back to my depleted soul.

"I have ordered you my favorite coffee, a mélange, and a warm treat they serve only on the cold days of winter. It will warm our insides," Gwen announced with a delightful, pleased-with-herself smile.

We sat and sipped and chatted and giggled for three hours, almost without stop. The treat had been *Milchrahmstrudel,* a sort of sweet cottage cheese–filled pastry smothered in warm vanilla sauce, and it had indeed warmed me—but not as much as being with Gwen did. One of the deepest friendships of my life had been nurtured over a cup of something hot and some honest conversation.

Cafés are sprinkled all through the city of Vienna, and each is filled to overflowing every day as friends stop amidst the busyness of their days to share some moments of rest and to sip a steaming cup of tea or coffee together. I found this custom irresistible and adopted it for myself. And when we returned to the States, I looked for new ways to make it part of my life. Because I've always been a bit of an Anglophile, I eventually added the English tradition of afternoon tea to create my own personal approach.

Over time, my teatime habit became a foundational discipling tool for me. Taking time in the middle of a busy day to focus on a real live person and share our hearts over tea or coffee became a way of connecting with other women, with neighbors, and especially with my children—and even with my swirling, hurried self.

Eventually, I developed the practice of hosting people in my home for tea. To say, "You are welcome at my table. I have prepared for you. I would like to know you" was a way of inviting people into my life in a personal way. Teatime discipleship became a habit of stopping, looking someone in the eye, and making a space that says, "I care about you." It was also an unthreatening way to begin getting to know them, asking them questions, and gaining access to their hearts. And it was an unparalleled way to build and nurture friendships.

Teatime Friendship

Striking up conversations on dusty roads and by public wells, discussing every kind of important and trivial issue at dinner parties, sharing fire-grilled fish at the seashore, sipping wine around a table of friends after a long, wearying day—these are pictures I've garnered from the Gospels as I studied the ways Jesus taught, loved, and befriended those along His path.

Initiating friendship by inviting someone to table bridges the gap between our hearts and those we want to encourage. It reflects a grid of life that says, "Because I am to be the love of God to those He brings into my life, I need to reach out to them as Jesus reached out to us, to share His love, grace, and redemption." Such thinking establishes a pattern of living where we naturally look for opportunities to establish friendships.

Friendship isn't always easy to find at this time in history, when people move frequently (we certainly have), when polarized attitudes divide populations, when electronic "communication" so often substitutes for face-to-face relationships. But friendships can be built by our intentionally purposing to serve others through our words, our meals, our conversation, our leadership. Teatime offers an ideal venue for doing this.

Teatime discipleship might begin by seeking out spiritually strong women who will feed my soul so that I have something to give to others in turn. I was recently remembering how many times I have felt alone or dry both spiritually and emotionally, but when I entered into the company of several particular friends, I always left feeling stronger, encouraged, with more true thoughts about life and the Lord with which to feed my soul. These women have an intentionality about their spiritual lives, and I know that when I invest time with them, I am investing in my own spiritual well-being.

Many years ago, I made it a habit to surround myself with such godly friends, who help keep me accountable with my spiritual ideals. I arrange my schedule carefully to include time with these women, call them regularly, find ways to make memories together. Treasured friendships have grown out of my commitment to make these times happen by inviting these special women to my tea table on a regular basis.

Next, befriending others, including my children, comes from having my sensors out to see when there is a need to be encouraged, when trials or stresses come across the paths of my loved ones, those dark places that descend like a cloud for many that God brings across my path.

God designed us all to need community on a regular basis. But community doesn't just come about by fate. It must be developed by planning and intention and invitation. And for me, at least, teatime has become an invaluable community-building tool. I have often extended an open invitation to my friends, husband, and kids to join me for my regular afternoon teatime just to connect—or reconnect. And I try to make a point to reach out more specifically to make new friends and to offer words of encouragement for those who need it.

Teatime Encouragement

Words have such power—power to devastate, to inspire, to encourage, or to tear down. Learning to use words aimed at the heart to soothe and encourage is a skill I have been learning over many years in ministry. Those who are discouraged, feeling hopeless, empty, or insecure, can come out of a teatime with a sense that their lives matter, that God sees them, that they are loved, and that there is hope for their future. Becoming an intentional encourager of those who join me for tea is a way to help them feel and believe in the love of God.

Developing an intentional value for passing on hope comes with a way of thinking. Most people do not need more guilt, more pressure to be perfect, or more to do. Instead, they need messages of hope to fill the empty corners of their lives, to keep them growing and moving forward.

Think about these verses:

- "Therefore encourage one another and build up one another, just as you also are doing" (1 Thessalonians 5:11, NASB).
- "Do not let any unwholesome talk come out of your mouths, but only what is helpful for building others up according to their needs, that it may benefit those who listen" (Ephesians 4:29, NIV).
- "Rejoice with those who rejoice; mourn with those who mourn" (Romans 12:15, NIV).

Teatime discipleship, then, is our invitation for someone to come to us for a few moments of rest, restoration, friendship, comfort, or just time to talk. The point is, if you can't make time for a whole day, you can still find a few moments to reach out to those who need some joy or happiness or companionship. Over time, those daily few moments add up. I believe it was through the accumulation of thousands of teatimes over many years that I was able to secure the trust and intimacy of my children's hearts.

Expect Interruptions

Slam, bang, stomp—the sounds accompanied one of my children as she entered the front door. Peeking out to see who was there, I was met with a loud sigh and a brooding face that seemed shadowed by a dark cloud of emotion. Ducking back into my bedroom, I breathed deep to let my own sigh escape.

The small flame of the candle flickered wildly as air from the opening bedroom door fanned it. My frazzled child peeked through the door and asked if we could talk for a few minutes. Her quiet voice told me she did not want to attract the attention of anyone else in the house.

I had come to my bedroom to be alone. A fire glowed in the fireplace, a cup of tea steamed at my side, and a melancholy Celtic tune played softly in the background—this was the perfect setting I had planned for a short, one-woman retreat by myself on a few stolen minutes of a

Sunday afternoon. But I could see she needed to talk about something that was important to her.

The tears began to overflow her dark eyes as she sat down. The past year had been hard and lonely for her. We had moved to a new city, and no friend her age was to be found. Several of her Christian acquaintances had been dabbling in sex with boys they were dating, and Christian leaders we knew had split our church over an immoral relationship, leaving many broken relationships behind.

On top of this, a variety of countries had experienced terrorist attacks the week before while Clay and I were gone on a brief anniversary trip, and she had been forced to work through the trauma without us. All of these issues plus the questions of what to do with the rest of her life combined to trouble her heart and mind.

"Mama, I've been having such doubts in my faith. So many believers seem mediocre and compromising, and our world seems to be falling apart, and it's just hard for me to make sense of it all. Have you ever felt like this?"

As I surveyed my own very demanding day and need for time alone, I quickly brushed aside my expectation of the next quarter hour and said, "How 'bout a quick, private teatime right here in my room. I would love to hear about all that is simmering in your heart."

Hurrying down to the kitchen, I quickly placed a slice of bread into the toaster and poured another cup of tea. When the toast popped up, I buttered it and sprinkled it with cinnamon sugar, then lit a little candle. In just five minutes I was carrying a tray to my bedroom so my child and I could share our private teatime while she talked about her doubts.

Having lived through all the seasons of raising four children from birth into adulthood, I had come to understand that doubt is something all thinking people must face at one time or another. Yet I had seen the hand of God leading me faithfully through all the fear-filled times, and He had whispered secrets to me through His Word about how we can make it through such times with our souls intact, our spirits healthy and strong. Through experience and grace, I had acquired a legacy of faith and hope to pass on to my child in the quietness of my room. After listening to her words and hearing her soul pleas, I assured her that seasons of doubting God are normal to most mature believers and that God would be able to stand true to her even in these struggles. I was able to gently point her to the foundations of God's love, His ways, and His plan to use her at this time and in her world to live a faithful story.

A tiny smile began to form at the corners of her mouth. "I am so glad you love me as I am and still believe in me—in spite of my doubts. Loneliness has felt like a weight wrapping itself around my feelings with a palpable darkness."

I have learned over the years that if I want my children (and my husband and friends and the women involved in my ministry) to feel a place of priority in my life, I must regularly set aside time to invite them into my space, to lay my table, and to give whatever the moment needs. Ministry rarely happens at convenient times. Preparing myself with an expectation of being interrupted has helped me host at my teatime table many who needed to feel the touch of God and hear the words of God in their moment of need.

Now that my children are all adults, I'm aware of a constant barrage of temptations, disappointments, and expectations invading their lives and the lives of most people I know. There's a limit to what I can do to protect them from what the world throws at them. But I can listen to them and help them sort out their thoughts and feelings—if I choose to make myself available when they need me.

And so availability became a habit of my life over many years. Making myself emotionally available to them when they needed it was a choice I learned to make again and again—a choice that helped forge a deep connection with each of them. I became the confidant for my children and others, so that as they grew older, they would still have the habit of coming to me. Availability in attitude and time has been the key to opening deeper relationships among us.

Who taught me this? Jesus did. Immediate availability was the way He operated. He answered questions when they were asked. He made a point of going off alone with His disciples to provide them with focused attention. And often He did this over food. In fact, He gave the most strategic talks of His life as His best friends and most devoted disciples were filling their stomachs with warm food (what could be better than fish over an open fire?), and they sat listening to His wisdom as their ease and comfort opened their hearts.

We do well, I think, to follow His example.

Planning for Teatime Discipleship

Because I consider teatime discipleship to be a strategic and invaluable part of both my ministry life and my personal one, I have developed habits of preparing to be able to celebrate these moments any time of day. Cultivating and creating beauty as a daily habit helps me to be prepared at a few minutes' notice for those who need some focused time and a little bit of encouragement.

A memory burnished into my values as a small child still serves me in my preparation efforts today. When I was nine years old, my mother asked me if I would like to enter a local flower show alongside her. Mom loved gardening and kept a varied and prolific rose garden as well as many kinds of irises. Her invitation sent me on an hour-long quest through our garden. I was to pick one of the loveliest flowers in our yard to arrange in a vase for the elementary competition at the flower show. A freshly bloomed dark purple iris called my name. Being allowed to choose a simple crystal vase of my grandmother's from our closet filled me with pride at being grown up enough to be trusted with this treasure. A blue ribbon fluttered over my arrangement when I walked into the fragrant room of displays, and instantly I fell in love with the lure of flowers.

Though not a gifted or skilled florist, I still delight in bringing flowers into my rooms as a reflection of God's own creativity. More important, I have learned that keeping fresh flowers on hand helps me to quickly create an atmosphere of beauty for my teatimes.

Last night, I perused the array of inexpensive flowers at my local grocery store and chose those that would stay fresh for up to three weeks. Wanting to keep fresh flowers around the house on a limited budget has taught me to find the "deals" our local store displays each season. A bunch of carnations with baby's breath or a sleeve of colorful mums costs very little but still communicates a message of preparedness and value for those who I hope will breathe beauty at our table. And sometimes a large bunch of flowers, carefully divided into different vases, will provide up to five arrangements, spread throughout my house. (Daisies—what a deal!) And what a simple way to add something special to my teatimes.

Keeping flowers is only one way I've learned to prepare myself for "instant" teatime. I also keep a supply of small, medium, and large candles and restock them regularly so I'll have one to light whenever I want to make an occasion of friendship over a mere cup of tea. Cookie dough balls are a staple in my freezer, and I can bake them two or three or a dozen at a time on a moment's notice. (See instructions in chapter 8.)

I always have a simple woolen pashmina scarf, a pretty place mat from a secondhand store, or even a fabric remnant on hand to add a touch of grace to whatever table I choose for tea, and I keep my phone loaded with all sorts of favorite music for a special ambience. Naturally, I also keep my teakettle, teapot, teacups, and mugs close at hand—not to mention a supply of delicious teas. (I prefer strong black English tea, but I keep a collection of herbals always at hand.) I even travel with a portable "tea kit"—scarf, candle, my small speaker, and some cups and tea. This way almost any room can provide an opportunity for impromptu teatime discipleship.

It doesn't take much. A match lighting a candle, a teapot warmed, a bit of music, and something pretty for the table make teatime an instant possibility when someone in my life needs a little focused time. Preparing ahead of time speaks to others of my love and their value. It's an open invitation for them to share life with me.

Time for Tea, Anyone?

Teatime is an art for some, and that's true for me, too, I suppose. I do love (and need) to make the teatimes I host for others and for myself times of beauty as well. But teatime is more than just a spot of beauty in my day. It's also a means of sharing my love and my concern and understanding. And for me and my teatime guests, it's an island of peace and rest in a sea of busyness and stress.

Teatime has become a daily habit for me, my husband, my children, and a number of our friends, and we've become quite evangelistic about sharing its benefits. In fact, I suspect there are people all over the world whose lives are more civilized and peaceful because we've passed along this little custom of taking time to breathe in peace and joy a few moments of every afternoon.

Whether it's simple or elaborate doesn't matter. It doesn't even matter if you drink coffee or tea (or something else). Even the busiest of people should have the space to take a few minutes every day to breathe out the stress, to breathe in peace, to sip peace along with your beverage, and to share your life with someone else.

What do you think? Are you ready for another cup?

Something to Ponder

Romans 12:10

> Love each other with genuine affection, and take delight in honoring each other.
>
> ROMANS 12:10

What does the phrase "genuine affection" mean to you?

- I love the phrase "take delight in honoring each other." This sounds so lovely, to think of someone else "delighting" in me as a friend. What does that look like in real life? What does it take to honor one another? What is your definition of honoring someone?

1 Thessalonians 5:11

> So encourage each other and build each other up, just as you are already doing.

Encouragement means to give courage to someone, and it is such a strong reason to help each other keep going strong in the Christian life.

What does the verse above reflect about our stewardship to invest in people this way?

- What does it look like to build one another up? How does one do that?

Something to Try

Write a love note to each of your children, telling what you especially love about him or her. Leave the notes under their pillows or send them in the mail. (If you don't have children, choose someone else to receive a letter of appreciation.)

- List three people in your life who need encouragement. Plan on having each of them over to your home for a personal teatime (or meet them at a cute little coffee shop) and take initiative to use words of life to encourage them and to show them their value to you. Consider doing this with your husband (if you are married) or your roommate.

Recipes for Your Teatime Table

✳ Clay's Best Cinnamon Toast

One of the most satisfying teatime treats our family enjoys is a quick round of cinnamon toast. It is now even a favorite of my Dutch son-in-law, who had never heard of it before! After many years of chomping down this treat, Clay came up with what we believe is the perfect ratio of cinnamon and sugar. We mix it together and keep it in glass Parmesan-cheese dispensers for sprinkling. These look like big salt shakers with extra-large holes and usually have a metal lid that screws on. They can be found online, at department stores, and in discount stores.

Sliced bread (We prefer homemade, but you can also use English
      muffins or the bread of your choice.)
Softened butter
Cinnamon sugar, mixed 1 part cinnamon to 6 parts sugar of your
      choice (I use fine turbinado, or "raw," sugar), and a few dashes
      of sea salt

Toast bread until it is browned to your satisfaction. Spread butter
on toast while it is still hot, then sprinkle on the cinnamon-sugar
mixture to taste. We prefer heavy sugar so that it makes a crust.

✳ Sarah's Best Cream Scones

Scones are rich little biscuit-like pastries popular with tea in the United Kingdom. We love them with clotted cream (or a substitute), raspberry or blackberry jam or jelly (our favorite), or marmalade. Lemon curd is also wonderful on scones. Spread the toppings on the scones in layers—first the jam or lemon curd, then the cream. Smashing!

2 cups unbleached all-purpose flour
3 teaspoons non-aluminum baking powder
¼ cup sugar

½ teaspoon finely ground sea salt
6 tablespoons cold butter
Nuts, chocolate chips or cinnamon chips, fresh or dried fruit
    (whatever you like), optional
1 cup heavy whipping cream (the kind that comes in a carton in the
    milk section), plus a bit more if you need it
Jam, lemon curd, and clotted cream for serving (If you can't find real
    British clotted cream, see below for some good substitutes.)

Heat oven to 425°F. Mix flour, baking powder, sugar, and salt in mixing bowl and whisk together until mixed thoroughly. Cut in the butter with whisks in your mixer, two knives, or a pastry blender. Keep working the dough until the mixture is coarse, with only a few larger lumps of butter. At this point you can stir in nuts, chocolate or cinnamon chips, fresh or dried fruits, or anything that suits your fancy. (One of my favorites is 2 tablespoons each of dried cranberries, white chocolate chips, and chopped pecans. But we actually prefer these scones plain because we use wonderful raspberry jam with them.)

Stir whipping cream into flour-butter mixture until the dough sticks together. Spray a place on the kitchen counter with cooking spray and then dump the dough onto this space. (Doing this keeps the dough from sticking to the counter.) Press the dough with your hands or fists until you can form it into a nice round lump.

Like a biscuit dough, scone dough can seem to be dry and crumbly, but I usually manage to pat down the mixture with my hands and squish it into a rectangle or round. If you absolutely cannot do this, add a little more whipping cream. Sarah likes to roll the dough out thinner, about ¾ inch thick, while I prefer it a little thicker—up to 1½ inch. Cut out scones into whatever shape you prefer. I like to use my heart-shaped cookie cutters to do this, but you can also use a juice glass to cut rounds, or biscuit cutters (you can buy them in any cooking shop). You can also roll the dough into a circle and cut wedges, like pie pieces. Squish any scraps together and roll out again to cut more scones.

Carefully place scones on an ungreased cookie sheet and bake for about 12–15 minutes, until set and slightly golden. Don't overbake; you want them to be flaky. Cool on a rack for about 10 minutes until easy to handle.

Makes about 12–15 scones, depending on the size of your cutter.

✳ Faux (but Delicious!) Clotted Cream

In the United Kingdom, scones are traditionally served with jam and clotted cream, a thick cream made by steaming whole milk until it thickens into a sort of a thick custard with clots of cream that stick together. Authentic clotted cream is often difficult to find outside the UK, so we have come up with two fairly satisfying substitutes to serve with our scones.

Cream Cheese "Clotted Cream"

1 part cream cheese, softened
1 part vanilla yogurt
Vanilla extract
Salt

Mix cream cheese with yogurt until totally smooth. Add a splash of vanilla extract and a pinch of salt. You can make this in large quantities or small, depending on how many scones you are serving. We usually make a large batch because we tend to serve it when we have crowds of people for a luncheon or friends over for tea.

Whipped "Clotted Cream"

This is a simple way to pretend you have clotted cream. Our friends all love it and ask for our secret recipe! It's basically just a good homemade whipped cream.

1 8-ounce carton whipping cream
2–3 teaspoons granulated sugar
½ teaspoon vanilla extract

Using a whisk or a hand mixer, whip cream and sugar together until mixture forms soft peaks. Add a capful of vanilla extract. Voila! It is ready for your scones—or anything else that would benefit from a dollop of rich homemade goodness.

CHAPTER 11

THE GIFT OF US
A Family Day Celebration

❈

*Perhaps nothing helps us make the movement from our little selves to a
larger world than remembering God in gratitude. Such a perspective puts
God in view in all of life, not just in the moments we set aside for worship
or spiritual disciplines. Not just in the moments when life seems easy.*

HENRI NOUWEN

*I will remember the deeds of the LORD;
yes, I will remember your miracles of long ago.*

PSALM 77:11, NIV

Table-Discipleship Principle:

Developing a sense of history and
roots helps cultivate a sense of living
our part in God's megastory.

THE HEAT OF FRESHLY BREWED COFFEE radiates through the ceramic mug and warms my fingertips. But there is another warmth lighting up my morning mood: All of my children are back in my home, sleeping in their beds. This is a rarity now in our family. In the last few years our family has been spread across the country and the globe. My heart goes with each child everywhere they go, and sometimes it feels like my heart is stretched thin as my love travels over the globe with my dear children. But for this morning at least, all of my dear ones are safe, close, and about to wake up.

I set my mug on a coaster and make my way to the kitchen to continue preparations for the day. Bustling around the kitchen, I pull out our special-occasion pottery and start the water boiling for a big pot of tea. As I pass the oven, I am greeted by the wafting fragrance of the nearly finished cinnamon rolls. (Do you see a pattern here?) Time to grate the potatoes for the Polish eggs.

Everything has to be special. It is Family Day.

For thirty-two years our family has celebrated this original Clarkson holiday. It doesn't have a specific spot on the calendar, but is scheduled anew every year, usually in August before everyone dives back into the rush of jobs and school. We even got one in last year at Oxford, two days before Sarah's wedding there—although we did have to make a few modifications to the routine!

As you may have picked up, most Clarkson celebrations involve food, and this one is no different. Our day starts off with cinnamon rolls and Polish eggs, a recipe from my missionary days in Poland. Then we pack our cooler to the hilt with Family Day delicacies for a picnic in the mountains: homemade fried chicken, paprika-dusted deviled eggs, generously iced Texas sheet cake, crunchy kettle chips, and natural sparkling fruit juice as a special treat.

But the food is only an exclamation point on the true celebration of Family Day—the celebration of God's faithfulness to our family.

Sleepy faces arrive one by one in the kitchen. I hug them close, tempt them with just a taste of the feast to come, and then set them to work. Thirty minutes later finds us devouring savory eggs and spicy-sweet rolls and laughing as if we'd been together all along.

I am sometimes amazed that my children still tease each other the way they did when they were ten. I send a warning look in the direction of a particularly jubilant teaser, then laugh and shrug it off. When forks begin to scrape the icing off our empty plates and coffee mugs are raised to catch the last drops, we begin our transition to the living room for our "remembering time"—but not without grabbing fresh cups of coffee.

Settled in our favorite corners of couches, we are ready. Clay has come armed with a Bible, a manila envelope marked with the year, blank paper, and a pen. He leads us in prayer and then opens the Bible to the familiar chapter: Joshua 4. He reads the ancient words that inspired our tradition:

> Now when all the nation had finished crossing the Jordan, the LORD spoke to Joshua, saying, "Take for yourselves twelve men from the people, one man from each tribe, and command them, saying, 'Take up for yourselves twelve stones from here out of the middle of the Jordan . . . and carry them over with you and lay them down in the lodging place where you will lodge tonight.' . . . So these stones shall become a memorial to the sons of Israel forever." . . . [Joshua] said to the sons of Israel, "When your children ask their fathers in time to come, saying, 'What are these stones?' then you shall inform your children, saying, 'Israel crossed this Jordan on dry ground.' For the LORD your God dried up the waters of the Jordan before you until you had crossed, just as the LORD your God had done to the Red Sea, which He dried up before us until we had crossed; that all the peoples of the earth may know that the hand of the LORD is mighty, so that you may fear the LORD your God forever." JOSHUA 4:1-3, 7, 21-24, NASB

Clay closes his Bible and removes his glasses. "And that is why we have this day every year—to remember what God has done in our lives, to thank Him for it, and to anticipate in faith how He will continue to work. So let's get started. Who wants to go first?"

And so we proceed around the circle, one by one. Clay is the traditional scribe of this custom and sits ready to record all with his pen and paper. First we simply recall what has happened in the last year— the good, the bad, the joyful, the painful. Then we consider the ways in which God has provided, moved, helped, comforted, and generally been at work in our lives. Clay writes it all down and then tucks the piece of paper neatly away in the manila envelope. (In the early days we had our children draw pictures of their remembrances and write thank-you notes to God. We kept them in a three-ring binder at first, but we quickly outgrew it and moved to the envelope system.)

Once everyone has spoken, I ask what they hope to see God do in the next year. What are the desires of their hearts? We close our time with prayer, thanking God for each other, for what He has done in the past and for what will happen before the end of the next year.

Hardly has "amen" escaped my mouth when everyone bounds off to don their family-picture garb—solid colors (required) and blue (optional). This practice evolved over the years. Blue is the never-officially-agreed-upon-but-almost-always-worn Clarkson family picture color. We all roll our eyes realizing that, once again, we match.

Now it's time to head off on our picnic. Packed into the car that is slightly too small for our many long limbs (our children are all very tall, and so is our son-in-law), we put on our favorite music from their childhood and sing at the top of our lungs as we drive up the winding mountain roads. Arriving at our favorite picnic stop, we all pile out. My kids may all be adults, but I still hear a chorus of mock-whining: "I'm hungry!"

And so we eat. Again. And talk and laugh, cherishing this rare time with the whole clan reunited. Finally, we pack up our picnic and set out on a small hike. And this is the time we take our famous through-the-years photos—lots and lots of them. After many years of capturing the day with our cameras, we all have favorite sites in the high mountains of the Rockies with backdrops of pine trees, rock outcroppings, wild-flower meadows, and panoramic views from the high advantage of our mountainside trail.

Our picnic and photo time usually takes at least a couple of hours. These pictures have shown up on album covers, book covers, blog posts, Facebook, and of course in frames in my living room. The photo time is a big deal to our ritual Family Day and has taken on a life of its own.

Clay and I walk slowly as we all hike toward favorite sites chosen for past photos. And even now, as adults, the kids run ahead. I love to watch them as they stride on ahead of us.

Sarah, with her gentle loveliness and iron-willed passion for beauty and truth, holding hands with her new husband as they whisper secrets and saunter along.

Joel with his long-legged gait and thoughtful idealism.

Nathan, my outside-the-box, blue-eyed boy with a heart steeled by conviction.

Joy, my free-spirited hard worker, a delight like her name, outrunning us all.

I squeeze my sweet Clay's arm as we watch our pack of offspring gallop ahead. What gifts they are. Look what God has done in our lives.

Much later, back in the car, we weave down the curvy mountain roads. But now everyone is quiet, tired out from the long day and our physical exertion. I'm tired, too, but I'm also deeply happy.

Look what God has done. I wonder what He will do in the future.

When Clay and I first started celebrating our Family Day, it was because we wanted, just like the tribes of Israel in that foundational passage in Joshua, to create a memorial. In our journey through the year, we wanted to place a marker, our own version of a stack of stones, where we could stop and remember how God had moved, worked, and provided in our lives.

Every year—hard or easy, prosperous or full of loss—our Family Days have brought us back to the essential truth: God is working, and we are not alone.

Our family cherishes our tradition of Family Day with cinnamon rolls, mountain walks, fried chicken, and remembering together. You and your family can create your own cherished day full of traditions and tastes that are specific to you. Whatever the method, I encourage everyone to create spaces in their lives to take stock, thank God, and renew their faith. I believe such times are important because they culti-vate a heart of thankfulness, create in us a sense of identity, increase our fortitude in times of darkness, and give us faith to approach the future.

Cultivating Hearts of Thankfulness

Thanksgiving is intimately tied to remembering. If you can't remember what someone has done for you, how can you be thankful?

The Bible uses various forms of the word *remember* more than 170 times, and very often the idea of remembering is tied to thanking God. The Psalms in particular make this frequent connection. Over and over the psalmist encourages the Israelites to remember God's cov-enant to them and to remember what He has done for them, so that they might know His faithfulness and in turn live faithfully according to His covenant.

Take, for instance, Psalm 66. The psalmist calls the people to "shout joyful praises to God," then engages in a jubilant recollection of what God has done for the house of Israel—delivering them from Egypt through the Red Sea, testing and purifying them, giving them leaders, bringing them "through fire and flood" to "a place of great abundance."

Why all the reminders?

Because, quite simply, people forget. And when they forget or don't notice, they tend to whine or complain.

The Israelites forgot again and again about God's faithfulness and His plans for them, and they complained a *lot*. We *all* do that. I've heard that goldfish have bad memories, but I sometimes wonder if human memories are much better.

So many times in my life I have seen God work, felt His presence, heard Him speak directly to the desires of my heart. And then, only a few days later, I find myself pouring out my exasperated heart, feeling like my prayers are hitting the ceiling, wondering if there is a God in the universe.

When it comes to God's work in our lives, we fall so easily into spiritual amnesia. This is why, from time to time, we need to stop the busyness in our lives and *remember*. Even better, we need to create *reminders* of God's faithfulness. Reminders like the stones in Joshua 4. And reminders like our Family Day.

God reminded His people so many times to remember His works because He knew that remembering shapes the way we live. Remembering naturally leads to thankfulness. And a heart of thankfulness connects us to an essential truth: Everything we have has been given to us for a reason. Living in this knowledge helps us to walk with purpose, knowing that God has given us this year, this family, this body, these skills, and we ought to use them to His glory.

Creating a Sense of Identity

Having celebrated Family Day for more than thirty years, we now have a file full of manila folders holding our Family Day remembrances. Tucked inside that file, in Clay's neatly recorded notes and the crayon-scrawled pictures and thank-you notes from the children's younger years, I find stories of our family's most heart-wrenching periods and stories of God's provision that can still bring a thankful tear to my eye. All together, those manila folders tell a larger story, the story of God's faithfulness in the story of the Clarksons.

This record has created in my children an incredible sense of identity and belonging that has lasted them into adulthood. Having grown up with a consciousness of how God had worked in the story of our family, they went into the world with the expectation that God would continue to work in their own stories. When they felt lost, that sense of story and identity kept them anchored. We Clarksons may have our quirks and frustrations with each other, but at heart we know we are each other's people, part of the same story.

A sense of identity is essential for our children to stand strong in their generation. Modern technology has created a world where thousands of voices call out to them every day, telling them who they are, how they ought to act, what they ought to love. The voices of our culture try to overwrite their family stories, leaving them lost and isolated. If our children are to weather the cacophonous onslaught, they must be able to hear a strong, beautiful, harmonious voice singing the song of who they *really* are, who they belong to, and what story they are telling.

When you intentionally make times to remember God's work in the life of your family, you give your children a story to be a part of. You give them a context for their actions, encouragement to write their own stories faithfully and beautifully, and a sense of identity to help safeguard their hearts from the onslaught of competing voices. In moments of weariness, temptation, and decision, they can remember the joyful story they are part of and move forward in faith.

A Reason to Keep Going

There were years when Family Day fell smack dab in the middle of weeping seasons for us. How did remembering God's faithfulness help us then?

If you've lost someone, remembering all of the ways God has been faithful does not bring your loved one back, and indeed it might make you ache even more for his or her presence. Sometimes remembering can cause a sense of dissonance; you can remember times when God was working, but He doesn't seem to be doing anything now. In fact, He may seem to be noticeably absent. So in seasons of grief or difficulty, remembering seems exactly like the thing you *don't* want to do.

Remembering does not make suffering easier, but it makes it endurable. Joyful seasons of God's abundance do not negate seasons of pain and scarcity; good times and bad times cannot cancel each other out. No, the sorrow in our lives is real, but so is the joy. So we remember in order to hold on to our faith that sorrow will not have the last word, that a current season of darkness will not last forever.

One thing our Family Day ritual has taught us as well is that God is still active in those dark seasons of life, even when we can't see His work or feel His presence. Almost always, as we've looked back at a difficult past year, we have been amazed at the ways our generous, gracious God was actively working in our circumstances. His faithfulness was there all along. We just didn't notice until we took the time to look back and remember.

Remembering helps in difficult times because it draws us out of the cloud of our distress and helps us see the big picture. God will give grace again as He always has. Hearts can find strength in knowing that He has worked before, and He will again.

The writers of the Psalms understood this. In Psalm 77, the psalmist identified as Asaph pours out his heart before God, sparing no words to express his deep distress. This in itself is a good reminder that it is okay to be profoundly out of sorts and tell God about it. Yes, God promises a peace that passes understanding, but the Bible is full of people who had moments when they were broken, confused, and didn't know what to pray. But I love the psalmist's reaction to this pain. Right in the middle of this literary version of weeping and wailing, he says,

> I shall remember the deeds of the LORD;
> Surely I will remember Your wonders of old.
> PSALM 77:11, NASB

And then the psalmist does a wonderful thing. He goes on to remind himself of all the ways God has worked in the past and of God's mighty power in both human affairs and the natural world. The implied conclusion is that while, yes, this moment is difficult and terrible, God will rescue and save again. This darkness is not forever. We will experience the redemption of God, even if it is not in this life.

Family Day reminds me of this true fact every year. No matter what comes, I can look back on six decades of God's tender care of me and my family and find hope. We may be weary, sad, or confused, but God will always come to our rescue again.

Approaching the Future with Faith

The future is always a mystery. No matter how old I get, I keep finding myself wishing I knew what is to come. This is the tension of living by faith, not knowing what is to come, but living as though our actions matter—because they do!

For me, a glance at the past helps me face the future more fearlessly. When I page through thirty years of manila folders and remember God's faithfulness, I am filled with a tenacious optimism. My life has not been at all what I imagined; it has been infinitely better because it was guided by the steady hand of my gracious heavenly Father. I choose not to be afraid of the future because I have seen God's work all the days of my life. As King David puts it,

> Once I was young, and now I am old.
> Yet I have never seen the godly abandoned
> or their children begging for bread.
>
> PSALM 37:25

It is not enough for me to just live life without fear; I want to live it courageously, for the Kingdom, with faith. When I think back on my life so far, I am amazed and thankful that I've had the privilege of being a little part in God's work in the world. And I don't want to stop now! I want to give my all in looking for more ways to be a part of what God is doing. And I want to challenge you to do the same.

But living by faith requires a good spiritual imagination and a good memory. To make sound faith decisions, you have to believe that God will provide and that the decision you are making will mean something in the end.

This can be so difficult when you are in the thick of living life. But I find it helps me to look to Hebrews 11 for my model. Sometimes known as the "Hall of Faith," this passage recalls people from the Bible who made decisions based on their calling from God rather than taking the easier, more pleasant path. Many if not all of them had to keep going without seeing the immediate benefits of making faith decisions. But theirs are the stories we cherish as examples of brave lives and faithful living.

The author of Hebrews sums it up by saying, "All these people were still living by faith when they died. They did not receive the things promised; they only saw them and welcomed them from a distance, admitting that they were foreigners and strangers on earth" (Hebrews 11:13, NIV).

Hebrews 11 is a practice in remembering. It looks back at all the stories God has woven faithfully together, and then looks straight in the eyes of the reader and says, "Therefore, since we are surrounded by such a huge crowd of witnesses to the life of faith, let us strip off every weight that slows us down, especially the sin that so easily trips us up. And let us run with endurance the race God has set before us" (Hebrews 12:1). We remember God's faithfulness in the past so we can walk—or run!—into the future with strength and hope.

What Next?

The last table we share on Family Day is at a favorite coffee shop in town that is part of a Greek Orthodox church and an outreach ministry to the community. It is halfway home from the mountains where we hike. We all order chai lattes made from their special mix—the smoothest we have ever tasted, or maybe they just taste that way served in artisan ceramic mugs after we've exhausted ourselves hiking. The conversation is sweet, the tradition goes on, and all are happy as we finish one more year of remembering who the Clarksons are, what we stand for, and how God has worked His faithfulness through our lives over many years.

I always find it bittersweet when my children go back to their corners of the world. My mama heart wants to hold on to them forever, cherishing their hearts in my home. But I am so thankful to see them going out into their world, bringing beauty, goodness, and truth through their lives and living out their love of Jesus. Family Day helps me hold these feelings in what feels like a healthy balance. I look to the past, remembering the sweet gifts God has given me, and this helps me walk forward in faith. So though I may wipe away a tear as I wave good-bye to my dear ones, in my heart I thank God for His faithfulness and smile into the future.

What will He do next?

Something to Ponder

Hebrews 11:1-2, 39-40

Faith shows the reality of what we hope for; it is the evidence
of things we cannot see. Through their faith, the people in days
of old earned a good reputation. . . .

All these people earned a good reputation because of their
faith, yet none of them received all that God had promised. For
God had something better in mind for us, so that they would
not reach perfection without us.

Hebrews 11 is a chapter full of hero tales, stories of those who practiced
faith in God as they were living real-life stories. Read this chapter and
dwell on the stories.

Which stories stand out to you? Why?

- The author of Hebrews thought it was important to impress upon
  his readers the stories of faith. Why do you think this was empha-
  sized?

Psalm 43

Declare me innocent, O God!
  Defend me against these ungodly people.
  Rescue me from these unjust liars.
For you are God, my only safe haven.
  Why have you tossed me aside?
Why must I wander around in grief,
  oppressed by my enemies?
Send out your light and your truth;
  let them guide me.
Let them lead me to your holy mountain,
  to the place where you live.
There I will go to the altar of God,
  to God—the source of all my joy.

I will praise you with my harp,
    O God, my God!

Why am I discouraged?
    Why is my heart so sad?
I will put my hope in God!
    I will praise him again—
        my Savior and my God!

The author of this psalm finds himself in distress and writes this psalm as a prayer, hoping to return to faith in God.

Read this psalm over twice. What stands out to you?

- Within this psalm, count how many times the author reminds himself to "remember," "look for," or "think" about God's work in his life.

Something to Try

Get out a journal and write your own "Hall of Faith," thinking about the ways you have seen God work, trusting Him for the promises you haven't yet seen fulfilled.

- At your dinner table, lead your family in remembering ways that you have seen God's faithfulness in your life.

- Organize your own version of Family Day. Pick treats and activities your family will love. Take time to sit down together and think through the ways you have seen God working in your life. Pray and commit your year to God. Then do it again next year.

Some Recipes That Are Really Us

Polish Eggs

Many years ago, when I lived in Poland, it was controlled by the Russian Communist regime. During those austere years, meat was very difficult to come by. The stores offered mainly potatoes, eggs, butter, milk, cheese, and very few vegetables or fruit.

One of our ministry partners, who had grown up in a Polish neighborhood in Chicago and spoke fluent Polish, had moved back to his native land to work underground with us to reach the country for Christ. One day as my roommate and I were getting ready for our language classes, our friend showed up at the door and announced, "Have I got a treat to spoil you girls today."

He came into our kitchen, dumped onions and potatoes onto our counter, and then, like a magician, pulled a chunk of ham from the bag.

"I found this in the store today and it was vanishing quickly, so I grabbed some for us," he told us, a wide grin painted across his face. "I will make you a dish my grandmother made us for all of our holidays."

I brought the recipe back home with me. Ever since, my family has called this wonderful dish Polish Eggs, and we gobble it up whether for breakfast or dinner. So tasty.

10 eggs
2 tablespoons milk or half-and-half, optional
Vegetable oil to cook potatoes and meat in
2 large or 4 small potatoes, grated
¾ cup cubed ham or 8 slices of bacon
1 medium onion, chopped
2 tablespoons butter or oil to cook the eggs
1 cup grated cheddar cheese
2 tablespoons sour cream
Salt and pepper to taste
More grated cheese for garnish

Crack the eggs into a bowl. Add milk or half-and-half, if using, and mix with a fork or whisk. Set bowl aside.

Pour vegetable oil of your choice into a large skillet—enough to cover the bottom of pan about ¼ inch deep. Place on burner and turn heat to low. While oil is heating, peel the potatoes if you prefer (we like ours with the skin on) and then grate them. Gently place potatoes into the skillet so as not to splash the hot oil. Cook until light brown on the bottom and then flip to cook on the other side. When potatoes are cooked to the crispness you desire (some like them crisp and some like them a little bit softer), remove from skillet and place on a paper towels to drain.

Add a little more oil to the same skillet—just enough to barely cover bottom of pan. Place the ham or bacon in the skillet and also add the onion. Cook until the meat is slightly browned and seems to be cooked through. I stir the mixture to flip the meat on its two sides. The onions will be translucent when ready. Empty meat-onion mixture onto a paper plate.

Wipe the skillet to clean out any bits of food and put in 2 tablespoons butter to melt over medium heat. Pour the eggs into the pan, stirring constantly to keep them soft and moist. When eggs are almost cooked, take pan off the stove. Crumble in the potatoes, sprinkle in the meat and onion mixture, and sprinkle the cheese on top. Place skillet back on burner and gently fold the eggs, potatoes, meat, and cheese together. Add sour cream and lightly toss mixture again. Remove from heat, salt and pepper to taste, garnish with a little more cheese, then feast immediately while the eggs are hot.

Serves 6–10 people, depending on appetite.

❇ Sally's Special Fried Chicken

Many years ago, when I was a young teen, my very sophisticated Aunt Margaret came to babysit my brother and me while my parents were on an anniversary trip. One night I walked in from school to find my aunt bedecked in her apron. The house smelled promising, and sizzling noises were coming from the kitchen. "Now, finish your homework quickly and set the table," said Aunt Margaret, "or you will miss my famous fried chicken."

Not one to be denied, I set the table especially fine and even picked flowers from our yard to grace our feast. Flying through my schoolwork, I came back to the kitchen just as she was putting the final touches on mashed potatoes, gravy, and a plate piled high with crisp, golden chicken.

For some reason, that meal grew larger than life in my life. Great homemade fried chicken was already one of my favorite meals. But Aunt Margaret had a special twist. She never told me a specific recipe, but she said one had to dip the chicken in milk and add a touch of sugar to the coating. I spent many years perfecting my own recipe based on that little bit of information.

I'm happy with the results, and so is my family. I do not allow myself this high-calorie treat very often. But when I do, I enjoy every morsel and stuff myself full. This is our go-to entrée for Christmas Day and our Family Day celebrations. We enjoy it with mashed potatoes, gravy, and tiny peas or a seven-layer salad (a recipe for another book).

As I may have mentioned before, I am a "seat of the pants" sort of cook and work mostly by intuition. So if you want to change this recipe to your own taste, feel free. I put in the basics, and you can add the rest.

Canola oil or vegetable oil of your choice
2–3 pounds boneless, skinless chicken breasts or thighs
2 cups unbleached all-purpose flour
2 heaping teaspoons sea salt
1 tablespoon turbinado (raw) or white sugar (the secret!)
Pepper to taste
1 cup crumbs (bread crumbs, crushed cereal, or whatever you like)
2 eggs
1 cup milk (whatever variety you like)
Additional salt and pepper to taste

Place about ¼ inch of oil into a skillet and place on low heat to warm. Rinse chicken and pat dry with a paper towel. Slice the chicken pieces into strips about half an inch wide. Mix flour, salt, sugar, pepper, and crumbs in a gallon-size zippered plastic bag. In a medium-sized bowl, whip eggs into milk.

Dip each chicken piece into milk and egg mixture to coat, gently shake off excess moisture, then place into bag of flour mixture. You can place five or six pieces into the bag at a time. Zip the bag closed, hold it at the zip (for extra security), and shake until all chicken pieces are totally covered.

Check to see if oil is sufficiently heated to fry chicken. (You can tell if it's the right temperature if you flick a drop of water in it—just a drop!—and it bubbles.) Gently lay breaded chicken pieces into the warm grease. Fill the whole pan with chicken pieces. (For 2 pounds, I usually use two frying pans.) Cook until crisp on one side (check the bottom) and turn over to crisp on the other side. Then remove from pans onto paper towels to drain. Add additional salt and pepper if desired and serve.

Serves 6–8.

❋ Larla's Brownies

My best friend from missions in Poland and Austria, Gwen, always had these incredible fudge-topped brownies to share every time she came to visit me. Gwennie got the recipe from her amazing mama, Anna Laura, called Larla by her grandchildren. Later, when I was a mama of three little ones and lived in Nashville, Tennessee, far away from my family, Larla would invite me and my wee three to visit for several days at a time so that I could get a break. Always she had these brownies waiting for us—a recipe she had perfected over eighty-seven years. (She lived well into her nineties!) We made many happy memories at Larla's table.

Vegetable oil or nonstick spray to grease pan
5 tablespoons butter
2 ounces (2 squares) unsweetened baking chocolate
2 eggs, well beaten
1 teaspoon vanilla

1 cup granulated sugar

⅔ cup unbleached all-purpose flour

½ cup chopped nuts (Larla used English walnuts.)

2 squares unsweetened baking chocolate

3 tablespoons unsalted butter

1½ cups confectioner's sugar

1 teaspoon vanilla

2 tablespoons hot water

Preheat oven to 325°F. Grease a 7 × 11 inch pan or spray with
nonstick spray for easy cleanup. (Note that this is a smaller size pan
than the more common 9 × 13.) Melt together 5 tablespoons butter
and 2 squares baking chocolate in the top pan of a double boiler
over warming water. Cool mixture to lukewarm, mix with eggs and
1 teaspoon vanilla, then add granulated sugar, flour, and nuts. Pour
batter into prepared pan and bake about 25 minutes. Watch carefully
so that the edges do not begin to harden.

For the icing, melt together 2 more squares of chocolate and
3 tablespoons butter in the top of the double boiler. Remove from
heat and add confectioner's sugar, 1 teaspoon vanilla, and about
2 tablespoons of the hot water from the bottom of the double boiler.
Stir well and spread immediately over warm brownies in the pan.
It will melt and cool to make a fudgelike topping. Cut into squares
or rectangles.

Makes 9-12 brownies, depending on how large you like them.

CHAPTER 12

STEPPING INTO THE STORY
A Shepherds' Meal for Christmas Eve

People who love to eat are always the best people.

JULIA CHILD

That night there were shepherds staying in the fields nearby, guarding their flocks of sheep. Suddenly, an angel of the Lord appeared among them, and the radiance of the Lord's glory surrounded them. They were terrified, but the angel reassured them. "Don't be afraid!" he said. "I bring you good news that will bring great joy to all people. The Savior—yes, the Messiah, the Lord—has been born today in Bethlehem, the city of David! And you will recognize him by this sign: You will find a baby wrapped snugly in strips of cloth, lying in a manger."
Suddenly, the angel was joined by a vast host of others—
the armies of heaven—praising God and saying,
"Glory to God in highest heaven,
and peace on earth to those with whom God is pleased."

LUKE 2:8-14

Table-Discipleship Principle:

Celebrating the feast days and historical events
in Christianity together builds a sense of
community with believers throughout the ages.

As I GAZE BACK over the decades of my life, pleasant memories float through my mind, comforting me and wrapping around my thoughts like a warm blanket. And one of the warmest of these is of a Christmas Eve dinner in our crooked little house in Vienna, the occasion of our very first shepherds' feast.

We encountered a variety of faith-stretching lessons daily back in those days as we were confronted by the challenges of living in a foreign culture. My idealistic, conviction-driven husband was working as a junior pastor at the International Church in Vienna, Austria. Because Vienna was one of the most expensive cities in the world at that time, we searched for a proper place to live with a two-and-a-half-year-old princess and the expectation of a baby boy yet to be born. Clay and I finally found a house we could afford. We moved in just in time for Joel to be born—delivered by an Austrian midwife in the hospital down the street on a cold, windy November night.

So that Christmas found five of us—Clay and I, toddler Sarah and newborn Joel, and a young friend who was having an adventure on a break from college and living with us for six months—squished together in a tiny (nine-hundred-square-foot) gray stucco bungalow. The foundation had settled, leaving the basement steps slanted and uneven, with a bit of effect on the rest of the house. Most of the rooms were about as big as a large walk-in closet. Rain would pour down our walls—inside!—when it rained. Pigeons often found their way into the attic and then got stuck there. But the energy of young love, youthful ideals, toddler glee, and discoveries every day with a newborn son sang happiness and vibrancy into our lives.

Joel had a funny way of crying when he was hungry—a kind of a growl. That gave us pause; we had never heard of a baby who growled instead of crying. But we thought he was adorable, and Sarah was absolutely smitten. She toddled around telling everyone who would listen that "Dod dave us a baby boy—just like Desus was when He came to Mary on Christmas!" Having heard the nativity story in the dark of our chapel one evening, she was sure that Joel was our own Jesus, and she would watch by the window each evening for the angels to appear to sing him a song.

Maybe it was her childlike love of the story that inspired me to host our first Shepherds' Meal that Christmas Eve. To be honest, I can't remember. But I'll never forget the evening itself.

We thought our little orphan home had never looked more beautiful. Flames on crimson candles shivered and waved each time visitors rang our bell to signal their arrival and pushed open the front door. Our tiny antique table was laden with winter bounty—red apples, golden pears, and large polished hazelnuts—that gleamed in the candlelight. Seven of us in mismatched wooden chairs crowded around a table built for four, content to share in the friendly companionship of a festive evening. No one wanted to be alone on this frigid Christmas Eve.

We were something of a motley crowd, but so happy to be together—a young Austrian woman whose spouse had just abandoned her for another man, a Taiwanese secretary who worked at the United Nations headquarters, a refugee from the Middle East, and a young missionary from England, lonely on his very first time away from his family. Sarah sat chattering in my lap and talking about the angels. The friend who was living with us helped me serve the simple meal, and we all sang "Silent Night" as a prayer, because it was the only carol everyone knew.

Four different languages were our mother tongues. As to religious conviction, we had one Catholic, one *Evangelisch* (Lutheran Reformed), an Asian Baptist, a British Anglican, and one agnostic who looked on and listened with curiosity. But hearts were opened by the simple beauty of bread, cheese, and warm herbed soup as we spoke of the shepherds who had found and worshiped Jesus on that first Christmas so long ago. And my own heart was warmed by the gathering of friends from such different cultures who shared our table and celebrated the love that whispered His reality through the moments of the evening.

I remember thinking that this was what heaven would be like—all unified, all tied together by the sharing of friendship and food as we celebrated Jesus' first coming, each worshiping from our own traditions, but grateful for the divine Love that had kissed our evening with His presence.

There was something so special about that first Shepherds' Meal that we couldn't wait to "do it again next year." And so we have. In the thirty-plus years since then, our family has enjoyed a Shepherds' Meal every Christmas Eve, no matter where we lived. Even the preparation has become a tradition—a family affair.

Forward through the Years

Sautéing onions and fresh rosemary and thyme fill the air with alluring fragrance, waiting to be added to my old recipe for onion-herb bread. Kneaded bread dough takes on a sheen, marking its readiness to be placed into bread pans, as strong hands shape it into loaves. One of our boys has taken on the challenge of putting together the rich potato soup that we long ago christened White Christmas Soup, making sure to add the right amount of butter, salt, and milk to keep it creamy but not too thick.

Sarah unwraps the soft cheeses—always Gouda, Camembert, and Boursin—and decorates an elaborate plate with tiny orange slices, grapes, apples, and pears. Dark roasted Worcestershire pecans from an old recipe from Clay's mom or my own buttered pecans (see recipe in chapter 6) accompany the cheese. Joy sets the table with crystal goblets passed down through the family and Christmas plates that show the wear and tear of many celebrations. Candles crowd the table since all the electric lights will be off for our feast. All ears are tuned for the doorbell; our guests for the evening will be arriving soon to share our much-loved, traditional celebration of shepherds and angels and a baby and the meaning of it all.

My desire from the beginning was to have a simple meal, no fuss, so that we could focus on the story of the night when Christ burst into the world. Our Shepherds' Meal, as it has evolved, is still simple, but so delicious and rich in meaning for all of us. Each year we gather in deep anticipation of good food shared over the marvel of God coming to ordinary people like those long-ago shepherds—and to us as well. His heart reaching out to ours because He understood that we, like the sheep on that long-ago hillside, are in dire need of a Shepherd.

The Heart of a Shepherd

One of my favorite verses in all of Scripture is Matthew 9:36: "When he saw the crowds, he had compassion on them because they were confused and helpless, like sheep without a shepherd."

Our Jesus, our God, sees us when we are confused, helpless, and weary, carrying so many burdens in our private worlds. He does not react with disdain or criticism, thinking we should be stronger or more perfect. Instead, He sees us as people who were made to be shepherded. We need direction, instruction, help, and guidance in order to live well into the lives we have been given.

Truth is, sheep are easily overcome. They are hardwired to need guidance, protection, someone to look out for their needs and welfare. And that's definitely true of us human sheep. We were never meant to just buck up and do life without help. We were made to need and to long for our Shepherd's guidance and help and love and joy in our lives.

We hunger for what He came to give us. "I came that [my sheep] may have life, and have it abundantly," He said (John 10:10, NASB).

And oh, how we need the redemption He offers us through His life and death and resurrection: "I am the good shepherd; the good shepherd lays down His life for the sheep" (John 10:11, NASB).

As we ponder the coming of Christ amid a delectable meal, crunching on roasted nuts, savoring melted butter on soft, warm, herbed bread, gathered around a candlelit table, it is easy to imagine Jesus coming among us as a good Shepherd, the One who gives us of His abundance, who lays His very life down for us.

Familiar verses memorized together at this same table come to mind:

The LORD is my shepherd;
I shall not want.
He makes me to lie down in green pastures;
He leads me beside the still waters.
He restores my soul;

He leads me in the paths of righteousness
For His name's sake.
PSALM 23:1-3, NKJV

So we reflect once again on the fact that even as Jesus came to the world to redeem us on this Christmas evening, so He takes full responsibility for our lives. He leads us, comforts us, protects us, restores us, and helps us make righteous choices.

The generous provision and love of our serving, sacrificial God pours over our hearts and soothes our thoughts. Anxiety melts away. Reassurance comes. Wherever each of us is, our Good Shepherd finds us and gives us Himself. And this, too, is what we celebrate around this Christmas Eve table.

These Are My People

Christmas is a time for the life of the One who is come to invade our hearts with delight. And for weeks now, the celebration has been picking up momentum. Flickering candlelight; shimmering multicolored lights on a real tree inside the house; familiar songs that beg for swaying and dancing; delectable aromas of pine, vanilla, spices, hot bread, and coffee warm our hearts as we steal away from the onslaught of cultural messages.

This evening is just what I hoped it would be—simple, peaceful, precious to us all. I did not want to kill myself cooking elaborate dishes and messing up the kitchen one more time for a grand night of scrubbing pots and pans. Instead, my hope was for a tradition that would bring peace of heart and warmth of spirit to each one—a Mary time instead of a Martha time for our Christmas Eve remembering.

Friends and family gather with hugs and kisses and celebration and presents. Shared stories about angels, babies, wise men, young mothers, and animals speak to the minds and hearts of young and old, collecting new layers of meaning every year. And all these are wrapped in one short period of a few weeks that fill the heart and stir the imagination to new dreams.

What's not to love about Christmas?

And on this night we now see even more how the delights of home—the very intentionally laid table, the familiar recipes prepared with care, the games and fun and making of memories, the music filling every day, the cherishing of Christ together—can give our children, family, and friends even more love for Him.

We Clarksons so love this special time together. For my children who live far away, coming home to celebrate together—to celebrate all that is profoundly important—is something they can hardly wait for. It is another of the invisible strings that tie our hearts so strongly together.

Recently, as I was planning our December, I called one of my children to find out when he could make it home for Christmas. I supposed his visit would be short because of his heavy work schedule. Instead I heard, "Mom, I don't think you know how much being together with all the kids builds me up. I am lonely a lot—working, paying bills, being responsible. But I want to be with everyone as long as I can. I have saved my vacation time just so we can all be together. These are my best friends."

And from another: "This has been such a challenging year to all that I believe. To feast together daily to discuss all that matters to us—the ideals, our faith, our values, our decisions—keeps me wanting to be faithful. I receive so much strength and accountability to keep going. This is my tribe, and they remind me of all we have held dear over the years."

As I write this, Christmas is fresh in my mind. This year we had all four adult children and one new spouse home for fifteen days. Fifteen days of feasting together, carols around the piano, gifts opened and exclaimed over, walks together in the snow, talking and more talking. Fifteen days of meal preparation, kitchen cleanup, messes galore, and countless empty mugs and cups from countless servings of hot chocolate with whipped cream, tea, and coffee.

And yes, those fifteen days wore me out, but they were also deeply satisfying. The rousing discussions filled my heart with gratitude. All of these precious ones have a passion for God. They care so deeply about the world, are so intent on having a Kingdom impact. As our Christmas season unfolded, I saw so clearly, once again, how profoundly strategic our family table has been in building strong faith and convictions through the camaraderie and community of being together and belonging to one another.

On the last day of our time together, right before everybody piled into the car headed to the airport, someone snapped a quick selfie with the seven of us crunched together on the stairs that climb to our bedrooms. It popped up on Instagram before they were out of the driveway with this text accompanying it: "These are *my* people! Where they go, my heart goes. Here's to the next time we're all on the same continent!"

There is a foundational influence that rituals of celebration bring as anchors to our lives. These practiced rhythms and traditional feasts remind us what we believe, why we nurture our faith, how God has been faithful over history and through our own lifetimes. And gathering together to document and celebrate these profoundly important feast days does make us all feel connected, a part of something bigger than us all.

Celebration and Sharing

Our heavenly Father was the first to celebrate. He was the first one to document the birthday of Jesus—supernaturally, with music performed before humble shepherds and faraway kings. And long before that, He was encouraging His people to feast together as a way of remembering His goodness and His willingness to walk with us every day in blessing.

When I think about the wonders of the first Christmas—astonishing, bewildering, unimaginable beings appearing on the earth, extraterrestrial choirs filling the sky, a heretofore unknown star rising in the heavens, learned kings traveling from afar, a virgin birth in the midst of a love story, an old woman and an old man marveling and speaking of the Messiah as the baby is dedicated—I can't help but think they were part of God's plan to help us celebrate Jesus' arrival.

Christmas is a time when we bring friends and family into our home to be refreshed. It is a time of personal worship and a time of joy. It's a time of work and preparation, but all to say "I love you" and "God loves us and is worthy of our celebration of Him." In these traditions we understand that God wanted us to put aside special times for the passing down of His story and His love.

I think that sometimes people are afraid to have too much fun or to celebrate life. Yet it is only when we do this fully, from the heart, that we understand the joy of the Lord, the God who gave us the ability to be satisfied, to laugh merrily and play games and eat to our hearts' content.

So our family makes time to delight together. It is part of the organic life of Christ—the tastes, smells, fun, love, and theology that give us the whole picture of this baby become Shepherd and Savior and King. In our home, through our Shepherds' Meal, we celebrate His coming to earth fully and happily. And best of all, we share our celebration—with each other and with others God sends our way.

I have long loved this quote from a dear friend, Elizabeth Foss.

> Make hospitality your prayer. Seek to comfort and to serve.
> Look for ways to lighten someone else's load. In every guest,
> no matter how cranky, no matter how demanding, see Christ.
> Open your heart wide; risk allowing people to see your
> weaknesses. For it is in that very weakness that His power
> is made perfect.[1]

I try to think of this, too, at Christmas. As we approach the holidays, I ponder how to make my home a place where people can see Christ more easily. Small children who need cool sips of juice and small bites of food and one more story (maybe something about shepherds). Teens who rage with hormones and moods but still need a cup of thoughtfulness and a few cookies prepared on their behalf. My adult children, hungry for a familiar taste of home and family. My weary husband, who needs patience and compassion served along with a favorite treat. My friends and neighbors and even the random stranger who needs somewhere to be over the holidays. I want my home to be a place where, through the giving of hospitality and love, the Lord Jesus Christ becomes incarnate.

The older I get, the more I see that the age-old traditions, the rituals of life that remind us who we are, what our roots and heritage have been, bind us to a faith that will be passed down through generations. And so we put aside the secular call of the world for a while to be amazed once again that God became a vulnerable baby, placed in a real family like ours. We listen once more to the old, old story of shepherds on a hillside serenaded by singing angels. And we are reminded once more of our part in it all:

To live faithfully under the guidance of our Good Shepherd.

And to pass the stories on, so that all may believe in the miracle that took place in Bethlehem so long ago.

Something to Ponder

Isaiah 40:11

> He will feed his flock like a shepherd.
> > He will carry the lambs in his arms,
> holding them close to his heart.
> > He will gently lead the mother sheep with their young.

There are so many beautiful Scriptures that depict Jesus as a Shepherd who cares diligently for us. Reflect on this amazing passage written hundreds of years before Christ's birth but given as a foreshadowing of His deep love for us, His children, His personally chosen flock.

Do you believe that Jesus loves you so much that He cherishes holding you close to His heart? What does that mean to you? How does it change the way you think of yourself and live day to day?

- The second half of the verse reveals a shepherd being very patient with the mother who is caring for her children. What does this verse tell us about the way Christ interacts with us as mothers? What are some of the ways you believe you have been "gently led"?

- When we ponder these verses, we understand that Christ is gentle in His handling of His sheep. Do you expect gentleness and patience from Him in your own life?

Matthew 18:3

Then he said, "I tell you the truth, unless you . . . become like little children, you will never get into the Kingdom of Heaven."

Children are caught up in the miracle of the Christmas story and delight in the sparkles of the lights on the tree, learning the familiar Christmas songs, delighting in company, treats, gifts, and celebrating.

How does this verse help you to calm your spirit and to seek to see Christmas anew each year with the innocent faith of a child?

- What do you think it means for us, as adults, to "become like little children"? What characteristics do you think Jesus was talking about in this passage? What would have to change in your life for you to develop these characteristics?

Something to Try

Take time to reflect on several of the "Good Shepherd" verses listed in this chapter. (If you like, use a concordance or an online Bible search engine to find more.) Give any burdens you are carrying to your Shepherd, Jesus, and write your thoughts and prayers in a journal. (You might even want to keep a Christmas journal that you can go back to every year.)

- Plan a time with your family to be together over a simple candle-lit meal, with the intention of having a night of peace together. Check your heart before you start the evening that you are at peace with the Lord. Resolve that no matter what tensions come, you will be the peacemaker, like our own Prince of Peace.

- Pick one of the classic Christmas passages (Isaiah 7:14; Isaiah 9:6; John 1:14; Luke 2:8-12) to memorize as a family, a little each night.

This is a great activity for Advent, the four weeks before Christmas, but you can do it throughout the year. When Christmas comes, you will each have a piece of the story tucked away in your hearts, something that will speak to you each Christmas you celebrate.

Recipes for Shepherds and Friends

✳ White Christmas Soup

Our family could eat potato soup every day of the year because it tastes so amazingly wonderful, but we especially enjoy it on Christmas Eve. We associate it with the candlelight meal, the quiet, beautiful time together every year. The soup we make at Christmas is a simple one in honor of the kind of food the shepherds probably ate. Actually, I am pretty sure those Middle Eastern shepherds did not eat potato soup! But it was our own original attempt to keep the meal simple.

8–10 sizable red potatoes, peeled and chopped or sliced into small
      pieces (Red potatoes are a little bit sweeter and have a lower
      glycemic count, but use whatever potatoes you prefer.)
3 tablespoons olive oil
1 medium onion, diced
1 clove garlic, minced (can substitute ½ teaspoon garlic powder or
      1 teaspoon garlic paste)
¼ cup (½ stick) butter
2–3 cups milk, half-and-half, or a combination of the two (We use
      1½ cups of each for our special Christmas meal!)
1½–2 cups grated aged cheddar cheese (more cheese at Christmas,
      less for daily soup)
1–2 teaspoons fine sea salt
½ teaspoon black pepper
Sour cream and chopped fresh dill for garnish
Cooked, chopped bacon, optional

Place the potatoes in a pan of water. Bring to a boil and cook until tender. As they cook, place the oil in a pan and sauté the onion with the garlic until onion is translucent.

When the potatoes are cooked, drain the water and add the butter in small pieces so it will melt quickly. Add the onion mixture. Mash all of this together well with a potato masher.

Slowly stir in the cream or milk, adding ½ cup at a time until the soup looks like the right consistency. (Potatoes soak up liquid over time, so usually I need to add the full amount.) Stir in 1½ cups of cheese plus the salt and pepper. Keep soup warm until ready to serve.

Just before serving, ladle soup into your favorite bowls. Sprinkle about a tablespoon of the remaining cheese over each, add a small scoop of sour cream, and then sprinkle the dill on top for a festive look.

We do not add bacon to our Christmas soup because the Jewish shepherds would never have eaten pork. But when we make this soup throughout the rest of the year, we definitely use a sprinkle of bacon, and it's delicious.

Makes about 7 servings.

✳ Christmas Sticky Toffee Pudding
(from my sweet friend Stephanie Wilbur)

Nathan paid to have a DNA study made on our family and found out that we are just about 75 percent from the United Kingdom in lineage. This was no surprise to us since we feel it in our bones. We all love tea, literature, long walks and hikes, civility of living, and great conversations over meals—plus, we love British history.

Consequently, we have adopted a favorite English recipe for our Christmas dessert. It is so much more delicious than you can even imagine, with the warm caramel sauce on top and whipped cream as garnish. I hope you will try it.

I do have to admit that there's another reason I'm partial to this dessert. The first time we tasted it was on a visit to Prince Edward Island, where Anne of Green Gables is set. We ate it at the inn where part of the TV miniseries and its sequel were filmed in the 1980s—a big deal to us because those were family favorites!

Seconds of this sweet treat may be required. But everything is legal at Christmas, right?

Butter for greasing pan
2½ cups water
2 cups pitted dates, chopped very fine (I use about 30 largish dates.)
2 teaspoons baking soda
2½ cups unbleached all-purpose flour
2 teaspoons non-aluminum baking powder
½ cup (1 stick) unsalted butter, softened
1½ cups dark brown sugar
2 large eggs, beaten
1 tablespoon vanilla extract
2 cups (1-pound package) unsalted butter
1 pint heavy cream
4 cups packed dark brown sugar

Preheat oven to 350°F. Butter a large baking dish—mine is 9 × 13 inches. Bring the water to a boil in a small saucepan and then add the dates and baking soda; set aside. Whisk flour together with baking powder and set that aside as well. With an electric mixer, beat ½ cup butter with sugar until fluffy. Add eggs and vanilla extract, and beat until blended. Gradually add flour mixture. Fold in soaked dates (with liquid). Stir until blended. Pour batter into prepared baking dish. Bake until set and firm on top, approximately 40 minutes.

For the sauce, combine 2 cups butter with cream and dark brown sugar in a medium-heavy saucepan. Bring mixture to a boil, stirring constantly. Boil gently over medium-low heat, stirring constantly, until mixture is thickened, about 10 minutes.

Preheat broiler. Poke holes into the cake. (I poke a lot of holes. We want that sauce to get way in there!) Pour about 1½ cups or so of sauce over the cake, spreading evenly. Place under broiler until top is bubbly, 1–3 minutes.

Serve dessert warm with extra sauce drizzled over, with ice cream, or in a bath of heavy cream.

Makes at least 16 servings, depending
on how you cut this very rich cake.

CHAPTER 13

CREATING KINDRED SPIRITS
A Christmas Tea for Friends Old and New

I would rather walk with a friend in the dark than walk alone in the light.

HELEN KELLER

Two are better than one because they have a good return for their labor. For if either of them falls, the one will lift up his companion. But woe to the one who falls when there is not another to lift him up.

ECCLESIASTES 4:9-10, NASB

Table-Discipleship Principle:

Celebrating life and creating joyful memories through the seasons creates deep wells of accountability.

It was Christmas, and we didn't have any friends.

Sarah, my oldest, was nine years old. The walls of our new home in Texas were still partially bare, and random corners still held cardboard boxes filled with the remnants of our old life in Tennessee.

As a veteran globetrotter, I well knew the period of adjustment that comes with moving to a new place. But there is nothing quite so "achy" as the lonesomeness of a solitary Christmas. Somehow, when my three children were younger, they had felt the loneliness of a new town less keenly. But Sarah had now reached an age where she was acutely aware of our isolation and longed for friends. My mama heart yearned alongside her. I knew that building friendships in a new place takes time, but I shared her deep sense of disconnection.

This longing was deeper than a desire simply for people to pass the time with. I also longed for true kindred spirits and godly community. Perhaps worse than the loneliness of a new town was the ache of experiencing broken or shallow friendships. I worried that my longing for spiritual friendship would always be frustrated by our constant moves and by the general difficulty of being a sinful person trying to relate to other sinful people.

One rainy afternoon I sat in my new Texas home with its barren walls, a cup of tea in my lap, and felt the tears seep out from beneath my weary lids.

Lord, I am lonely, and my children need godly friends. I know You love me, and that knowledge is what I need most, but if I am going to move forward faithfully in life and in love of You, I really wish I could do it with kindred spirits by my side.

I wiped an indecorous tear from my nose and tried to gather myself. In a few minutes the sound of patting feet would alert me that it was time for breakfast and the whirlwind that is a day with three children under the age of nine. As I sat silently, watching streams of water wash down my window from the gloomy Texas clouds, an answer came to me.

If you are lonely, so are others. Create a space for friendship in your home. You be the facilitator.

With this burst of inspiration and the urgency created from knowing all my children were about to wake up, I set to dreaming, and by break-fast time I had an idea that would become a cherished tradition in our home: a mother-daughter Christmas tea. We would not be alone that Christmas season.

I realized that if I longed for community, probably others did too. Wallowing in my loneliness would not cure it; I needed to become a creator of community. So I made a list of mothers and daughters I had met and wished I knew better. I also listed some interesting women who weren't part of a mother-daughter pair but who had friendship potential. And I invited them all to a Christmas tea where we could celebrate the meaning of Christmas while (I hoped) creating some new friendships. I set our simple table with candles and festive napkins, tried a few new recipes (including our now traditional raspberry soup!), and opened my home.

The event was such a success that we decided to do it again the next year. And the next. Every year brought a different array of guests. Not everyone invited came; not everyone who came knew each other. In fact, our teas have often included a motley crew of people with diverse backgrounds who might not otherwise have met each other—mothers and daughters from church, a barista from our favorite coffee shop, a wise but lonely recent widow, a cousin living in town that year, an attendant at our favorite natural food store, and more.

Each tea was different in attendance and unified in spirit. As we sipped and munched together, we created fellowship during a season that for many people is filled with loneliness. Several years even saw some of our friends who weren't Christians encountering believers and Jesus for the first time.

Flash forward twenty-three years to my blue-walled kitchen in Colorado. Sarah is home on a rare and cherished visit from her life in England. Our family "girls' club" (Sarah, Joy, and I) gather in the kitchen and settle into a productive bustle—after twenty-three years we have our Christmas tea prep down to a well-ordered dance. Joy runs the cold raspberry soup through a strainer, catching all the seeds to ensure Clarkson-brand creaminess. Sarah taps the tops of the scones to see if they are appropriately crispy yet. I place a Christmas ornament at each place setting as a party favor. We pass around a tube of lipstick, and we are ready.

As I walk to the door to welcome our first guest, I breathe a prayer of thanks. God answered my prayer that rainy Texas morning, and He has answered it a thousand times since. How could I have known all those years ago what sweet friendships would blossom because of that one moment when I chose to respond to His prompting?

We are made to love and be loved. Friendship can be one of life's greatest delights and most sturdy supports. Any theology or method of discipleship that avoids this truth is simply out of touch with our identity in Christ. Living in relationship with God and with others is at the core of our identity and our experience of life. Discipleship always takes place in the context of relationships: our relationships with God, with those who walk with us in faith, and with those who walk behind us as we follow Jesus. In my life, friendship has been one of God's primary conduits of spiritual conviction and inspiration. I have come to see the necessity of friendship and continue to seek ways to develop deeper, more meaningful friendships.

The Context of Community

God works through relationships and community. The history of our faith is one of God's interaction with us personally and in the context of relational communities.

When you think of it, in fact, community and relationships are intrinsic to the very nature of God. As Christians, we understand God in terms of the Trinity: Father, Son, and Holy Spirit. And as mysterious and hard to understand as the Trinity may be, it's clear that the Trinity is inherently relational. Nowhere is this more evident than in the book of John, which speaks of Jesus' relationship with the Father and the Holy Spirit in the most intimate of terms. They were all involved at the beginning, working together to create the world (John 1:1-4). And after Jesus came to earth, they continued to communicate, love, and serve each other.

If God, therefore, is a relational being and we are made in God's image . . . then we are made to be relational! God created us to delight in our relationship with Him, but also to delight in relationship with each other. There should be a stream of lifegiving love running from our relational God to us, to each other, and back to God again—a vibrant community of love.

Having deep, meaningful relationships is not just a pleasant addition to our lives, but an element essential to our identities. In the beautiful, sweeping story told in the first chapter of Genesis, God looks at solitary Adam and says, "It is not good for the man to be alone" (Genesis 2:18). While this is often used to promote the idea that people ought to get married, I think it is a far deeper statement. We humans were not created to live in isolation, but in relationship.

Even modern psychology promotes the idea that when we are separated and isolated from meaningful connections and communities, our personality, health, and resiliency diminish. The writer of Proverbs even goes so far as to see isolation as a sign of sin, saying that "he who separates himself seeks his own desire" (Proverbs 18:1, NASB). Surely it's a sign of the Fall that our sin so often causes us to feel isolated, ashamed, and separated from those we love.

The history of our faith is one in which God always worked in communities. The Old Testament tells the story of God's consistent faithfulness to the nation of Israel. His intention was always to show His righteousness and kindness to the world through this chosen community, His nation of priests. And His expressed concern was always for the community, not just for the "special" or "more spiritual" individuals. His people were to celebrate God's work together, inspire each other to righteousness, and call one another to holiness. Yes, He worked in and through the lives of individuals like David and Moses, just as He works in our individual lives, but their lives were always a thread in the tapestry of the greater story and a deeper community.

And then there was Jesus. He started His earthly ministry by gathering a group of disciples around Him—twelve imperfect men who would spend the next three years in close relationship with Him, traveling together, talking together, sharing meals, sharing their lives. At their last meal together, Jesus made a point of saying, "Now you are my friends, since I have told you everything the Father told me" (John 15:15).

Over the next few years, Jesus added others to His band of followers. A group of women traveled with Him and supported Him and the disciples. Friends like Mary and Martha and Lazarus of Bethany hosted them in their homes. Curious people dined with Him and asked Him questions, and some eventually followed Him too. And through it all He remained close to His family, including them in His circle of friends. (Don't forget that family can be friends too.) Like us, Jesus maintained friendships at different levels—a close inner circle as well as a broader community of relationship. But community and relationship remained integral to His entire ministry.

Then, after the dramatic events of His crucifixion and resurrection, Jesus gathered His friends around Him once more. And in His final instructions to them before He ascended, He did not say, "Now go and live a solitary life, praying by yourself all day." He told them to go and make disciples, which was actually to say, "Create a community of people committed to loving and following Me."

The gospel would be spread through relationships—relationships with God and with each other. It was through God's work in the community of the early church that Christianity was disseminated throughout all the world.

And around what did they build that community? Acts 2:42 tells us: "All the believers devoted themselves to the apostles' teaching, and to fellowship, and to sharing in meals (including the Lord's Supper), and to prayer." The early church bonded over meals together as the context for discipleship, and so should we. That is the essence of the lifegiving table.

If we want to live meaningful lives and be a part of bringing God's Kingdom into our world, we must invest in community, because God does most of His work through community.

Friendship is the context in which discipleship often takes place.

Witnesses to Our Lives

I will never forget Joy's twenty-first birthday. After graduating early from college, she had moved back to Colorado for a year to work before pursuing further studies. It was a quiet year in her life, a time of being faithful in important but nonglamorous ways. I was very proud of her, and I wanted to do something special and memorable for her birthday. So I reserved the back room of her favorite coffee shop.

We invited twenty people who were dear to her—family friends of various ages, some friends from high school, and some who had participated with her in speech and debate or other activities, and of course two siblings who happened to be in town for a few days. It was a mixed crowd—young and old together—but almost everyone who came had known Joy for the majority of her life.

At one point in the evening, I opened up the conversation for each person to share a story, a memory, or a word of encouragement for Joy. (We had sent out an e-mail to prepare everyone to be ready to speak.) Every single person ended up contributing something, then we ended with prayer and cake. As the evening ended, I felt like Joy's own cloud of witnesses had surrounded her with a sense of the values and faith all held dear.

As we walked out to the car, Joy looked over at me:

"My heart is so full, Mama. It's so good to know I've had people to walk with me in life and that I will have them as I grow older."

This is one of the most valuable aspects of friendship. We need friends to witness life with us.

When I was a young teen, I remember going out with one of my best friends to watch the sunrise. She lived near a large field where we could enjoy the moment without buildings or telephone wires to block the view. We bundled up and took flasks of coffee to keep us warm in the early morning chill. Picking a soft spot of grass, we watched in awe as the sun rose in all its golden glory. Something about its beauty caused us to think about true and beautiful things, and we ended up sharing our dreams of what life might be.

I remember thinking that while the sunrise would have been just as beautiful if I had watched it on my own, it would not have been as meaningful. Having someone to share the beauty with sealed the experience as a moment of significance in my life.

I believe this is how true friendships impact our lives. In friendship we share beauty, acknowledge significant moments, and cherish memories that sustain us through life. In friendship we become companionable witnesses to God's goodness—witnesses who can later remind one another who we are—and to whom we belong.

We all need people to be with us on the significant days of our lives—the birthdays, the graduations, the marriages, the births, the losses. We need people in our lives who know our story and speak love, encouragement, and truth to us when our vision grows cloudy. Anyone who has experienced a lack of connection in such significant times can testify to the ache of a life without friendship. Life's joys are sweeter with friends who celebrate with us, and its sorrows are easier to bear.

Helping One Another

Friends give us strength as we walk through life. The author of Ecclesiastes revealed a profound and necessary truth when he wrote, "Two people are better off than one, for they can help each other succeed" (Ecclesiastes 4:9).

We are so much more vulnerable to attack when we are alone. It is easier to become depressed, defeated, or prideful without friends who cheer us, correct us, and fight for our good. When we reach points of deep discouragement, convinced we can never progress, true friends lift our heads and say, "Remember who you are! God has worked, and He will again." We need people with us to remind us of what is true when we forget. And we need to be those people for others.

Another way that friends support each other—one that has been vital in my own life—is by loving and discipling each other's children. What a gift to have someone to speak into their lives, especially during those seasons when children do not want to listen to parents.

We had friends like that who sort of became family to us through many years of shared meals and investing in each other's lives, and they were instrumental in our children's growth and faith. They listened to my kids, met with them, and counseled them in very natural moments of our shared life through the years, so it wasn't just Clay and me doing all of the table talk and discipleship. And of course we did the same for their children.

Some of us are fortunate enough to have grandmas and grandpas, aunts and uncles, and other extended family who can take on that support role, so that children can say, "Mom and Dad believe this, and Uncle Fred and Cousin Chris—all of us stand for this legacy of faith." But for those who don't live close to family or don't have that kind of heritage, family friends can take that place. And even those who *do* have extended family can benefit from the loving support of friends.

Friendships Expand Our Understanding

Friendship opens our eyes to the complexity and beauty of God and life. To be good friends, we must learn to open our hearts, to see differences as beautiful and similarities as worth celebrating.

Every individual you meet has a completely unique background, personality, and story. Even people from very similar backgrounds have been shaped by their specific family, personality, and experience in life. This means that there will never be one friend who completely understands every nook and corner of our souls; only God can do that. But it also means that friendships can expand our vision and help us embrace the diversity of God's world.

If we look for perfect friends, we will be lonely. If we look for friends who are just like us, we won't find them. Instead, we should look for kindred spirits who introduce us to what we wouldn't otherwise experience.

This principle is reflected in all of the recipes I have collected from friends throughout the years—soups, pies, cookies, breads, roasts, with dozens of different flavors, spices, and textures. Some of those recipes are in this book.

Without friends to suggest recipes, my family would have missed out on many a scrumptious meal. And the same is true of our lives if we don't open our hearts to the beauty of difference in others. When we have friends who are different from us, we get to experience life more fully and in ways we couldn't have without their friendship. Wouldn't we be missing out without them?

However, I do believe that friendship must be based on some similarities. We are called to be loving and kind and fair in all our relationships. But we are not called to be close friends with everyone.

True friends are kindred spirits, people with whom we have something in common. It could be a shared or similar upbringing, similar interests, or shared values. But what binds me most closely to my good friends is a dedication to being a disciple of Jesus. In this kind of relationship, I find that although I may disagree with my friend from time to time or have personality differences, I can still trust him or her to follow Jesus, so the deepest parts of our hearts are in unison.

I am blessed to have a tapestry of such friendships spread across the nation and the globe, many of whom I met doing ministry internationally. While sometimes this is lonely because we cannot always be together, I cherish my far-flung network of kindred spirits.

One of the greatest gifts my international friends have given me is the ability to see God outside of my box; they remind me that He is not American. The way I see the world is limited by my personality, background, and even nationality. But through my friends, I am exposed to truths about God, humanity, and even food that I could not experience on my own.

Friendships expand our souls and help us to see that God is not Polish or American, extroverted or introverted, extravagant or simple. He is the God of the universe. When I look into the eyes of my wonderful, diverse circle of friends, I gain a broader understanding and view of Him.

When Friendship Goes Wrong

In an ideal world, we would all be surrounded by throngs of people who want our best, know our story, share our deepest convictions, and are willing to walk with us through life. However, as so many of us are keenly aware, this is not usually the case. Unfortunately, the common reality of our world is isolation, loneliness, and superficial, fake, or damaging friendships.

I am all too well acquainted with this reality. I'm sure you are too. Even the early church had its squabbles and parting of ways (see Acts 15). But giving up on community and friendship is not the answer to this issue. Rather, we ought to pursue godly friendships with tenacious intentionality. Seek out godly friends, and when you find them, cherish them. Do everything you can to nurture these friendships, investing time and attention. And don't forget to invite them to share your table, because sharing food is one the very best ways to build relationships.

And what if a friendship brings pain? When two people with different personalities, backgrounds, and beliefs engage in a relationship, there are bound to be areas of friction. And when the two people involved happened to be sinners (as we all are), we inevitably end up hurting one another. A careless remark, an absence when we are needed, a philosophical disagreement, a petty betrayal—any of these can cause a painful rift between friends. Then there are those people we encounter whose lives have been so damaged in childhood that they have no idea how to relate in a healthy way.

When conflict happens with friends, we do well to be persistent in seeking to repair the relationship. Pray urgently about the situation. Try to see things from the other person's point of view. Seek forgiveness and be willing to offer it. Strive for reconciliation. A friendship is a precious thing, not to be lightly discarded.

But if the misunderstanding persists, the best advice I can give is this: (1) do your best to be a peacemaker, and (2) entrust people to God. Romans 12:18 says, "If it is possible, as far as it depends on you, live at peace with everyone" (NIV). But implied in that same verse is the reality that living in peace is not always up to us.

Not all friendships last a lifetime or remain at the same level of closeness. We should always seek to extend grace in our friendships, to be kind, to try to understand. But if, as happens to all of us, a friendship cools or ends, check your own heart to make sure you are walking in godliness and then release the situation to God. You can trust that the God of community and relationship can take care of your heart and your friend's heart too. Christian friends are not perfect, just redeemed, like us.

In Praise of Friendship

The years of my life have been marked by deep and diverse friendships. My committed group of friends in Colorado has been a great joy in my life as well as a significant element in the success of my ministry. And kindred spirits close and abroad continue to inspire and convict me. I am astounded by the sweetness and fruitfulness of those friendships, developed slowly over the course of many years and nurtured whenever possible through phone calls, e-mails, texts, and visits.

Relationships are foundational to our identity as humans and as Christians. We are relational beings created to be in friendship with God and those around us. Friends shape the way we see the world, helping broaden our perspective and deepen our understanding. Friends help us celebrate important moments of life, hold us up in times of trial, teach us about God and life, and spur us on in our walk with the Lord. They are a prize we should pray for and seek.

And who knows, maybe one of those friendships will begin with something as simple as a Christmas tea.

Something to Ponder

1 Samuel 18:1, 3-4, NASB

Now it came about . . . that the soul of Jonathan was knit to the soul of David. . . . Jonathan made a covenant with David because he loved him as himself. Jonathan stripped himself of the robe that was on him and gave it to David, with his armor, including his sword and his bow and his belt.

Read all of 1 Samuel 18, but consider the verses printed above especially. I have always found the strength of the language in this passage profound. We do not usually speak of friendship in such intimate terms, and yet Jonathan and David's friendship is one of the most profound examples of friendship in the Bible.

Have you ever had a friend to whom you could say your soul was "knit"? Whom you loved as yourself?

- What kind of commitment do you think that entails?

- Do you think your family can also be your friends? Why or why not?

- Is it important to also maintain close friendships outside of your family? Again, why or why not?

Acts 2:46-47, NASB

Day by day continuing with one mind in the temple, and
breaking bread from house to house, they were taking their
meals together with gladness and sincerity of heart, praising
God and having favor with all the people. And the Lord
was adding to their number day by day those who were
being saved.

When I ponder the atmosphere I would love to celebrate at my table, this description of the early church seems like a wonderful goal. To share meals together with such glad hearts and praise God together sounds like a little bit of heaven.

What elements of community do you see in this passage? What did the early Christians do together? What were their relationships like?

- Consider your own friendships, community, and church. Are your friendships marked by similar qualities? What qualities do you tend to slack on? How might you build such qualities into your relationships?

Something to Try

Write a list of what you wish for in a kindred-spirit friend. Do you have such a friend? Is it a desire of your heart?

- Write down how you would be that sort of friend to another person. Pray for God to bless the friendships you have or ask Him for a kindred-spirit friend.

- Plan your own friendship tea—at Christmas or another time of year. When choosing people to invite, think outside the box. Is there someone you think you might click with but have never reached out to? Be brave and invite that person. When choosing your menu, consider making something you've never made before. Think about making your guests feel special by the dish you choose. Choose a favor to give each guest. This doesn't have to be something expensive. It could even be a card handwritten to each person, thanking them for coming.

- Build relationships around your dinner table or tea table by preparing questions for everyone to discuss. Here are just a few ideas:

  "If you could give only one gift to each person you know, what gift would you give this year?"

  "What is one of your happiest memories from this past year?"

  "What one way do you want to be intentional about celebrating life in the coming year?"

  "What is a lesson of wisdom you have learned this past year?"

Recipes for Friends and Family

✻ Rosy Raspberry Soup

When each of my children turned fifteen, we took him or her on a trip to the places where I invested my early single years in ministry. Sarah's trip at age fifteen took us to several countries in Eastern Europe. One warm day we met some friends in a tiny, quaint, wood-paneled basement café. The place was packed with people—romantic couples, students from the nearby university, and visitors like us—with tables almost touching in order to squeeze in even more. We literally squished into a green velvet–cushioned booth with four of our new friends.

"You must try the cold raspberry soup on this very hot day," they urged us. "It is tradition in our neighborhood."

And so we did. The beautiful rose-colored potion, with whipped cream swimming atop the cool bowl, invited us to swallow down every delectable bite. We have served it as a first course at our Christmas teas ever since.

3 cups fresh or frozen (unsweetened) raspberries (18–20 ounces)
1½ cups water—or 1¼ cups water plus ¼ cup sweet wine such as
      white zinfandel
1 cup cranberry-apple or cranberry-raspberry juice
½–¾ cup granulated sugar
1½ teaspoons ground cinnamon
¼ teaspoon ground cloves
2 tablespoons seedless red-raspberry jam
1–2 tablespoons lemon juice
1 cup vanilla yogurt
Canned (aerosol) whipped cream from the dairy case (not "whipped
      topping," which tends to be full of chemicals)
Fresh mint leaves for garnish, optional but pretty

Thaw raspberries if frozen. (I do this in my fridge the day before.) Place raspberries, water, and wine (if using) in a blender and puree. Taste to see if mixture is the right consistency for you—some like it thick, some like it thin. Add juice or more water if you want it thinner. Transfer to a large saucepan and add the juice, sugar, spices, and jam. Stir to dissolve sugar and jam, then taste to make sure mixture is sweet enough. (It will depend on the raspberries.) If the mixture is too sour, stir in a bit more sugar and blend in thoroughly. Then cook the mixture over medium heat just until it begins to boil.

Remove pan from heat. Strain mixture through a sieve to remove any seeds, and allow to cool. Whisk in lemon juice and yogurt. Cool in refrigerator.

To serve, pour into small bowls or custard cups. (I use pedestaled cut-glass custard cups that I bought many years ago for a dollar apiece at a thrift store.) Top each with a squirt of whipped cream and some fresh mint leaves if you have them.

Serves 4–6, depending on the size of your serving dishes.

❋ Mama's Chicken Salad

I used to beg my mama to make this sweet-and-salty treat during summer days at home when I was a teen. Great as an appetizer, a sandwich, or a filler for pita bread. Easy and a crowd pleaser, especially on a hot summer's day, though it is also regular fare at my Christmas teas.

About 4 cups cooked, diced chicken (I boil 4 boneless, skinless
    chicken breasts and cut them up, but you can substitute
    a whole rotisserie chicken from the grocery store, skinned
    and boned.)
½ cup mayonnaise
½ cup vanilla yogurt
2 teaspoons granulated sugar
2 teaspoons curry powder (Add more if needed when tasting at end.)
1½ teaspoons salt
Pepper to taste

Several squirts of real whipped cream (not "dairy topping") from an
aerosol can
½ cup green onion, minced
1½ cups grapes (purple or green or both!), sliced in half
¾–1 cup chopped buttered pecans (Look in chapter 6 for the recipe.)
⅓ cup dried cranberries, optional but beautiful, especially for
Christmas
Warm pita bread or flour tortillas, optional

Drain and pat chicken dry so salad is not wet. Shred or cut into small
chunks.

Mix together mayonnaise, yogurt, sugar, curry powder, salt,
pepper, and whipped cream. Stir in chicken, green onion, grapes,
buttered pecans, and cranberries (if using). Mix thoroughly.

I love serving this mixture with warm pita bread or flour tortillas.
Cut up or tear the bread or tortilla into small triangles and pick up
salad with bread for bite-sized portions.

Serves 5–6.

CHAPTER 14

LIFEGIVING ON THE GO
Cultivating an Influence to Last a Lifetime

✦

Eating and reading are two pleasures that combine admirably.

C. S. LEWIS

I recommend having fun, because there is nothing better for people in this world than to eat, drink, and enjoy life. That way they will experience some happiness along with all the hard work God gives them under the sun.

ECCLESIASTES 8:15

Table-Discipleship Principle:

Learning to see ourselves as people
who reach out and meet the needs of
others, everywhere, all the time, is at
the heart of a lifegiving ministry.

Snow fell all week. Below-zero temperatures kept us inside. Even our golden retriever, who usually loved to frolic in the snow, would not stay outside. Checking my iPhone to see if there would be any reprieve, I was so happy to see that today's temperature will climb all the way up to twenty-eight degrees. Practically sweltering!

I went to bed happy last night, anticipating a much-needed soul time with Joy, my now twenty-one-year-old. Having graduated from college at nineteen, she worked at home for a year and then began attending the University of St Andrews in Scotland to get her master's degree. But now she is home for winter break. And I want to enjoy every moment, because when she's gone, there is always a hole in my heart from missing her.

Our custom, which I started first with her sister, Sarah, is to arise on Saturday mornings (before anyone else in the house finds us), dress quickly, and jump in the car to go downtown to our favorite coffee shop. Swirling hearts or swimming swans atop strong cappuccino delight us as we slowly begin to awaken to a morning together. Anticipation of a warm, cheesy egg quesadilla, a signature dish, has us ridiculously smacking our lips. Sides of raspberry-chipotle jam and salsa will complete our favorite Saturday morning treat. Our mouths actually began to water before we got out of bed, as we imagined getting to split our regular breakfast again. It has become one of our favorite things—a familiar treat, a sweet reverie away from our crowded household, and a deep anchor of comfort and connection in our week. Our lifegiving table away from home.

This morning I awakened early to prepare for our time together by writing down some questions I want to ask Joy, a verse I would like to share, and an outline for a new book I would like her input on. Preparation and planning for our times together always gives me direction to be able to pass on things I want to share and ways to open up conversation so that I can know what is on her mind and heart.

On our drive down, slipping and sliding along the snowy way, Joy takes over as DJ. This morning our prebreakfast atmosphere consists of classic oldies from my era (James Taylor, Jim Croce, Carole King, Simon and Garfunkel). We end with John Denver's "Sunshine on My Shoulders," belting the song out together in unself-conscious, intimate companionship. If anyone heard us, they would probably think we're crazy.

Escaping the cold, snowy sidewalks, we are happy to discover that our favorite two-person table is free. We get our coffee before ordering breakfast, laughing as we compare the designs in the foam that give us even more pleasure in our sips. We chat quietly, share tidbits from our week, breathe out stress, and get ready for a very memorable time together.

It's not home, but this little coffee-shop two-top is a truly lifegiving table for us both.

"Joy, I am thinking about writing a book about foundations that can't be shaken, from a biblical perspective. It feels to me like a lot of people in your generation and the women who follow me in ministry find their faith subjective, dependent on what is happening in culture at any given time. But many feel like they are drifting, and they don't know how to follow Christ. I would love to do a Bible-based book. Can you help me come up with the areas I should include in the book? I don't want it to be preachy, but captivating and soul-filling. I am always inspired when I pick your brain."

Our conversation flows from feminism to worldview, loving good and hating evil, world events, a funny story she has heard, and some great ideas about what I should include in my book. After an hour, reluctant to leave, we both sigh, don our heavy winter coats, and head out into the cold.

Our usual custom after our "date" is to walk the tree-lined streets and admire the stately Victorian homes in this area of downtown. And even though the cold is still bitter and we both have a million things to do, we decide it will be an adventure to roam our old familiar pathways together.

I hold her arm close as we saunter along for half an hour. And we both are renewed, ready to plunge back into the fray.

It's Not Just about the Food

Right now I have a new book deadline in ten days. I am in the process of launching a new book on social media, coordinating with forty bloggers (all friends) in relation to the launch, recording six podcasts with other people and four more on my own website, conducting countless interviews and promotions, corresponding with a launch team of 350 people, and preparing for five national conferences, one of them in Europe—all of this in the next eight weeks.

I don't know how I ended up in this place. I am a dreamer, an introvert, a lover of people at heart, and I resist this bigger arena by nature. It happened slowly from just being a mama, a wife, and a friend, and writing about it. I guess there are a lot of people like me who want to know that our lives and struggles, our faith, our desire to live a steadfast life are the same and who appreciate that I write about my normal life, struggles, and joys.

However it happened, the pressure is on, and for this season at least I need to work eight to twelve hours a day just to keep up. And yes, I am making plans to put up more boundaries, to slow down and enjoy my days more—soon. But in the meantime, even in the midst of my current crazy schedule, I am determined that nothing will get in the way of time that I have prioritized for my inner circle—my husband, my children, and my closest friends.

I know that for me to keep my marriage alive and growing, to invest in my friendships, and to pass on a legacy of faith, mentoring, focused love, and training in the lives of my children, I have to plan my time carefully and make sure there is room in my schedule for what matters most—my people! And much of this time comes from our habit of celebrating life together every day at our lifegiving table.

To make sure this happens, I have prepared a kind of grid in my mind through which I view the rest of life, a tool for scheduling and decision making: *These relationships trump all other tasks. No matter how busy I am, I will always take a break for what God has said are my Kingdom priorities—people He has ordained for me to love, serve, and encourage.* I have also set my mind to *prepare* for these times so as to make the most of them—to look for things I want to say, plan for questions to ask, consider ahead how best to offer friendship and encouragement.

The lifegiving table, remember, is not just about food and feasting—although food and feasting are deeply important. And it's not just about home, although it definitely begins at home. What makes a table lifegiving is what happens at the table!

The table is a vehicle for spiritual influence, godly mentoring, true connection of hearts and minds. And that can happen anywhere, but it will not happen by accident. We must be prayerful and intentional about preparing for the table, then reaching out, encouraging, teaching, showing interest through our questions, teaching, loving as we enjoy meals, coffee, tea, or a snack with others every day, every year, all the time.

It starts with developing a lifegiving self-image, seeing ourselves as mentors and ministers. We are not just cooks and servers and fellow diners. Instead, we are called and commissioned to be the hands of God's love to those He brings our way, the voice of God's words in our messages and conversations, the touch of God's love in initiating friendship and seizing the moments given to us each day. Every coffee shop, café, restaurant, dorm room bed, cup of tea, smoothie, or hot chocolate can become a place where hearts and minds meet when we see ourselves that way and train ourselves to look for opportunities to mentor and minister.

I am not suggesting that every conversation has to be about the Kingdom or something serious or important. But if we are committed to the value of being purposeful in our relationships, ready to use our moments to build others up, we will be much more likely to have a significant spiritual impact with those God brings our way.

Best of all, we'll be able to have that influence wherever we go.

The Portable Lifegiving Table

My ministry to women all over the world means that I travel many weeks of the year. Sometimes it is a weeks-long international trip, but often I travel to speak at weekend conferences. One night I was dreading a weekend engagement because I had been away from home for several weeks in a row. A brilliant thought popped into my head: *Take home and table with you wherever you go. Make a table for friendship and mentoring by taking everything you need with you. Create a table of friendship and influence that is portable.*

So now, these many years later, whenever I go on the road I bring along everything I need to create a lifegiving table moment, either alone or with someone who needs my love and encouragement. This helps me create some peace wherever I am and sets up my times with the Lord and with my sweet ones.

While visiting China on my book tour in seven cities a couple of years ago, I purchased several beautiful pashmina scarves for a song. Now I take them everywhere I go. A pashmina works as a shawl over my shoulders when the plane is too cold. But it also brings added loveliness to a coffee table in my hotel room—a perfect setting for an impromptu teatime.

Candles in tiny jars or cans (plus matches!) also accompany me wherever I go. Their flickering lights automatically create a soft atmosphere. My iPhone and computer are always stocked with a variety of background music, easily played on my tiny portable speaker.

I always travel with my very own tea—always a strong English Breakfast blend, with Yorkshire Gold being my favorite—and a china teacup or mug because china keeps tea and coffee warmer longer. This is a necessity to keep me centered on the road. Being able to continue my daily habits of creating islands of beauty and civilization makes me feel I have a little touch of home when away.

For snacks, I carry a zippered plastic bag of toasted, salted, sprouted walnuts and almonds, sometimes salted dark-chocolate almonds or tiny wrapped rounds of Gouda cheese. Fruit or veggies are available wherever I go, so I can have a tiny feast for whoever visits me.

And it goes without saying that I travel with my Bible, whatever book I am reading, and my most current study journal. I may even stuff in my newest *Victoria* magazines. (My Sarah and I love perusing them, as the old ones are collector items and have lots of articles about authors we love.) These are beautiful to look at and fun to page through—food for thought and ideas for recipes and decor and travel and more. Therapy for my eyes and soul without having to contemplate too many stressful subjects.

Looking for opportunities to deepen friendships, to counsel women, to have fun and invite someone in so that I do not feel alone has provided me with countless sweet and memorable moments from setting my table in my hotel rooms.

It can happen nearer to home as well, of course, and I don't even have to pack my bag. I have been known to create a lifegiving table in restaurants and coffee shops, at picnic tables in the woods, in local hotel lobbies, and in the houses of friends. Sometimes I serve the food and drink; sometimes it's served to me. But as long as I carry with me the vision of table ministry, I can almost always make something happen.

Once again, it's not about the food. It's about what happens at the table.

Preparing *Me* for Table Ministry

Preparing to be a lifegiving presence wherever I go also involves preparing my heart and mind and even my body to reach out in relationship. If I want to be a vessel of life from which others can draw, a resource from which they can learn about God or pick up some wisdom, I must make time to fill my heart and mind with wisdom, encouragement, and strength.

Most women I know are taxed every day, all the time. Whether the pressure comes through spouses, children, other family members, bosses or colleagues at work, or our own ambitions and ideals, we give and give and give endlessly. But unless we create a plan for filling ourselves up—our hearts, our minds, our strength—we will eventually run dry and be unable to bring much to the table.

I strive to deepen my own soul, mind, and heart on a regular basis because I always want to grow, learn, and pursue excellence in all areas of my life. This is a personal goal of mine. And I have devised several strategies to keep myself moving toward that goal. And the first and most vital of these is setting aside daily table time alone with my heavenly Father.

Setting a Table for God and Me

Many years ago, I was intrigued to understand God as my Father in Scripture. I came to realize that my sense of Him as a divine Spirit somewhere in the heavenlies who looked at me with scorn for my shortcomings was neither biblical nor healthy. Cultivating a personal knowledge of Him as my compassionate heavenly Father (Psalm 103:13) who was aware of my frailties (Psalm 103:14), whose love would never end (Romans 8:31-39), and whose generosity caused Him to send His only Son to save me (John 3:16-17) helped me begin to relate to Him from the depths of my heart.

Most mornings since then, I have shared my early-morning table with God and invited Him into fellowship with me. I have a cozy quiet-time chair in my room with the table beside it holding a candle and usually a cup of something warm. Favorite music also calms my spirit and takes me more easily into His presence.

Thanking Him for His love and acknowledging His generosity in my life starts out our time together. Pouring out my heart and thoughts, dreams and wishes and complaints is a part of my freedom with Him.

I learned this from King David, whom God cherished as a man after His heart. David wrote,

> Surely I have composed and quieted my soul;
> Like a weaned child rests against his mother,
> My soul is like a weaned child within me.
> PSALM 131:2, NASB

Something about that description of innocently and wholeheartedly laying his whole life before God and resting against Him as a baby does with its beloved mother touched me deeply. And so gradually I began to practice living in relationship with Him as a child, trusting Him with the whole of who I am and bringing all of me to the table when I meet with Him.

Because I am something of a book nerd, with a mind and heart shaped by stories and Scripture, it's only natural that I bring books to my table time with God. My Bible is a must, of course. So is a journal to jot down notes, revelations, ideas, and inspirations. When I am alone in a room with the Lord and He speaks to me, I want to record my impressions to revisit later.

I choose from a pile of devotionals, depending on the day or my mood. And I am often working my way through a variety of good books to fill my mind, even if it takes me forever to finish them, so they also have a place at my table. (At present I am reading a biography of Oswald Chambers, a book by Phillip Yancey, one by Eugene Peterson, and a devotional by Brennan Manning.) I find that God often speaks to me through these as well, especially if I approach them with an open heart and a listening ear.

When others are coming to me on a regular basis, I want to have a soul that is full, inspired, engaged in great ideas so that others will be able to draw out what I have invested. Even as I am emptying out my heart, mind, and soul, I must purpose to fill them on a regular basis.

In Good Company

My daily table time with God is absolutely essential for sustaining me and preparing me to reach out to others. I literally could not keep going without it, and I would definitely not have the resources to prepare and maintain a lifegiving table. But I have found other ways to fill myself up as well.

One of my most satisfying of these is to put myself in the company of people I know who challenge me to be my best self. One of these, a dear friend, is approaching eighty. She has walked with God, studied His Word, and extended her teaching to people all over the world for more than fifty years. I know that if I make time to be with her, I will always leave wanting to love and serve God more.

My own children often fill this role for me as well. Three out of four of them have studied theology at the graduate level, and this has provided me with a unique learning opportunity—I always learn something when talking to them. My other child is an avid reader, engages every day with apologetics, loves great stories, and sends me the best book recommendations. All of my children motivate me to stretch my mind, to think more deeply, to look at the world, life, and Scripture in a holistic way. Perhaps their interest in theology came from those years of dinner-table discussions while they were growing up.

And here, too, my habit of reading sustains me, because I have long thought of my favorite authors as beloved and influential friends. What a privilege to spend time with the likes of Chambers and Yancey and Manning, not to mention great writers of fiction like George MacDonald, J. R. R Tolkien, and C. S. Lewis. I also find enlightenment and enjoyment from certain blogs and podcasts and some well-chosen films (often recommended by my children). Although there is no substitute for actual time spent with flesh-and-blood mentors, I have found there are many different ways of feasting my mind and filling my cup in preparation for serving others in my table ministry.

In It for the Long Haul

I have worked in ministry for forty-two years, have raised four children to adulthood, and have navigated thirty-six years of marriage. All this has meant learning to pace myself in this life's journey. I must take time to be centered, to make sure my own needs are met, or I will serve with resentment instead of purpose and will eventually burn myself out.

Learning to listen to myself has helped me to identify the danger signals when I am running low on resources and in need of refueling. Sudden outbursts of anger or feelings of impatience or frustration are sure signs that I have exceeded my body and mind's capacity to live life well.

When I find myself being especially grumpy or negative, I have learned to take stock and to figure out how to make sure I have what I need—emotionally, mentally, and physically as well. For we are not just souls or minds, remember. We also have bodies. And in order to be effective for the Kingdom, we must take care of ourselves as whole persons.

Here are just a few of the habits I have found essential to sustaining me for the long haul:

Nourishing, healthy, sustaining food is a basic. In fact, one reason table ministry is so fulfilling is that it feeds the body as well as the mind and spirit.

- Physical exercise helps build strength and burn off tension. I am an avid walker and find that outdoor exercise especially is therapy for my whole self.

- Getting sufficient sleep is essential to lasting well. Putting off my worries and fears and relaxing enough to sleep through the night is a habit I have had to learn.

- My daily private quiet times give me the opportunity to center myself and "fill my cup" as a daily routine.

- Setting aside the Sabbath for rest or at least building in some restoration spots helps me keep going. So does getting away from normal responsibilities by taking a weekend with a friend or family or going on a weekend trip.

- Planning regular table times with friends who fill me up and bring me joy is an investment that is necessary to keep going over many years.

- Making time to laugh, play, and celebrate life with my family and friends (ideally over a delicious meal) keeps me thankful and joyful as well as relieving stress.

I have learned, in other words, that to be that hostess at table and in life who brings beauty, wisdom, and encouragement, I have to regularly invest in those same gifts for myself as well. Replenishment and restoration must be a way of life, so that when I come to table, I will be working from an overflowing heart and not a depleted one.

I know that all the work and deadlines and demands of life will be piled up when I get home from a trip or just get up to face a day, but I will be better able to attack the piles of work and have more energy to deal with decisions if I live a sustainable life day to day. Now my body will have slept every night, because I make rest a priority. I will have refreshed my mind and soul, and I will have filled my memory bank with ideas, stories, and Scripture so that I can be a resource to those who need to draw from me. By investing in worthy resources, I am more able to bring a lifegiving self to my lifegiving table—at home or on the go, both now and for years to come.

From My Lifegiving Table to Yours

This book is coming to an end. I could have written so much more about dinners with neighbors who needed a haven of friendship, missionaries who needed a place to rest, Bible studies with literally hundreds of women through the years who have eaten and sipped and shared at my table, countless fun progressive dinners, outside barbeques, dinners in rocking chairs on the porch, children's parties—so many ways to celebrate at a lifegiving table. But these stories will have to wait. There's a limit to how much I can put into one book.

In conclusion, I would observe that there is no one kind of table, no perfect menu, no ideal occasion for sharing food together.

Hopefully in these pages you have been inspired, encouraged, and challenged to begin seeing more clearly the strategic nature of your table, the many ways it can be used to minister to others, and the many possibilities for using feasting and love to bring others in your life to a better understanding of what our Lord is like.

Someday we will all be together at the most wonderful banquet we could ever imagine, with the very best food, the most soul-enriching beauty, the finest in companionship. The occasion will be the wedding feast of the Lamb described in Revelation 19. Jesus, who taught us so much about table life, is preparing to celebrate that great future feast with us at His own table.

But until then, we can practice in our own homes and elsewhere to become a host like He is—to welcome others, to provide love along with nourishment, to share hearts and minds as we share food and drink, to cultivate and pass on a legacy of deep love and sturdy friendship. And as we gather around our own lifegiving tables, I know we will grow to love and appreciate Him more.

Grace and peace to your table!

Something to Ponder

1 Samuel 30:6, NASB

> Moreover David was greatly distressed because the people spoke of stoning him, for all the people were embittered, each one because of his sons and his daughters. But David strengthened himself in the LORD his God.

David's example here gives me a model of finding strength in God even when up against difficulties.

What rhythm of life do you prefer to set up so that you can invest in time with the Lord?

- How can you order your schedule to try to be as consistent as possible in spending time with the Lord?

Proverbs 27:17

> As iron sharpens iron,
>   so a friend sharpens a friend.

Finding people who cause you to want to follow hard after God, people who help you stay fast to your biblical ideals, is a worthy investment.

How do you think a friend can "sharpen" a friend? How have you experienced this in your life?

- How can we intentionally store resources of faith and conviction in our own hearts so that we have something to give to others?

Something to Try

Successfully hosting a lifegiving table over the long haul and in the midst of a busy life requires an intentional plan for yourself. Here are some questions and suggestions to help you get started:

What priorities do you believe God has given you in this season of your life? What kind of grid can you put in place to make sure your choices reflect those priorities?

- What is a time every day when you can dependably schedule time with God?

- What personality features and life preferences do you need to consider in order to invest in your own well-being?

- Who informs the way you think and the wisdom you bring? What leaders can you follow that will bring you to a more excellent place in mind, heart, body, and soul?

- What do you need in order to keep your body going in a healthy way? Do you need to schedule exercise? Plan a better diet? Go to sleep earlier?

- Place anchors in your week (like I did with Joy) that bring you delight, comfort, pleasure. Find a new café (or hotel lobby or park bench) to call your own place.

- Confess any negative attitudes you have cherished about your home or your family that keep you from being able to extend grace at your table when you are hosting people there.

- What can you read that might give you great stories to fill your soul? My son reads only thirty minutes every day, but with that time invested, he covers between eight and ten books a year. Small chunks regularly read equal a filled mind.

- Where in your home can you set up a space for private table time with God? Find a special cup or mug to use just for yourself and make this a set-apart time that pleases you and also finds favor with God because you have made time for Him and invited Him in.

- Who are the people in your life who tend to help you become your best self? Who helps you grow in faith and move toward excellence of character? Plan times in your schedule when you can regularly invest time and build memories with these friends. Choose a place where you can talk and enjoy some time together, and then make this friendship ritual a regular habit.

Recipes for Portable Feasting

❈ Oasis Wraps

A few years ago, the kids and I were on a speaking trip in the Middle East—out in the desert, way beyond Dubai. Each evening we ate at a retreat center, a sort of oasis in a very dry patch of desert. The food was delectable to all of us. Almost every night we had pita bread, freshly made hummus with a lemon flavor, grilled chicken, and chopped tomato and onion in a vinaigrette dressing. Our mouths watered every night when dinnertime approached. We enjoyed that meal so much that we did our best to replicate it at home. The result is one of our favorite portable meals.

1 package whole-wheat pita bread, naan, tortillas, or wraps

1 pound of boneless, skinless chicken tenders (As I mentioned earlier, sometimes I cook up to 5 pounds of chicken, cut it into small pieces, and store them in my freezer in individual bags I can use for many recipes.)

1 medium onion, chopped or sliced small

1 bell pepper, any color

1–2 tablespoons olive oil

1 container hummus (Homemade tastes best but is not necessary for wraps in a hurry.)

1 avocado, seeded, peeled, and mashed

1–2 cups cherry tomatoes, chopped

Salsa and/or sour cream, optional

Wrap the pita, tortillas, or other bread in aluminum foil to heat at 350°F. Sauté chicken, onions, and peppers together in the olive oil. Onions should be translucent when finished. (If you are using chicken that has already been cooked, it still tastes better if you sauté it with the veggies and oil.) When the poultry and veggies are cooked, take them off the grill or pan and make an assembly line.

Take a warm pita or tortilla, spread generously with hummus, and sprinkle some of the chicken and pepper mixture on top. Add a dollop of mashed avocado on top, pile on some chopped tomatoes, and then roll the whole thing up into a burrito-style wrap. Salsa or sour cream can be added if you wish. (Sometimes we just let everyone make their own since they all have different preferences.)

✵ **Homemade Hummus**
This simple recipe produces a fairly plain hummus, although I love the lemon zing. If you want more flavor, try adding minced garlic, cumin powder, or diced bell peppers. Garbanzo beans are basically a holder for other flavors.

1 15-ounce can garbanzo beans, drained (liquid reserved)
Juice of 1–2 lemons (depending on your taste—we love lots
        of lemon) or 2 tablespoons bottled lemon juice
4 tablespoons tahini (sesame paste), or to taste
2 tablespoons olive oil
½ teaspoon sea salt

Place garbanzo beans, lemon juice, and tahini in a blender or food processor. (We find that the food processor yields the best texture.) While machine is running, gradually add olive oil. If mixture is too dry or grainy, add more oil or a little water or bean liquid until it reaches a creamy consistency. Add salt, and your hummus is ready.

Makes about 4 servings.

✵ **Lots of Lemon Blueberry Cake**
A few years ago, I wanted to make a new dessert for a large group of friends. Blueberries are a staple in our home (for oatmeal, salads, munching, crisps) and were especially abundant that time of year. Plus I had just returned from a trip to Italy, where I'd taken a cooking class and actually picked

lemons the size of grapefruits fresh off the trees. With both blueberries and lemon on my mind, I started searching for recipes that combined those two great flavors. I looked up several recipes and have changed this and that to make one that is truly my own.

This cake is great to freeze in sections so that you can take out a little bit at a time for teatimes on the fly. I've even been known to tuck frozen pieces into my carry-on when I travel by plane. The cake thaws while I am en route and is ready to share with someone in my room the day I arrive.

Oil or cooking spray plus flour to prepare pan
3 cups unbleached all-purpose flour
1½ teaspoons non-aluminum baking powder
¼ teaspoon baking soda
¼ teaspoon salt
1 cup (2 sticks) salted butter, room temperature
1¾ cups granulated sugar
4 eggs
2 teaspoons vanilla extract
1 cup plain yogurt
½ cup sour cream
5 tablespoons fresh lemon juice (I love lots and lots of lemon juice.)
1½–2 tablespoons lemon zest, chopped
1¾ cups blueberries, tossed in 1 tablespoon of flour (Fresh blueberries
    work the best. If you are using frozen, use only 1½ cups.)
1½ cups confectioner's sugar
7 teaspoons fresh lemon juice
1 tablespoon maple syrup
Zest of 1 whole lemon to garnish, optional
⅓–½ cup blueberries to garnish

Heat oven to 350°F. Grease and flour a Bundt pan. (I cover the whole inside of the pan generously with cooking spray, then sprinkle 1–2 tablespoons of flour and shake it around until all the sides are equally coated.)

In a large bowl, whisk together flour, baking powder, baking soda, and salt. Set aside.

In another large bowl, beat butter until smooth. Add sugar and cream together for up to 5 minutes, until fluffy. Add eggs one at a time and beat well after each addition. Add vanilla extract, yogurt, sour cream, 5 tablespoons lemon juice, and 1½–2 tablespoons lemon zest. Beat until combined.

Add flour mixture to egg mixture in three batches, beating well after each addition. Then continue beating 3 or 4 minutes on medium-high until mostly smooth. Add blueberries and fold in very gently with a spoon so that the batter will not turn blue. Spoon into prepared pan and shake to even it out.

Bake at 350°F for 50–60 minutes, or until a toothpick inserted in the center of the cake comes out clean. If it still has batter on it, put the cake back in the oven for 10 more minutes and test again. (Because I live at 7,300 feet altitude, I sometimes have to cook it a little longer.) Cool on a wire rack for 8–10 minutes. Gently run a knife around the inside edges and along the inside rim of the pan to loosen cake. Turn out of the pan on a rack and cool completely.

For the glaze, mix together confectioner's sugar, 7 teaspoons lemon juice, and maple syrup in a small bowl until smooth. Drizzle glaze over the top of the cake and let it roll down the sides. If desired, sprinkle with lemon zest and fill the hole in the cake with fresh blueberries.

Sometimes I double this glaze recipe to freeze with the cake when I cut the cake in sections.

Sliced thinly, makes 20–24 slices.

Appendix
Table Talk Conversation Starters

IF YOU WANT TO ENCOURAGE discussion at your table but aren't quite sure what to talk about, maybe these conversation starters will help. Some are aimed at younger children, some are for older ones; many work well for anyone. I hope they'll inspire you to start your own list of appropriate questions to bring to the table.

General Questions and Icebreakers

1. Have adults share a story from their childhood. Then ask, "What is your favorite memory from your childhood?"

2. "Tell us about a book or story you are reading now."

3. "Who is your favorite book or movie hero? Why?"

4. "What is the best movie you've seen this year? Your favorite movie of all time?"

5. Talk about a favorite time you have spent in nature (for example, camping out under the stars, hiking, going on a picnic, skiing, a drive in the fall to see the changing leaves, playing in the snow, a trip to the beach or a lake). See what others remember. Plan another outdoor experience to enjoy together soon.

6. "What is one new thing would you like to try? Why?"

7. "Name one place you would like to visit. Why would you like to go there?"

8. "Tell about one of your proudest moments."

9. Ask guests to tell a story about the place where they live.

10. Start a story: "Once upon a time . . ." and then have the others continue it one by one. The last one has to come up with an ending!

11. "If you could be invisible for a week, what would you do?"

12. "If you could have a superpower for a week, what would it be and how would you use it?"

13. "What is your favorite thing in nature? What shows God's art the best?"

14. "What profession do you think you would like to pursue when you grow up?"

15. Talk about the advantages of living in a big city or a country town. Ask everyone which he or she would choose.

16. "What is the most important sense (seeing, hearing, smelling, tasting, feeling, touching)? Why? What would be the hardest to lose?"

17. "Who is the best friend you ever had? What are your favorite memories with that person? How do you think a friend should behave?"

Exploring Literature and Culture

1. Read a favorite poem (you can find many poetry sites online). Read it dramatically—especially if it's a funny one—and discuss its meaning.

2. Memorize the poem "If" by Rudyard Kipling and recite it together at the table.

3. After the meal is over, remain at the table and read one chapter from a great book aloud. Good possibilities are *The Lion, the Witch and the Wardrobe,* by C. S. Lewis; *Treasures of the Snow,* by Patricia St. John; and *Kidnapped,* by Robert Lewis Stevenson, but there are many more. We read the James Herriot series of animal stories for our Sunday afternoon teatimes, and our children loved them.

4. "What person in history do you most like and why?"

Exploring Faith and the Bible

1. Discuss the difference between faith and works.

2. Discuss a Bible story at least once each week. Ask questions like "Do you think what he said was wise?" "Would you have reacted that way to Jesus?" "What do you think this story teaches us?" Good stories include Caleb and the spies (Numbers 13), Joshua at Jericho (Joshua 6), David and Goliath (1 Samuel 17), Abigail and her foolish husband (1 Samuel 25), Esther (the book of Esther), Peter walking on water (Matthew 14:22-33), the angel appearing to Mary and her response with the Magnificat (Luke 1:26-56), Jesus healing the blind man (John 9), Jesus cleansing the Temple (Matthew 21:12-13), and many more.

3. Memorize a Bible verse together by repeating it out loud three times each night for a week. You can do this with individual passages (Psalm 1, for example) or a whole book.

4. "Who do you think was the meanest person you have read about in the Bible and why?"

5. Think of as many diverse animals as you can and how they look different. Discuss God's love for variety and what that says about Him.

6. Read the passage about the disciples telling the children to go away and Jesus taking time for them (Matthew 19:13-15).

"What does that tell you about His value for children? For your children?"

7. Read the Easter story each night for one week before Easter and ask your guests to discuss what they think the scenes of these stories looked like or what was going on in the background.

8. Read the story of the angels coming to the shepherds on Christmas Eve (Luke 2:8-20). Ask why God would first appear to shepherds and what it means.

9. Read Genesis 1:27. Discuss in what ways we were made in the image of God. Ask how we should represent Him through our image to others so that they can see God in and through our lives.

Questions for Christmas Tea or around the Holidays

1. "If you could only give one gift to each person you know, what gift would you give this year?"

2. "What is one of your happiest memories from this past year?"

3. "What one way do you want to be intentional about celebrating life in the coming year?"

4. "What is a lesson of wisdom you have learned this past year?"

Notes

CHAPTER 2: TABLEOLOGY

1. See the "Why Family Dinners?" link on The Six O'Clock Scramble: Dinnertime Unscrambled, www.thescramble.com/family-dinners-matter. A series of reports on family dinners conducted from 2003 to 2012 by the National Center on Addiction and Substance Abuse at Columbia University support many of these conclusions. They can be accessed at http://www.centeronaddiction.org with a search for "The Importance of Family Dinners."
2. Leonard Sweet, *From Tablet to Table: Where Community Is Found and Identity Is Formed* (Colorado Springs: NavPress, 2014), 9.
3. N. T. Wright, *How God Became King: Getting to the Heart of the Gospels*, reprint ed. (New York: HarperOne, 2016, orig. pub. 2012), 238.
4. Sweet, *From Tablet to Table*, 18.
5. Norman Wirzba, *Food and Faith: A Theology of Eating* (New York: Cambridge University Press, 2011), 110.
6. William S. Kervin, *A Year of Grace: 365 Mealtime Prayers* (Peabody, MA: Hendrickson, 2003).
7. That's according to a 2015 estimate by the Population Reference Bureau. See Paul Ratner, "How Many People Have Ever Lived on Planet Earth?" BigThink, May 1, 2016, http://bigthink.com/paul-ratner/how-many-people-have-ever-lived-on-planet-earth.
8. C. S. Lewis, *Prince Caspian*, Chronicles of Narnia series (New York: HarperCollins 1951, 1979), 212.
9. Henri J. Nouwen, *Life of the Beloved: Spiritual Living in a Secular World*, 10th anniversary ed. (New York: Crossroad, 2002).
10. Jeffery Overstreet, "Babette's Feast (1987), and Other Food-Related Films," *Looking Closer* (blog), October 8, 2012, http://www.lookingcloser.org/blog/2012/10/08 /caille-en-sarcophage-hallelujah-a-tribute-to-babettes-feast-and-other-big-screen -cuisine.

CHAPTER 4: THIS IS WHO WE ARE

1. Sally Clarkson and Sarah Clarkson, *The Lifegiving Home: Creating a Place of Belonging and Becoming* (Carol Stream, IL: Tyndale Momentum, 2016).

CHAPTER 6: AN ANCHOR FOR YOUR WEEK

1. G. K. Chesterton, *Orthodoxy* (New York: Cosimo Books, 2007, orig. pub. 1908), 52. Accessed as a Google Book at https://books.google.com/books?id=PeiaPZOvU-oC&q =%2abounding+vitality%22#v=snippet&q=%22abounding%20vitality%22&f=false.

CHAPTER 7: FAITH, FUN, AND FEASTING

1. *English Oxford Living Dictionaries* (online), s. v. "phatic," https://en.oxforddictionaries .com/definition/phatic.
2. *Oxford Pocket Dictionary of Current English* (online), s. v. "emphatic," http://www .encyclopedia.com/humanities/dictionaries-thesauruses-pictures-and-press-releases /emphatic-0.

CHAPTER 8: LIVING OUT GRACE

1. Abraham H. Maslow, "A Theory of Human Motivation," *Psychological Review* 50 (1934), 370–396, http://psychclassics.yorku.ca/Maslow/motivation.htm.
2. Madeleine L'Engle, *Walking on Water: Reflections on Faith and Art* (New York: Northpoint, Farrar, Straus and Giroux, 1980), ch. 1.

CHAPTER 12: STEPPING INTO THE STORY

1. Elizabeth Foss, "Scriptural Hospitality: Inspired by Charity," Catholic Exchange, November 26, 2004, http://catholicexchange.com/scriptural-hospitality-inspired -by-charity.

Recipe Index

About the Author

SALLY CLARKSON is the mother of four wholehearted children, a popular conference speaker, and champion of women everywhere. Since founding Whole Heart Ministries with her husband, Clay, Sally has inspired thousands of women through her blog and podcasts. She is the best-selling author of numerous books and articles on Christian motherhood and parenting, including *The Lifegiving Home, Own Your Life, Desperate, The Mission of Motherhood, The Ministry of Motherhood,* and most recently, *Different: The Story of an Outside-the-Box Kid and the Mom Who Loved Him.*

Sally lives in Monument, Colorado, and loves Jesus, her family, reading, music, tea, traveling, long walks, and her golden retriever, Darcy.

Her passion is to mentor women and to disciple them to become the women they were created to be.

SALLY CLARKSON

Books and Resources to Help You Own Your Life

Sally has served Christ in ministry for four decades. She and Clay started Whole Heart Ministries in 1994 to serve Christian parents. Since then, Sally has spoken to thousands of women in her Mom Heart Conferences and written numerous inspirational books about motherhood, faith, and life. She is a regular mom blogger.

ONLINE

SallyClarkson.com—Personal blog for Christian women

MomHeart.com—Ministry blog for Christian mothers

WholeHeart.org—Ministry website, blog, and store

MomHeartConference.com—Ministry conference website

SallyClarkson.com/podcast—"At Home with Sally Clarkson and Friends" podcast

IN PRINT

Seasons of a Mother's Heart (Apologia Press)

Educating the WholeHearted Child (Apologia Press)

The Mission of Motherhood (WaterBrook Press)

The Ministry of Motherhood (WaterBrook Press)

Dancing with My Father (WaterBrook Press)

The Mom Walk (Whole Heart Press)

Desperate (with Sarah Mae, Thomas Nelson)

10 Gifts of Wisdom (Home for Good Books)

You Are Loved (with Angela Perritt, Love God Greatly)

CONTACT INFORMATION

Whole Heart Ministries | Mom Heart Ministry

PO Box 3445 | Monument, CO 80132

719.488.4466 | 888.488.4466 | 888.FAX.2WHM

Make your table a place
WHERE YOUR FAMILY AND
FRIENDS LONG TO BE.

Books by Sally Clarkson

OWN YOUR LIFE

THE LIFEGIVING HOME (with Sarah Clarkson)

THE LIFEGIVING HOME EXPERIENCE
(with Joel Clarkson)

DIFFERENT (with Nathan Clarkson)

A DIFFERENT KIND OF HERO (with Joel Clarkson)

THE MISSION OF MOTHERHOOD

THE MINISTRY OF MOTHERHOOD

YOU ARE LOVED BIBLE STUDY (with Angela Perritt)

DESPERATE (with Sarah Mae)

THE LIFEGIVING TABLE

THE LIFEGIVING TABLE EXPERIENCE
(with Joel Clarkson and Joy Clarkson)

Visit her online at SALLYCLARKSON.COM.

CP1190